J.R.R. Tolkien, Robert E. Howard
and the Birth of Modern Fantasy

CRITICAL EXPLORATIONS IN SCIENCE FICTION AND FANTASY
(a series edited by Donald E. Palumbo and C.W. Sullivan III)

1 *Worlds Apart? Dualism and Transgression
in Contemporary Female Dystopias* (Dunja M. Mohr, 2005)

2 *Tolkien and Shakespeare: Essays on Shared Themes and Language* (ed. Janet Brennan Croft, 2007)

3 *Culture, Identities and Technology in the* Star Wars *Films: Essays on
the Two Trilogies* (ed. Carl Silvio, Tony M. Vinci, 2007)

4 *The Influence of* Star Trek *on Television, Film and Culture* (ed. Lincoln Geraghty, 2008)

5 *Hugo Gernsback and the Century of Science Fiction* (Gary Westfahl, 2007)

6 *One Earth, One People: The Mythopoeic Fantasy Series of Ursula K. Le Guin,
Lloyd Alexander, Madeleine L'Engle and Orson Scott Card* (Marek Oziewicz, 2008)

7 *The Evolution of Tolkien's Mythology: A Study
of the History of Middle-earth* (Elizabeth A. Whittingham, 2008)

8 *H. Beam Piper: A Biography* (John F. Carr, 2008)

9 *Dreams and Nightmares: Science and Technology in Myth and Fiction* (Mordecai Roshwald, 2008)

10 Lilith *in a New Light: Essays on the
George MacDonald Fantasy Novel* (ed. Lucas H. Harriman, 2008)

11 *Feminist Narrative and the Supernatural: The Function of
Fantastic Devices in Seven Recent Novels* (Katherine J. Weese, 2008)

12 *The Science of Fiction and the Fiction of Science: Collected Essays on SF Storytelling
and the Gnostic Imagination* (Frank McConnell, ed. Gary Westfahl, 2009)

13 *Kim Stanley Robinson Maps the Unimaginable: Critical Essays* (ed. William J. Burling, 2009)

14 *The Inter-Galactic Playground: A Critical Study
of Children's and Teens' Science Fiction* (Farah Mendlesohn, 2009)

15 *Science Fiction from Québec: A Postcolonial Study* (Amy J. Ransom, 2009)

16 *Science Fiction and the Two Cultures: Essays on Bridging the Gap Between
the Sciences and the Humanities* (ed. Gary Westfahl, George Slusser, 2009)

17 *Stephen R. Donaldson and the Modern Epic Vision: A Critical Study
of the "Chronicles of Thomas Covenant" Novels* (Christine Barkley, 2009)

18 *Ursula K. Le Guin's Journey to Post-Feminism* (Amy M. Clarke, 2010)

19 *Portals of Power: Magical Agency and Transformation in
Literary Fantasy* (Lori M. Campbell, 2010)

20 *The Animal Fable in Science Fiction and Fantasy* (Bruce Shaw, 2010)

21 *Illuminating* Torchwood: *Essays on Narrative, Character and Sexuality
in the BBC Series* (ed. Andrew Ireland, 2010)

22 *Comics as a Nexus of Cultures: Essays on the Interplay
of Media, Disciplines and International Perspectives*
(ed. Mark Berninger, Jochen Ecke, Gideon Haberkorn, 2010)

23 *The Anatomy of Utopia: Narration, Estrangement and Ambiguity in
More, Wells, Huxley and Clarke* (Károly Pintér, 2010)

24 *The Anticipation Novelists of 1950s French Science Fiction:
Stepchildren of Voltaire* (Bradford Lyau, 2010)

25 *The* Twilight *Mystique: Critical Essays
on the Novels and Films* (ed. Amy M. Clarke, Marijane Osborn, 2010)

26 *The Mythic Fantasy of Robert Holdstock: Critical Essays
on the Fiction* (ed. Donald E. Morse, Kálmán Matolcsy, 2011)

27 *Science Fiction and the Prediction of the Future: Essays on Foresight
and Fallacy* (ed. Gary Westfahl, Wong Kin Yuen, Amy Kit-sze Chan, 2011)

28 *Apocalypse in Australian Fiction and Film: A Critical Study* (Roslyn Weaver, 2011)

29 *British Science Fiction Film and Television: Critical Essays*
(ed. Tobias Hochscherf, James Leggott, 2011)

30 *Cult Telefantasy Series: A Critical Analysis of* The Prisoner, Twin Peaks, The X-Files,
Buffy the Vampire Slayer, Lost, Heroes, Doctor Who *and* Star Trek (Sue Short, 2011)

31 *The Postnational Fantasy: Essays on Postcolonialism, Cosmopolitics and Science Fiction*
(ed. Masood Ashraf Raja, Jason W. Ellis and Swaralipi Nandi, 2011)

32 *Heinlein's Juvenile Novels: A Cultural Dictionary* (C.W. Sullivan III, 2011)

33 *Welsh Mythology and Folklore in Popular Culture: Essays on Adaptations in Literature,
Film, Television and Digital Media* (ed. Audrey L. Becker and Kristin Noone, 2011)

34 *I See You: The Shifting Paradigms of James Cameron's* Avatar (Ellen Grabiner, 2012)

35 *Of Bread, Blood and* The Hunger Games: *Critical Essays on the
Suzanne Collins Trilogy* (ed. Mary F. Pharr and Leisa A. Clark, 2012)

36 *The Sex Is Out of This World: Essays on the Carnal Side of
Science Fiction* (ed. Sherry Ginn and Michael G. Cornelius, 2012)

37 *Lois McMaster Bujold: Essays on a Modern Master of
Science Fiction and Fantasy* (ed. Janet Brennan Croft, 2013)

38 *Girls Transforming: Invisibility and Age-Shifting in
Children's Fantasy Fiction Since the 1970s* (Sanna Lehtonen, 2013)

39 Doctor Who *in Time and Space: Essays on Themes, Characters,
History and Fandom, 1963–2012* (ed. Gillian I. Leitch, 2013)

40 *The Worlds of* Farscape: *Essays on the Groundbreaking Television Series* (ed. Sherry Ginn, 2013)

41 *Orbiting Ray Bradbury's Mars: Biographical, Anthropological,
Literary, Scientific and Other Perspectives* (ed. Gloria McMillan, 2013)

42 *The Heritage of Heinlein: A Critical Reading of the Fiction
Television Series* (Thomas D. Clareson and Joe Sanders, 2014)

43 *The Past That Might Have Been, the Future That May Come:
Women Writing Fantastic Fiction, 1960s to the Present* (Lauren J. Lacey, 2014)

44 *Environments in Science Fiction: Essays on Alternative Spaces* (ed. Susan M. Bernardo, 2014)

45 *Discworld and the Disciplines: Critical Approaches to the Terry Pratchett Works*
(ed. Anne Hiebert Alton and William C. Spruiell, 2014)

46 *Nature and the Numinous in Mythopoeic Fantasy Literature* (Christopher Straw Brawley, 2014)

47 *J. R. R. Tolkien, Robert E. Howard and the Birth of Modern Fantasy* (Deke Parsons, 2014)

48 *The Monomyth in American Science Fiction Films: 28 Visions of the Hero's Journey*
(Donald E. Palumbo, 2014)

49 *The Fantastic in Holocaust Literature and Film: Critical Perspectives*
(ed. Judith B. Kerman and John Edgar Browninged, 2014)

J. R. R. Tolkien, Robert E. Howard and the Birth of Modern Fantasy

DEKE PARSONS

CRITICAL EXPLORATIONS IN
SCIENCE FICTION AND FANTASY, 47

Series Editors Donald E. Palumbo *and* C.W. Sullivan III

McFarland & Company, Inc., Publishers
Jefferson, North Carolina

Library of Congress Cataloguing-in-Publication Data

Parsons, Deke, 1971–
    J.R.R. Tolkien, Robert E. Howard and the birth of modern
fantasy / Deke Parsons.
        p.   cm. — (Critical Explorations in Science Fiction and
        Fantasy ; 47)
    [Donald E. Palumbo and C.W. Sullivan III, series editors]
    Includes bibliographical references and index.

    ISBN 978-0-7864-9537-5 (softcover : acid free paper) ∞
    ISBN 978-1-4766-1749-7 (ebook)

    1. Tolkien, J.R.R. (John Ronald Reuel), 1892–1973—
Criticism and interpretation.   2. Howard, Robert E.
(Robert Ervin), 1906–1936—Criticism and interpretation.
3. Fantasy fiction, English—History and criticism.
4. Fantasy fiction, American—History and criticism.
5. Fantasy films—History and criticism.   I. Title.

PR6039.O32Z78755 2015
823'.912—dc23   2014039516

British Library cataloguing data are available

Front cover image: Enchanted nature series—The golden
tree © 2015 Shutterstock

Printed in the United States of America

McFarland & Company, Inc., Publishers
  Box 611, Jefferson, North Carolina 28640
    www.mcfarlandpub.com

For Juliette

Acknowledgments

Thanks to:

Professor John Halperin F.R.S.L. for being the bedrock of my Ph.D. program, and for editing the dissertation which became this book on a subject far from Jane Austen.

Professor Donald Palumbo, East Carolina University, for making this book possible.

Professor Robert Dawidoff, Claremont Graduate University, for introducing me to many great films, and for working with me on my qualifying examination and the dissertation that led to this book.

Professor Mark Eaton, Azusa Pacific University, for his generous support of my academic career and the dissertation that led to this book.

Kathleen and Wayne Parsons, for many pounds of paperbacks and comic books.

The late Pat Allen, George Clements, the late Lou Fernandez, Zach Munzenrider, and Bob Newbury, for discussions of comics, fantasy novels, and films.

Barb Syvertson and the Murray Library of Messiah College, the Edward L. Doheny Jr. Memorial Library of the University of Southern California, Penn State Harrisburg Library, the Honold/Mudd Library of the Claremont University Consortium, the Ella Strong Dennison Library of Scripps College, the Dauphin County and Cumberland County library systems in Pennsylvania, the Hershey Library, the Middletown Library, and the Carnegie Library of Pittsburgh.

Table of Contents

Acknowledgments
viii
Introduction
1

I. J. R. R. Tolkien (1892–1973)
3
II. *The Lord of the Rings*
35
III. Robert E. Howard (1906–1936)
58
IV. Conan
97
V. Superman
132
VI. The Inheritors
162

Conclusion
169
Chapter Notes
171
Works Cited
175
Index
185

Introduction

Ronald Tolkien had achieved much by the 1930s: he had a wife, a family, a home, and a professorship at Oxford. Still, he had not forgotten his past. He lost both of his parents as a boy. He lost most of his friends in the First World War. He felt that his mother had been martyred by her conversion to Catholicism. He held to his adopted religion as he surveyed the world around him with disappointment. He had hoped to change England; but the England of the 1930s was less interested in both God and the cultural heritage of the Anglo-Saxons than were his friends at boarding school. Modern England was destroying even the rural landscape of forests and fields that he loved. He needed to remind people of what was being lost.

Tolkien conceived *The Lord of the Rings* (1954–55) in the 1930s as an elegy to an England past, and as a response to modernity. He built the novel upon a detailed fantasy world of his invention and in doing so created the genre of modern fantasy. The novel was the key piece in the development of the phenomenon of fictional fantasy worlds that dominates popular culture today. *The Lord of the Rings* was born in the 1930s, like the genre of modern fantasy; much like modern fantasy, it is more popular today than it was in its youth.

Robert E. Howard spent most of his time in the 1930s slamming battered typewriter keys in an alcove of his parents' house as he sweltered in the West Texas heat. He felt that the political events of the decade proved that civilization was rotten, and doomed to a deserved extinction. He suspected that he was, too. However, on the page, he dreamed of a clean past of barbaric heroism and vitality. He created the Hyborian Age as a setting for the adventures of Conan, and to support a life free from authority.

Introduction

He provided boys and young men not unlike himself with a fantastic escape. More than this, Conan was an act of defiance against the civilization which he felt had trapped him. Conan escaped from danger after danger, slipping out of Texas and into popular culture. There was no escape for Howard.

Jerry Siegel wandered the halls of his Cleveland high school in the 1930s. He enlisted his shy friend, Joe Shuster, in a bid to escape obscurity. Both were little sons of little fathers, Jews as ill at ease with girls as with the gentile world of the United States. They moved to New York City, and created a superman. This paragon did not scheme to rule the world like the Nazis but defended a progressive vision of truth, justice, and the American way. The hero was powerful. Jerry hoped his superman would be powerful enough to keep him from having to return to Cleveland as a failure.

Superman grew beyond all reason, harnessed by American business. He was powered not by the yellow sun of Earth but by generations of hero-worshipping readers. Siegel unintentionally sparked the creation of detailed fictional fantasy worlds—so immense that they had to be called universes—populated by tens of thousands of characters. Jerry's dream spawned corporate properties that generate billions of dollars in the twenty-first century through films and product licensing. Superman and his children still serve as a toy chest for the infinite generation of stories. No matter how corporatized, nor how much more complicated contemporary superhero stories are than Siegel's homely tales, Superman and his children still cast a glance of x-ray vision back to the decade of their birth.

The modern fantasy world established something that is only beginning to mature. The overwhelming number of the highest-grossing films today derive from the fantasy worlds of the 1930s, which remain as culturally significant as they are profitable. They were not offshoots of disposable popular culture, nor new mythologies dressed in the clothes of the Great Depression. They were, and are, literary creations of unusual vitality that grew organically from their time—and that are greatly influencing ours.

I

J. R. R. Tolkien (1892–1973)

The past isn't dead. It's not even past.—William Faulkner

John Ronald Reuel Tolkien lived through the great wars of the British Empire in the twentieth century: the Boer War, the First World War, and the Second World War. He was no bystander to these terrible conflicts. These wars shaped his life more than the other great forces that remade England in the twentieth century—more than the decline of the British Empire, the changes in the class system, or the rise of modernity. Along with his English Catholicism and his passion for philology, these bloody wars were the great influences on *The Lord of the Rings* (1954–55) and his other fantasy writing.

Tolkien was born in the Orange Free State which would later become part of the contemporary nation of South Africa. His father was a banker. Arthur Tolkien was part of a generations-long effort by Great Britain to secure the mineral wealth of southern Africa by seeding the land with middle-class Britons (Pakenham 12). This effort failed, partly because the rugged environment never attracted enough British colonists to provide a critical mass for British supremacy (Pakenham 12). Tolkien's mother, born Mabel Suffield, was a good example of an English subject who was not attracted to the landscape of southern Africa. Tolkien wrote to his son, who would be stationed in South Africa while serving in the RAF during the Second World War, "All you say about the dryness, dustiness, and smell of the satan-licked land reminds me of my mother; she hated it (as a land) and was alarmed to see symptoms of my father growing to like it" (Carpenter 90).

Humphrey Carpenter wrote the authorized biography of Tolkien—

still the main source of details about Tolkien's life four decades after its publication. It is not clear how much Carpenter knew about Tolkien's early life, but the biographer himself was "displeased" with his own account: after the Tolkien family rejected his first draft he felt that he "castrated the book, cut out everything which was likely to be contentious" (Anderson 222). The motives of Arthur Tolkien for taking his young family to Africa are obscure, as are Mabel Tolkien's motives for taking young Ronald (J.R.R. Tolkien) and his baby brother back to England a few years later.

The historical record shows that Ronald was baptized in the Anglican cathedral in Bloemfontein (Scull 2). His father died from rheumatic fever when Ronald was four. Today rheumatic fever is treatable by aspirin and antibiotics, but it was a deadly disease in 1896. The boy had been back in England for a year when his father died.

The Tolkiens lived in Bloemfontein during the build-up to the Boer War. The climax of this bloody war came only a few years after the death of Arthur Tolkien. The Battle of Paardeberg took place in 1900 not far from Bloemfontein (Nassan 94). The battle presaged the fighting in Tolkien's war (the First World War) and the war of his son (the Second World War).

The Boer Army at Paardeberg was caught on an exposed hilltop. A flooding river blocked its retreat (Nassan 94). In the end the British waited for a few days ("siege") until they were forced to surrender. However, before this could happen, Major-General Horatio Herbert Kitchener took the opportunity given by the illness of the commanding officer to order a "devastating" artillery barrage followed by "a frontal advancement" (Nassan 94). In other words, he ordered his men to walk up a hill directly into rifle fire. Kitchener's attack killed or wounded 300 Boers and 1,260 of his own men in an afternoon. He was promoted to overall military commander a few months later.

The Battle of Paardeberg was not an isolated instance of military tactics refusing to adjust to the widespread use of the rifle, but part of a tradition. The tactic of shelling an area and then charging into it had failed to work forty years before in Gettysburg. It failed on a massive scale fifteen years after the Battle of Paardeberg in the First World War with ruinous consequences for Tolkien's generation.

Kitchener was involved in a darker episode in the Boer War which also set the stage for Tolkien's century. As overall commander of British forces, he fought no more "great battles" like Paardeberg. He changed tactics. He attacked the Boer guerrillas by taking all of the women, children, and old men out of the South African countryside and putting them in "concentration camps." This concentrated the population for disease (Pakenham xxi). Twenty to 28,000 people died in the camps, mostly children (Pakenham xxi).

Arthur Conan Doyle, creator of Sherlock Holmes, covered the war as an embedded journalist. He strenuously defended the concentration camps in a book and in a propaganda pamphlet in which he claimed it was "the duty of the British, a civilized people, to form camps of refuge for women and children" (Conan Doyle n.p.). His arguments contradict themselves from paragraph to paragraph, but it is clear that he is aware of the deaths. His primary argument is that the British could not leave "women and children without shelter upon the veldt in the presence of a large Kaffir population" (Conan Doyle n.p.). The British won the war, but the Boers would soon have an independent South Africa, and the system of apartheid, to deal with their large African population.

Neither the charge at Paardeberg nor the concentration camps ended Kitchener's career. He had reached the rank of field marshal in 1910 when he inspected eighteen-year-old Tolkien's class of the King Edward's School Officer Training course. He was a prominent, if aging, figure in Britain during the First World War. We do not know what the young Tolkien thought of the whiskered Lord Kitchener. Tolkien does record his thoughts on the Boer War a few years later when he is preparing to fight in his war: "I no longer defend the Boer War! I am a more & more convinced Home Ruler" (Tolkien *Letters* 5).

Mabel Tolkien died of diabetes on November 14, 1904—insulin had not yet been invented. Tolkien was twelve. He became the ward of a Catholic priest because Mabel Tolkien had converted to Catholicism. The reasons for the conversion are obscure. The decision had far-reaching consequences for Tolkien, and for his writings. He chose to remain true to his mother's adopted religion. This ensured that he would live his life as a minority in a rapidly secularizing, traditionally Protestant nation. Tolkien would later write, "I imagine the fish out of water is the only fish to have an inkling of water" (Tolkien *Letters* 64). Tolkien would always be a fish out of water.

Scholars do not agree on the extent of the influence of Catholicism on Tolkien's fantasy world. Brian Rosebury finds the Catholic tradition central to Tolkien's Middle-earth and states, "There is no doubt we are in an Augustinian universe, in which all Creation is good, and evil is conceived in terms of freely-chosen negation" (Rosebury 35). Fleming Rutledge portrays the events of Middle-earth as almost an evangelical gloss on the gospels: "*The Lord of the Rings* is like the Bible in its narrative structure, for the Bible is above all a narrative of God's mighty acts of deliverance recalling the words of the virgin Mary after the angel came to her: '[God] has put down the mighty from their thrones, and exalted those of low degree' (Luke 1:52)" (Rutledge 4). Patricia Sparks has an opposing view: "*The Lord of the Rings* is by no means a Christian work" (Sparks 82).

Whether or not *The Lord of the Rings* is "a Christian work" (it is not an allegorical one), or appealing to evangelical Protestants, it is full of Catholic influences. Tom Shippey finds specific traces of not merely Catholic, but *Anglo-Saxon* (Catholic) Christianity. He notes that in the novel, Sauron is defeated on March 25, the traditional Anglo-Saxon date for the Crucifixion (Shippey *Road* 200).[1] The date is a passing detail. However, the themes of Tolkien's stories of Middle-earth show the influence of his Catholicism.

The extent of the influence of Catholicism on Tolkien's writings is not constant: it is obvious in *The Silmarillion* (1977), but slight in *The Hobbit* (1937). The influence of Tolkien's religion on *The Lord of the Rings* lies between these two poles. The example of the character Gandalf illustrates the importance of Catholicism to the novel.

Gandalf is a wizard, or, more accurately, a Wizard—in *The Lord of the Rings* the designation refers to a species rather than a fantastical occupation. Gandalf is more concerned with moral leadership than the casting of spells. He does blast the odd villain with fire, but it is eventually revealed that he can only do this because he possesses one of the three Elvish rings (not the plot-driving, evil One Ring). Most of the physical manifestations of his "magic" come from his possession of a magic ring, not any intrinsic power. He looks like an old man, but most of his companions seem to know he is not human.[2] Tolkien reveals in an appendix that Gandalf has lived not just many years, but many centuries.

Although Gandalf is superhuman in age, he has a human personality—especially in the first third of the novel. He is compassionate and testy. He often acts as a heroic version of a devoted professor—dedicated to mentoring his charges, but exasperated by their frequent displays of ignorance. He is not infallible. His oversights at the beginning of the novel put Middle-earth in peril, and suggest that he is either suffering from some sort of dementia or is extremely absent-minded. He returns from the dead later in the book, and becomes a more no-nonsense leader, but with a less-developed personality.

Gandalf is an angel (not merely angelic). This is irrefutable, if the reader considers the material in *The Silmarillion* and Tolkien's letters, but there is sufficient information in *The Lord of the Rings* for a careful reader to come to this conclusion. Much of this information resides in an appendix, and this fact could escape a casual (or disinterested) reader. It would take a leap of imagination to come up with this insight from watching the Peter Jackson films without reading the novel, but Ian McKellan's portrayal of Gandalf is consistent with this interpretation of the character (*The Lord of the Rings: Fellowship of the Ring*).

The quasi-theological environment of *The Lord of the Rings* is complex, but it can be easily summarized. The events of the novel take place mainly in northwest Europe's prehistory. This is not prehistory for the entire world: Abraham has already offered to sacrifice his son to Jehovah when the One Ring is forged by Sauron. Tolkien never establishes the exact correspondence between the events in the West (as Tolkien sometimes calls it) and the Biblical events of the "East." The important point is that *The Lord of the Rings* takes place in the same world as the Bible— there is a Christian God and Jesus will come to redeem humanity. However, since God has not yet revealed himself through the Ten Commandments, or his other Biblical appearances to the peoples of

Middle-earth (northwestern Europe), the word "God" is never used in *The Silmarillion, The Hobbit,* or *The Lord of the Rings.*

There is enough God in Tolkien's writings to please some Christian readers, and to alienate some atheist readers. *The Silmarillion* is difficult to understand without realizing that it is thematically a meditation on original sin, but even in this most theologically oriented example of Tolkien's work, the artistic impression of the book does not depend upon its theology. In any case, *The Silmarillion* is not a popular work, and was published posthumously only because of the success of *The Lord of the Rings.*

The Catholicism of Middle-earth functions as a setting, not a lesson plan. *The Lord of the Rings* is not a devotional work—despite the fact that Tolkien was devoted to Catholic teachings. Tolkien's friend C.S. Lewis refracted elements of the New Testament for the benefit of the English children of his time in *The Lion, the Witch and the Wardrobe* (1950). In this story the Christ-like lion is sacrificed in a scene reminiscent of the crucifixion by an evil witch who relies on the "deep magic from the dawn of time" (Lewis 150). This metaphor suggests an "eye-for-an-eye" interpretation of parts of the Old Testament. The witch is foiled by a New Testament–like resurrection that uses the "Deeper Magic from Before the Dawn of Time" (Lewis 153). Gandalf is also resurrected in *The Lord of the Rings* because Tolkien believes that this is how God works—in the Gospels and in Middle-earth.

The characters in *The Lord of the Rings* are not primarily concerned with preaching, but when there is a sermon, it is usually delivered by Gandalf. Perhaps these "sermons" could be more accurately described as "lectures." Nothing about Gandalf can be considered Catholic inside *The Lord of the Rings;* there has been no St. Peter or historical establishment of the Catholic Church. However, the content of Gandalf's utterances is always consistent with the Catholic doctrine of Tolkien's era. For example, Frodo laments the suffering that the character Gollum has caused and tells Gandalf that it is a pity that Gollum was not killed: the creature "deserves death" (Tolkien *Lord* 59). Gandalf replies, "Deserves it! I daresay he does. Many that live deserve death. And some that die deserve life. Can you give it to them? Then do not be too eager to deal out death in judgment" (Tolkien *Lord* 59). Gandalf's speech combines the values of the Biblical passages "Where wast thou when I laid the foundations of the earth?" (*Authorized,* Job 38:4) and "Be ye therefore merciful, as your father also is merciful" (Luke 6:36). Tolkien makes it clear that Middle-earth would have been lost had the heroes killed the evil and dangerous Gollum. This is one example of a major theme in *The Lord of the Rings:* characters repeatedly invite disaster by believing they know all things. In Catholic terms, this leads to deadly sins such as Pride, Despair, and Wrath. Denethor and Saruman, among others, bring about their own demises and cause great suffering by making this mistake. Gandalf saves Frodo (and, through Frodo, the world) by guiding the hobbit away from this error.

Phrases and concepts in *The Lord of the Rings* are sometimes reminiscent of Catholic dogma. Gandalf tells a demonic creature, "I am a servant of the Secret Fire" (Tolkien *Lord* 330). The term "Secret Fire" is never explained in the text, but it is reminiscent of the concept of the Holy Spirit. A reader could ignore the phrase as inconsequential to the action—or perhaps as suggestive of a secular metaphor for the idea of the inner resources of a hero opposing the physical flames of an evil creature. However, since Gandalf is about to die slaying the demon and later be resurrected, the Holy Spirit is a better reference than "inner resources."

Tolkien also uses the Catholic interpretation of free will in an important passage. Frodo is pursued by the presence of Sauron. He has stumbled upon an ancient ruin. Sauron wants to influence Frodo to put the One Ring upon his finger. The ring will act as a locating device if Frodo wears it in this sacred spot. This will enable Sauron to find Frodo, take the ring and destroy Middle-earth. Frodo is fixed by the "Eye" (presence) of Sauron, who is an antagonist so nebulous in the novel (as opposed to the computer-generated villain of the films) that in passages like this one, the Dark Lord is indistinguishable from a negative psychological "inner voice" of Frodo's psyche. Sauron's voice urging surrender is opposed by a voice reminiscent of Gandalf (whom Frodo believes dead at the time): "For a moment, perfectly balanced between their piercing points, he withered, tormented. Suddenly he was aware of himself again, Frodo, neither Voice nor Eye: free to choose" (Tolkien *Lord* 401). Tolkien keeps the passage short, possibly to avoid the appearance of the technique of allegory, which he disdained.[3] The scene is not representative of the action of the long novel, but it is the most concrete example of the influence of Catholic doctrine on the book.

Not all examples of Catholic influence on the novel are so clear-cut. A central relationship in the novel is between the tormented Gollum and the One Ring, which he possessed (or was possessed by) for many years before losing it. This loss drives the plot of *The Lord of the Rings*. Tolkien describes Gollum's feelings about the ring: "He hated it and loved it, as he hated and loved himself" (Tolkien *Lord* 55). Tolkien authority Tom Shippey writes that Gollum is analogous to a contemporary drug addict (Shippey 46). The screenwriters of the films take this insight past the breaking point. The Gollum of the films is a shifty, manipulative addict whom the Frodo of the films seems foolish not to kill (or, if one were available in the cinematic Middle-earth, to convince to attend an Alcoholics Anonymous meeting). The pathos of Gollum in the novel is a consequence of his moral failings (he killed his friend to get something he wanted, and has had to live with guilt), not a physiologically "addictive" One Ring.

Morality is important for Tolkien, but his works are not "moralistic" in a pejorative sense. *The Lord of the Rings,* in particular, is often misunderstood. C.S. Lewis wrote that in the novel Tolkien was interested in differentiating good and evil, but not in identifying inherently good and evil people (Lewis *Power* 12). This is correct. Ironically, this is also in contrast to Lewis's own method of writing. Tolkien's interest is not in championing authority—at least, earthly authority.

Poet Donald Davie argues that, although Tolkien seems to be almost a parody of a traditional Tory, even he is against authority, in line with all British writers of the era (Davie 94). Davie is disturbed that twentieth-century British writers all follow the legacy of the Sophoclean character Antigone (Davie 94). He means by this that these writers whine, and hector authority, while taking no responsibility for their actions. His iconoclastic view is that Middle-earth heroes (Gandalf and Aragorn) refuse power, while villains like Saruman are damned for rightly attempting to use power to back up their authority (Davie 94).

Davie's argument is suspect, but considering his example makes Tolkien's view on authority clear. The corrupted wizard Saruman is ignoring authority—he's an angel who (like Gandalf) was sent to help the peoples of Middle-earth by coordinating resistance to Sauron. Saruman decides that this is a losing cause, and also that it would be better for him to be ruling Middle-earth—so that he can set things right. He cooperates with the evil Sauron while hoping to recover the One Ring for himself (which will enable him to replace Sauron).

Tolkien does support authority in *The Lord of the Rings*—divine authority. Since God hasn't revealed himself to the Jews or manifested himself as Christ, the position of the heroes in Middle-earth is precarious. Their position has some similarity to Tolkien's as a Catholic in a traditionally Protestant (and rapidly secularizing) country. Like him, his heroes are in a defensive position.

Tolkien was influenced by much more than his religion. His life's work was the study of languages and the "Northern" literary traditions of England and Scandinavia. This love also led him to create Middle-earth. The process of creation started decades before he first conceived of a hobbit. While in basic training for the army in October of 1914, he wrote to his fiancée Edith Bratt, "I am trying to turn one of the stories— which is really a very great story and most tragic—into a short story somewhat on the lines of Morris' romances" (Tolkien *Letters* 7). Humphrey Carpenter calls this the "germ of the story of Turin Turambor in *The Silmarillion*" (434, n. 6). The romances of William Morris were more popular in 1914 than they are today, but it is still unlikely that many other recruits were writing their sweethearts about such things between marches.

He later wrote, "I do not personally connect the North with either night or darkness, especially not in England, in whose long 1200 years of literary tradition Chaucer stands rather in the middle than the beginning" (Tolkien *Letters* 39). He championed this literature his entire life and, in a sense, revived it. However, his primary passion was language. He wrote to W. H. Auden in 1955 that "language and names are for me inextricable from the stories. They are and were so to speak an attempt to give a background for a world in which my expressing of linguistic taste could have a function. The stories were comparatively late in coming" (Tolkien *Letters* 214).

Critic Jared Lobdell writes about Tolkien that, "for him, perhaps, recapturing the past is a kind of advance" (Lobdell *Rise* 138). "Perhaps" and "kind of" are unnecessary additions to this point—for Tolkien, recapturing the past is an advance. This attempt to recapture the past is part of the appeal of Tolkien's writing, but it has not endeared him to some critics. John Garth writes that Tolkien has been attacked by critics influenced by *The Great War and Modern Memory* (1975) by Paul Fussell (Garth 289). Garth notes that Fussell singles out the writer who most influenced Tolkien, William Morris, as one of the "tutors" of war propagandists (290). Garth argues that these critics are misapplying this concept when they use it to explain Tolkien's works, and are missing the legitimate theme of his work: "Tolkien's stylistic values reverse Ezra Pound's famous modernist exhortation to 'Make it new!'" (Garth 291).

Critics hostile to Tolkien may not be missing anything—they may resent Tolkien's "reversal" of a value of modernism. Garth's point may explain some of the venom of attacks on Tolkien throughout the years. Tolkien starts from a different starting point than modernists. It is reasonable for critics interested primarily in modernism to shun his work. However, any linkage of Tolkien's writing to war propaganda is suspect because it has to ignore the strong anti-war themes of his writing.

Apologists for epics were once less temperate than John Garth. Algernon Swinburne called Morris's *The House of the Wolfings* (1889) "singularly beautiful" and maintained it would seem so to "any creature above the intellectual level of a baboon" (May Morris xxvii). Morris influenced Tolkien more than any other author after the Norman Conquest. Tolkien took place names like "Mirkwood," and the "Mark" from *The House of the Wolfings*, and placed them in Middle-earth (William Morris 3). Compare some of Morris's chapter titles to some of Tolkien's: Morris—"The Dwelling of the Mid-Mark," "Concerning the Hall-Sun," "Tidings of the Battle in Mirkwood"; Tolkien—"Concerning Hobbits,"

"King of the Golden Hall," "The Battle of Pelennor Fields" (William Morris 4).

Tolkien borrowed more than a few words from Morris. Morris placed an extraordinary emphasis on descriptive passages of the natural world. He wrote many sentences like this: "The moonlight lay in a great flood on the grass without, and the dew was falling in the coldest hour of the night, and the earth smelled sweetly" (William Morris 29). This interest in the environment is not a necessary part of epics written in the nineteenth century. Sir Walter Scott wrote few descriptive passages of nature in *Ivanhoe* (1820). Morris's contemporary Robert Louis Stevenson wrote even less about the actual island in *Treasure Island* (1883). Tolkien inherited and intensified Morris's unusual focus (for an epic) on the natural world.

Roger Sale writes, "Tolkien tries in many different ways to bring ancient values to life, but by and large he fails to do so" (Sale 198). Tolkien probably saw "these values" (Sale does not explain what values he means) as eternal and did not feel they needed to be revived. Stories about men and elves were no more ancient than they were contemporary for him, just as the Catholic Church belonged as much to the twentieth century as it did to the first. He did not express a desire to go back to a romanticized past, but he also did not agree with most of his contemporaries that his passions were obsolete. In *The Lord of the Rings*, when he describes a civilization in decline from the past of Middle-earth, he does not write about its morals, religion or the sexual excesses of its people. Instead, he describes a people who have abandoned the present in favor of the past, and have failed in their responsibilities to their families: "Kings made tombs more splendid than houses of the living, and counted old names in the rolls of their descent dearer than the names of sons" (Tolkien *Lord* 678).

Philology, the academic discipline that was most vital in the nineteenth century and has been more or less superseded by linguistics, was Tolkien's greatest passion. The study of language took him from being an orphan in Birmingham to a chair at Oxford. It was the basis for the fantasy writing that transformed him from an obscure academic into a famous author.

Tom Shippey emphasizes the influence of philology on Tolkien's fiction. He gives an example of Tolkien's thought-process that reveals the type of thinking that led to the creation of Middle-earth: Tolkien disliked the word "elfin." Shippey explains that "elfin" comes from a gloss by Edmund Spenser on his first poem, "The Shepheardes Calender" (1579), which said that the word "elf" was a corruption of Guelph (an Italian political faction), and that the whole idea of an elf was a papist notion "spurred by bald Friers" (Shippey *Road* 56). Shippey writes that this must have offended Tolkien both because it is poor philology and because it was insulting to Tolkien as a Catholic (56). Tolkien was fascinated by the words in Old English and other Germanic languages that seemed to refer to creatures that no longer exist and for which the literary evidence was fragmentary—or non-existent. Tolkien never uses the word "elfin" in his fiction. This was no pedantic detail for Tolkien. The word "elfin" probably connoted a cuteness that was abhorrent to him: his elves are noble, dangerous creatures. He probably thought "elfin" denoted not the elves that he imagined existed based on words in ancient languages, and the scraps of Anglo-Saxon tradition that survived the aftermath of the Norman Conquest, but the denatured denizens of children's books that were remnants of the tradition of Spenser and Shakespeare. He was offended by Victorian winged fairies because his lifelong study of language suggested to him that there once were creatures nobler and more vital (even though mythical).

Shippey sees Tolkien as an "ethnic writer": "Tolkien was conscious of many centuries of discouragement which had suppressed native traditions in England more quickly, perhaps, than in any other European country" (Shippey *Road* 352). The contemporary formulation of "dead white men" would have meant nothing to him. He saw Anglo-Saxon England as a victim of the cultural extinction which started in 1066 and was completed by industrialization. A fictional reimagining and recreation of this culture was his life's work.

Tolkien was not a solitary academic. He had deep ties to small groups of friends in both his youth and adulthood. He named his group of friends at boarding school the "Tea Club and Barrovian Society" or "T.C.B.S." Humphrey Carpenter writes that this was "an allusion to their fondness for having tea in the school library illicitly, and in Barrow's Stores near the school" (Tolkien *Letters* 8). His friends meant everything to the boy with no family. As late as the First World War, he felt that this group of boys had a special destiny. He wrote to a member of the group from the front at the Allied offensive at Somme on July 1 of 1916 that "the TCBS had been granted some spark of fire ... that was destined to kindle a new light, or what is the same thing, rekindle an old light in the world" (Tolkien *Letters* 9).

The T.C.B.S. consisted of Tolkien, Christopher Wiseman, Rob Gilson, and Geoffrey Bache Smith (Garth 66). They shared an interest in Germanic languages and epics. Tolkien's son Christopher was named after Christopher Wiseman (Garth 281). Tolkien was part of a strikingly reminiscent group of lovers of "Northern" culture as an adult at Oxford. John Garth suggests that C.S. Lewis, a prolific writer and extroverted professor with a dominant personality, effectively filled the roles for Tolkien of all three of his friends from the T.C.B.S. (Garth 281). Lewis and Tolkien formed the Inklings, a group of academics interested in ancient "Northern" literature, writing, and drinking. Tolkien read early versions of his tales of Middle-earth to the group, who met regularly at the Eagle and Child pub in Oxford.

The group was important to Tolkien, and served as a sort of lesser version of the T.C.B.S. It lasted until the end of the 1940s. Tolkien's son and literary executor, Christopher Tolkien, recalled what may have marked the end of the group (Glyer 88). Hugo Dyson was a member of the group who could not stand Tolkien reading from stories of Middle-earth—he was more interested in drinking and joking than in elves. He started to heckle Tolkien as he read from his work. Lewis told him to shut up. Tolkien continued, but was mortified. Critic Diana Glyer believes that repetitions of this incident led to the end of the Inklings (Glyer 88).

These groups were not the only significant personal relationships in Tolkien's life. He was married for decades, until his wife's death in 1971. His wife shared neither his passion for Catholicism nor his intellectual interests. They focused as a couple on their four children. He was a devoted father (Carpenter 72). He was particularly close to his younger son, Christopher. Tolkien wrote that Christopher's love provided consolation for him, "opening at once almost as soon as you were born" (Tolkien *Letters* 76).

The First World War was the second of three major wars Tolkien lived through, and was the event that most influenced his life and his works. Critic Janet Brennan Croft characterizes *The Lord of the Rings* as "World War I literature" (Croft *War* 65). She describes "World War I literature" as writing that concentrates on homoerotic friendships, is written in polite language, is religious, and does not contain sex. She contrasts this with "World War II literature," which she maintains concentrates on heteroerotic couples, includes coarse language, is secular, and portrays sex. Croft's system may not be accurate, but she makes a strong point that *The Lord of the Rings* recalls works written in the aftermath of the First World War more strongly than those written after the Second World War, even though the novel was published in the 1950s.

The form of *The Lord of the Rings* suggests that it was influenced by novels written several decades before the Second World War (although long after medieval romances). Critic Brian Rosebury argues that the structure of the novel is no different from that of *Little Dorrit* or any other Victorian novel (Rosebury *Tolkien* 27). Scott Lobdell claims that the book belongs to the Victorian tradition of three-decker novels: "*The Lord of the Rings* was not and is not a trilogy. It is a novel in six books that was published in three volumes for convenience's sake—in other words, quite precisely, a three-decker" (Lobdell *Rise* 142).

The Lord of the Rings is not a trilogy—it is one novel. However, after establishing this basic fact, trying to place Tolkien in any literary school (other than that of the modern fantasy genre, which he created) is counterproductive. His life experiences, such as service in the First World War, are the best guide to his literature.

Tolkien did not romanticize war even before he saw combat. He wrote about officers while in training: "Gentlemen are non-existent among the superiors, and even human beings are rare indeed" (Garth 94). He wrote of military life that "the worst features are unnecessary, and due to human stupidity" (Garth 94). His experience of combat led to a life-long hatred of war. He wrote to Christopher during the Second

World War, "The utter stupid waste of war, not only material but moral and spiritual, is so staggering to those who have to endure it. And always was (despite the poets), and always will be (despite the propagandists)" (Garth 290).

Most of the deaths in his unit of the Lancashire Fusiliers at its defining action in the massive Battle of the Somme were caused by British artillery shells (Garth 290). The artillery units tried to time their barrages so that the shells would strike the enemy just before the infantry reached them—so that the shells would stun or kill the enemy soldiers manning machine-gun positions. This was supposed to give the infantry a chance to avoid being slaughtered by enemy fire as it charged fixed positions (as had happened decades before in the Boer War at the Battle of Paardeberg, and was happening on a massive scale on the Western Front). Unfortunately for the Fusiliers, their artillery barrages often missed and landed directly on them (Garth 296). Those who survived this friendly fire were either allowed to retreat or shot by the enemy. Tolkien was spared being involved in these infantry charges because he was a communications officer. He would pass among the bodies of the victims of these assaults as his signals post was moved to different positions during the battle.

Geoffrey Bache Smith, a member of the T.C.B.S., wrote to Tolkien from the trenches in 1916, "May God bless you, my dear John Ronald, and may you say the things I have tried to say long after I am not here to say them, if such be my lot" (Garth 308). An artillery shell wounded Smith—he died from gangrene on December 6, 1916 (Garth 308).

Of the members of the T.C.B.S., only Tolkien and Christopher Wiseman survived the war. Tolkien froze the four young men forever as the four young hobbits of his novel. Compare the language of Smith's letter to the passage in which Frodo tells Sam that there is no need to conserve provisions because they will not survive to make a return journey: "But Samwise Gamgee, my dear hobbit—indeed, Sam my dearest hobbit, friend of friends—I do not think we need give thought to what comes after that.... If the One goes into the fire, and we are at hand? I ask you, Sam, are we ever likely to need bread again? I think not" (Tolkien *Lord* 624). C.S. Lewis felt that *The Lord of the Rings* caught the essence of his experience in the First World War. He later recalled "the horribly smashed men still moving like half-crushed beetles, the sitting or standing corpses, the landscape of sheer earth without a blade of grass" (Lewis *Surprised* 227). Lewis also had a relationship that in some ways recalls the bond between Frodo (a gentleman), and Sam (his servant) in *The Lord of the Rings:* "Dear Sergeant Ayres, who was (I suppose) killed by the same shell that wounded me. I was a futile officer (they gave commissions too easily then), a puppet moved about by him, and he turned this ridiculous and painful relation into something beautiful" (226).

Lewis wrote a review of the third part of *The Lord of the Rings* in 1955: "This war has the very quality of the war my generation knew. It is all here: the endless, unintelligible movement, the sinister quiet of the front when 'everything is now ready,' the flying civilians, the lively, vivid friendships ... and such heaven sent windfalls as a *cache* of tobacco 'salvaged' from the ruins" (Garth 311). These are minor elements of the book, and similar situations have existed in wars other than the First World War. However, it is significant that a man who was familiar with Tolkien, drafts of *The Lord of the Rings,* and combat in the First World War associated the fantasy novel with the First World War.

Garth argues that, unlike writers like Thomas Hardy and Wilfred Owen, Tolkien ascribed the evil of war to the devil or satanic figures in his works rather than an uncaring God (Garth 266). This is an interesting idea, but it is more to the point to note that Tolkien believed in orthodox Catholicism—unlike Hardy or Owen. This is an essential difference between Tolkien and most English writers of the twentieth century. Tolkien did not blame God for anything, nor was he an atheist or agnostic. Nor was Tolkien in any sense a Manichean: evil exists and does horrible things to people both internally and externally in *The Lord of the Rings.* However, evil in the novel is a corruption of good, not its equivalent.

Tolkien comments on war through his characters of *The Lord of the Rings.* Boromir is a heroic man who joins the fellowship representing the free peoples of Middle-earth. He is like Beowulf, but from a culture that is based in a massive stone city rather than a primitive wooden mead hall. He is a proud, valiant, and good man. However, he and his martial city are overmatched by the forces of the evil Sauron. He is too focused on glory, and war, to accept that there is no way to defeat evil by force of arms. He believes "the fearless, the ruthless, these alone will achieve victory" (Tolkien *Lord* 398).

Boromir slowly goes insane while accompanying the hobbits and the rest of the fellowship in their mission to destroy the One Ring. He wants to take the ring back to his city and use its power to destroy the armies of Sauron. He knows that the ring was created by Sauron to corrupt the people of Middle-earth, and that it has destroyed his great ancestor who tried to claim the ring's power for himself—but, to Boromir, a weapon is a weapon. His proximity to the malign influence of the ring leads to his undoing.

Boromir represents the heroic "Northern spirit" that Tolkien admired. However much he admired these figures, Tolkien also felt they were too focused on war. Boromir is a "Northern" hero without the resources to see through the delusions of modernity. The ring inspires visions of glory and power in which "he drew plans for great alliances and glorious victories to be; and he cast down Mordor, and became himself a mighty king, benevolent and wise." Tolkien felt that Beowulf's way was not appropriate to resist evil in the modern world.

Boromir confronts Frodo in a climactic scene. Frodo has possession of the One Ring. The more powerful, good characters fear to take it because they are wary of its corrupting influence. Boromir and Frodo are separated from their companions when Boromir presses Frodo to give him the ring so he can relieve the hobbit of the terrible burden of carrying it—and heroically take the war to Sauron. These are delusions fostered by the ring itself. Frodo replies that he would give the ring to Boromir but for the warning of his heart. Boromir is offended, and demands to know to what Frodo is opposed. Frodo replies, "Against delay. Against the way that seems easier. Against refusal of the burden that is laid on me. Against—well, if it must be said, against trust in the strength and truth of Men" (Tolkien *Lord* 397).

Fortunately, Middle-earth has characters on the side of the angels who are better than heroes: it has Englishmen. The hobbits are a romanticized and gently ridiculous race abstracted from myths of the salt-of-the-earth common Englishman. Until the climax, when their suffering is so brutal that all pretense is stripped away, the hobbits of the Fellowship maintain their characteristically English interest in regular meals and bourgeois values. These "soldiers" have much in common with the popular conception of British soldiers in the less fantastic wars of the West with the East today. A contemporary soldier responded to a reporter's question about the worst part of military life in Afghanistan with the quip, "The breakfasts" (Macintyre n.p.). Samwise Gamgee of Hobbiton would have answered no differently.

Tolkien describes Boromir's brother Faramir as having a more appropriate view of warfare than Boromir. Faramir says: "I do not love the bright sword for its sharpness, nor the arrow for its swiftness, nor the warrior for his glory. I love only what they defend" (Tolkien *Lord* 672).

The people of the last bastion of humanity opposed to Sauron have forgotten what a king is supposed to be. They believe that the responsibility of a king is to lead the people in war. A folk-saying remembered only by a superstitious crone foreshadows the return of kingship to the people of Minas Tirith: "The hands of the king are the hands of a healer" (Tolkien *Lord* 860). Aragorn, the eventual leader of the fellowship, becomes king by self-denial rather than feats of arms.

The fellowship is directly menaced by the cannon fodder of Sauron: the orcs. The orcs are moronic militarists—not "dehumanized" enemy soldiers. They are a distinct race rumored to have been fashioned by Sauron from elves (since, in Middle-earth, only the off-stage deity can create life) through torture and manipulation. The manipulation was possibly done through genetic engineering, but the cause is never explained—this is fantasy, not science fiction.[4] The orcs do not represent lower-class workers, or any other real-world constituency. They have no free will, and are suitable only for war and pillaging because they were designed that way by an evil power. They are automatons, not dupes. In the films produced in New Zealand, they sound like thugs from a dive bar in Auckland or Sydney. This is far from Tolkien's concept of the orcs. They speak coarsely in *The Lord of the Rings* because they do everything coarsely—they are organic robots whose only capacity is for cruelty.

Frodo succeeds in his mission, but is destroyed by war. He tells Sam, "I tried to save the Shire, and it has been saved, but not for me" (Tolkien *Lord* 1029). Frodo never shows an interest in fighting or in power, which is why he can bear the ring for as long as he does before succumbing to its corrupting influence. By the end of the novel he has become a pacifist. He will not fight, even to save his beloved Shire: "I'll bear no weapon, fair or foul" (937).

The scene that most characterizes Tolkien's view of war takes place in the Dead Marshes. Frodo, Sam, and the feral creature Gollum march through a swamp that has covered an ancient battlefield. The corpses of beautiful elves, men, and foul orcs are joined in death beneath the waters. The spectral bodies glow, and beckon to the living to approach. If people get too close to the corpses, they will be pulled under into the realm of the dead—which recalls a flooded trench from the First World War. Gollum whispers, "Many faces proud and fair, and weeds in their silver hair" (Tolkien *Lord* 628).

The tone of the novel looks back to an era before the stoicism of the British people during and after the Second World War. Fantasy author Marion Zimmer Bradley writes that the emotions of the characters of *The Lord of the Rings* "are *not* the stiff-upper-lip unemotional ones of the modern English-speaking peoples.... Legolas trembles with terror and wails aloud.... Boromir weeps in passionate repentance after his attack on Frodo, and when he is slain, Aragorn kneels at his side so 'bent with weeping' [that his companions think he is dead]" (Bradley 109–10).

Sam looks at Frodo and thinks: "I love him" (*Tolkien* Lord 652). Frodo addresses Sam as "my dear hobbit—indeed, Sam my dearest hobbit, friend of friends" (624). When there is nothing more to do at the end of the quest, Frodo says to his friend: "I'm glad you are here with me. Here at the end of all things, Sam" (947). When Faramir says farewell to Frodo and Sam, he does not just give them a manly goodbye but stoops to kiss their foreheads (695). Even Gandalf says to his friends: "I will not say 'do not weep'; for not all tears are an evil" (1030). This emotionalism survived into the film adaptations of the novel and is one of the traits that distinguished the films from standard blockbusters. *The Lord of the Rings: Return of the King* (2003) was the first film from the modern fantasy genre to win an Academy Award for Best Picture.

Fantasy has not been a celebrated genre in films (or in mainstream culture). A few winners of the Academy Award for Best Picture of the Year have had some affinities with fantasy: the modern historical romances of *Braveheart* (1995) and *Gladiator* (2000) are the best examples. Some Best Picture winners have had more or less related sensibilities: the sports film *Rocky* (1976), and the magical-realist *The English Patient* (1996). However, fantasy has been a minor mode in Hollywood film.

Many critics dislike fantasy because they perceive that it abandons or devalues "the real world." C.S. Lewis and Tolkien, as well as some contemporary critics, have tried to answer this charge. Lewis wrote that a reader of fantasy "does not despise real woods because he has read of enchanted woods: the reading makes all real woods a little enchanted" (Gray 137). In other words, fantasy attempts to alter "reality," not reject it. Another criticism of modern fantasy, which can be applied to many other genres, is that the dangers within these stories are false—the heroes are going to win. Tolkien shared this objection to a point: "A safe fairyland is untrue to all worlds" (Tolkien *Letters* 24).

Lewis, unlike Tolkien, was a natural polemicist. Many of his works are Christian apologies, and he marshaled a bit of the fervor he shows in these books to defend the genre of fantasy, stating that "a given reader may be (some readers seem to be) interested in nothing else in the world except detailed studies of complex personality. If so, he has a good reason for not reading those kinds of works which neither demand nor admit it.... We must not allow the novel of manners to give laws to all literature" (Hunt 22). Tolkien seems to have had little interest in commenting on literature outside of fantasy (and his academic field), but he may have agreed with this sentiment.

Critics often have difficulty evaluating fantasy literature. Jargon that may apply to related genres like science fiction falls flat when applied to fantasy. For example, this attempt at analysis is of *The Lord of the Rings:* "The density of Tolkien's description of the hobbits and Middle Earth might be said to naturalize his fantasy to the point where cognitive estrangement does not operate" (Booker 257). If this is so, it is for the obvious reason that Tolkien has no interest in estrangement, cognitive or otherwise. The density of his descriptions lies in his attempt to create (or, as Tolkien would have it, "sub-create"—because in his view only God may create anything) a fantasy world that the reader can enter into. If Tolkien succeeds in drawing the reader into a different world, not a different aspect of this one, then he can suggest all sorts of themes.

Some critics who are kindly disposed towards Tolkien seek to place his fantasy works in the literary mainstream, noting that "his works are as suffused with the spirit of the age as any by Eliot, Joyce, or Hemingway" (Mortimer 113). The "spirit of the age" is a nebulous concept. Tolkien himself was grounded in the Oxford of the 1930s when he had the epiphany that led to the development and popularization of his influential view of fantasy literature in *The Lord of the Rings.* His works look back to the past of the ancient Anglo-Saxons, and to other ancient cultures, though many critics overemphasize this point. *The Lord of the Rings* is written from the point of the 1930s: Tolkien is looking back at the horrors of the First World War and fearing the coming horrors of the second. Rural, pre-industrial England is glorified, although not canonized—the hobbits can be foolish as well as dangerously parochial. Many of the results of the industrial revolution are deplored, and a post-industrial future is awaited with anxiety—but not despair. In this sense, Tolkien could be said to partake in the spirit of the 1930s.

Some critics have been puzzled by Tolkien's popularity. Roger Sale wrote in 1968 that "the young show no signs of admiring Anglo-Oxford as such and generally have no positive response to the Old and the old heroic ways" (Sale *Tolkien* 247). This admiration may have been a simple case of "the young" disdaining the literature of their parents and appreciating the literature of their spiritual grandparents, rather than an academic conundrum. In addition, the "old heroic ways" were likely receiving approbation from many students even in 1968—they certainly do today. Most contemporary readers of *The Lord of the Rings* are not English, and are not likely to know anything about "Anglo-Oxford."

Critic Ann Swinfen decried "the attitude of the majority of contemporary critics ... that the so-called 'realist' mode of writing is somehow more profound, more morally committed, more involved with 'real' human concerns than a mode of writing which employs the marvelous." She notes that "the real world—that is, the world of empirical experience—was for many centuries regarded as the world of 'appearances.' To our ancestors ... the ultimate real lay in spiritual otherworlds. It is with the reality of such otherworlds that fantasy very largely deals" (Swinfen 2). This is a legitimate view, but it is more antiquarian than Tolkien's perspective.

Many critics have not seemed to notice that Tolkien believed that one could not (and should not) hold onto the past. The point is made many times in his fiction. The character of Denethor in *The Lord of the Rings* is a personification of this view. Denethor is the steward of the great, embattled human city of Minas Tirith. He is wise but bitter. Sauron has infected him with despair through a device that appears to show the future, but is actually just another technological tool which Sauron uses to co-opt foes. Denethor goes mad, and nearly takes his city with him when he commits suicide. Gandalf confronts him, asking what he seeks to gain by destroying everything around him before Sauron's armies reach the city. Denethor answers, "I would have things as they were in all the days of my life." If he cannot live in the past, then he "will have *naught*: neither life diminished, nor love halved, nor honour abated" (Tolkien *Lord* 854).

Tolkien makes a related point in the early part of *The Lord of the Rings*. Frodo complains, "I knew that danger lay ahead, of course; but I did not expect to meet it in our own Shire. Can't a hobbit walk from the Water to the River in peace?" An elf who has lived for thousands of years deflates this lack of perspective: "But it is not your own Shire... Others dwelt here before hobbits were; and others will dwell here again when hobbits are no more" (Tolkien *Lord* 83).This is a major theme of *The Lord of the Rings*.

Tolkien is not concerned, as Swinfen may be, with refuting empiricism. The *Catholic Encyclopedia* tells us that Catholic teaching holds that "sense experience is a source, and indeed the primary source, of human knowledge, but it holds that there are other sources beyond sensations" ("Empiricism" n.p.). Tolkien, a devoted Catholic, would have agreed with this. He was a spiritual man, but not especially mystical. He did not support materialism, but the primary idea that he objects to throughout *The Lord of the Rings* is modernity's embrace of Protagoras's claim that "Man is the measure of all things."

From Tolkien's point of view, this is reductive—it leaves out God, trees, food, and English literature before Chaucer. He also saw a sinister side to this attitude. Sauron is eventually revealed to be a prisoner of his own creation (the One Ring). However, he is immensely powerful and destructive. Sauron is far less human than Gandalf or the elves. He is an age-old entity—metaphorically, he is Satan's technologically oriented apprentice. (The Satan figure in Middle-earth cosmology is revealed in *The Silmarillion* to have been imprisoned in an earlier age of the world.) Sauron has a monomaniacal focus on destroying everything that is not himself. This works as a metaphor for Tolkien's view of modernity. To put it another way, if "man is the measure of all things"—which "man"? Tolkien sees a sole focus on the affairs of humanity as opening the door to totalitarians like Sauron and Hitler, who are more than happy to make themselves the measure of all things.

Swinfen sees the danger of the all-absorbing self as a major concern of many writers of twentieth-century fantasy: "It is a form of ultimately self-destructive egoism—the desire to make oneself the very centre of life, to which all else is subservient" (Swinfen 96). Tolkien sees this as the greatest failing of his own time. He applies this belief beyond the areas of religion and politics. For example, he is particularly concerned in *The Lord of the Rings* with the effect this thought-process has on the environment of the natural world.

Lee Oser, perhaps a spiritual descendent of Swinburne in his approach to defending fantasy, reverses the common charge against fantasy that it is childish. He turns the charge back upon its perceived source (critics in the thrall of modernism). He calls the derisive modernist attitude toward fantasy "the manner of the disillusioned child, for whom all wonder is a trap, for whom the goodness of the world must be entirely re-created, because the world has so badly failed to live up to expectations" (Oser 152).

Regardless of the merits of that statement (and statements of this kind both for and against fantasy are popular), there is no reason to believe that the modernists are alone in not being particularly fond of fantasy. Of course, the modern fantasy genre is based on the works conceived in the 1930s like *The Lord of the Rings,* and did not exist commercially until the 1960s. However, even allowing for the anachronism, were Chaucer and Shakespeare interested in fantasy in the manner of Tolkien? Are contemporary authors of literary fiction who are not "modernist"? It seems unlikely. Even writers working in genres that are sometimes linked with modern fantasy, like magical realism, do not share the interests of the modern fantasy genre. Jorge Luis Borges told an interviewer that he liked Lewis Carroll, but was baffled by Tolkien (Hadis 116).[5]

Tolkien was aware of many criticisms of fantasy. He used the opportunity of a special lecture at the University of St. Andrews to answer them. He wrote "On Fairy-stories" in 1938, soon after he started *The Lord of the Rings.* The lecture was an annual event that commemorated Andrew Lang, the Scottish poet who published collections of fairy tales in the late nineteenth and early twentieth centuries. Tolkien was probably invited because of the success of *The Hobbit* (1937). His lecture is the most important twentieth-century piece of criticism of fantasy.

Not everyone likes "On Fairy-stories"—not even all Tolkien scholars appreciate it. Tom Shippey is disturbed by its "lack of philological core." Even worse, the essay is at times "perilously close to whimsy." Still, Shippey is sympathetic to one of the implied arguments of Tolkien's essay. Shippey writes, "Probably at the bottom of the confrontation between LOTR and its critics there lies some total disagreement over the nature of the universe" (Shippey *Road* 136).

Tolkien begins the lecture by quoting Andrew Lang on "contemporary" (Edwardian) fairy tales: "They always begin with a little boy or girl who goes out and meets the fairies of polyanthises, and gardenias and apple-blossom.... These fairies try to be funny and fail; or they try to preach and succeed" (Tolkien "Fairy" 36). Tolkien approves of this comment—in fact he is disturbed by almost every aspect of the popular conception of fairy tales in his time. Tolkien is reluctant to use even the word "fairy": "It is probably irrecoverable for several generations because it has been made a sniggering, derisive synonym for homosexual" (Tolkien *Hobbit* 22).

He writes that one of the worst misconceptions about fairy tales is that they are about fairies. "Most good 'fairy-stories' are about the *adventures* of men," he notes. "Naturally so; for if elves are true, and really exist independently of our tales about them, then this also is certainly true: elves are not primarily concerned with us, nor we with them. Our fates are sundered, and our paths seldom meet" (Tolkien "Fairy" 38). This is the sort of language to which Shippey objects, but Tolkien is not being whimsical or delusional. He states that fantasy is based on recognition of fact and truth of the real world (75). His approach to fantasy creatures throughout his writings is like the approach of a method actor to a part: he takes them seriously and treats them as if they are real, but is not asking his audience to clap if they believe in fairies.

Tolkien next attempts to redefine the genre. "A fairy-story is one which touches on or uses Faerie, whatever its own main purpose may be: satire, adventure, morality, fantasy" (Tolkien "Fairy" 39). "Faerie" is the place where fantasy can take place: not in the here-and-now, but still real. The contemporary way of gaining entrance to this state of mind is art. His definition is an attempt to disassociate literary fantasy from popular misconceptions about what a fantasy story contains. He feels that it is not only tiny, winged fairies that are not an essential part of fantasy, but magic in the popular sense.

Tolkien links magic to language by redefining the concept of spells, which he says "might indeed be said to be only another view of adjectives, a part of speech in mythical grammar. The mind that thought of light, heavy, grey, yellow, still, swift, also conceived of magic that would make heavy things light and able to fly, turn grey lead into yellow gold, and the still rock into swift water." For Tolkien, magic is "the desire to wield that power in the world external to our minds" (Tolkien "Fairy" 48). Magic is language, and magic is desire. Tolkien's own work is consistent with his theory. There are almost no spells in *The Lord of the Rings.* Manifestations of magic in the novel are the result of an as-yet unrevealed God, or technology clothed in demonic form.

Tolkien emphasizes that fantasy—or, at least, the fantasy he prefers—is not primarily concerned with replicating the conflicts of ordinary life: "An essential power of Faerie is thus the power of making immediately effective by the will the visions of 'fantasy' … This aspect of 'mythology'—sub-creation, rather than either representation or symbolic interpretation of the beauties and terrors of the world—is, I think, too little considered" (Tolkien "Fairy" 49).

In the twenty-first century magic is often viewed pejoratively: "magical thinking" is shorthand for a personality defect in pop psychology. The "magic" Tolkien is interested in is a method to gain perspective, not a delusion or alienation. However, unlike Lewis (who hoped to gain converts), Tolkien will not even attempt to align his rhetoric to the mainstream perspectives of his era. He does not make concessions to contemporary conventions in order to be taken seriously. He has his way of expressing his ideas, which the reader is free to accept or reject. For example, he sums up his view of fantasy as stories that "open a door on Other Time, and if we pass through, though only for a moment, we stand outside Time itself, maybe" (Tolkien "Fairy" 56).

"On Fairy-stories" also lays out the history of Victorian and Edwardian fantasy. It is not an inspiring one for Tolkien: "Fairy-stories have in the modern lettered world been relegated to the 'nursery,' as shabby or old-fashioned furniture is relegated to the play-room, primarily because the adults do not want it, and do not mind if it is misused" (Tolkien "Fairy" 58). He sees this disregard as having roots in the class (and, implicitly, gender) bias of Victorian society. He writes that nannies and domestic workers preserved the oral folk traditions that were mined for academic fairy tales. He explains that this is because these workers were often from Scotland or Ireland. Unlike England, which experienced the industrial revolution first, these nations had not had their folk traditions destroyed by industrialization. So, in England, fairy tales were the province of lower-class females and the children they amused with survivals of the old Northern tradition. Tolkien makes the case that class bias and the historical association of fairy tales with children has tainted literary fantasy (66).

Tolkien does not believe that children have any particular interest in fantasy, and believes that fantasy should not be limited to children. He writes that fantasy offers "Recovery, Escape, Consolation, all things of which children have, as a rule, less need than older people" (Tolkien "Fairy" 67).

Above all, he feels that (good) fantasy does not require suspension of disbelief. Samuel Taylor Coleridge wrote in his *Biographia Literaria* (1817): "My endeavours should be directed to persons and characters supernatural, or at least romantic; yet so as to transfer from our inward nature a human interest and a semblance of truth sufficient to procure for these shadows of imagination that willing suspension of disbelief for the moment, which constitutes poetic faith" (Coleridge, *Biographia*, chapter xiv, paragraph 3). Tolkien writes, "What really happens is that the story-maker proves a successful 'sub-creator.' He makes a Secondary World which your mind can enter.... The moment disbelief arises, the spell is broken.... You are out in the Primary World again, looking at the little abortive Secondary World from outside" (Tolkien "Fairy" 61).

Tolkien finds suspension of disbelief "a substitute for the genuine thing, a subterfuge we use when condescending to games or to make-believe, or when trying (more or less willingly) to find what virtue we can in the work of art that has for us failed." It is a concept he feels may apply to drama, but does not work for narrative literature (Tolkien "Fairy" 61).

He cites the domination of English literary criticism by Shakespearean scholars as a contributing factor to critical misunderstanding of literary fantasy. If you prefer drama to narrative literature, he writes, "you are apt to misunderstand pure story-making, or to constrain it to the limitation of stage-play. You are, for instance, likely to prefer character, even the basest and dullest, to things. Very little about trees can be got into a play" (Tolkien "Fairy" 72).

The Birth of Modern Fantasy

The most striking passage of the lecture is Tolkien's response to the charge that fantasy is an irresponsible and childish escape from reality. "In real life [escape] is difficult to blame unless it fails; in criticism it would seem to be the worse the better it succeeds.... Why should a man be scorned if, finding himself in prison, he tries to get out and go home? Or if, when he cannot do so, he thinks and talks about other topics than jailers and prison-walls?" (Tolkien "Fairy" 79). This is the best explication of the psychology of those who appreciate the modern fantasy genre ever written.

Tolkien's fantasy is not a rejection of reality but a criticism of his era: "The bridge to platform 4 is to me less interesting than Bifrost guarded by Heimdall.... From the wildness of my heart I cannot exclude the question whether railway-engineers, if they had been brought up on more fantasy, might not have done better with all their abundant means than they commonly do" (Tolkien "Fairy" 81).

The Silmarillion (1977) is the work of Tolkien closest to Bifrost, and furthest from the bridge to platform 4. After his father's death Christopher Tolkien published selections from the vast private mythology that Tolkien had started during the First World War and was never able to finish. It is not a direct expression of the "spirit of the age" of the 1930s, as is *The Lord of the Rings*. It is not a book for children, as is *The Hobbit*; it is not even suited for adolescents or young adults, or anyone mainly seeking entertainment. It is not as popular or influential as either of these books. It has the unique distinction of being the raw material that shaped Tolkien's fantasy world, being itself shaped after the creation of that fantasy world in *The Lord of the Rings*.

Tolkien wrote in 1944 to his son Christopher, who was stationed in South Africa, "All we do know, and that to a large extent by direct experience, is that evil labours with vast power and perpetual success—in vain: preparing always only the soil for unexpected good to sprout in" (Tolkien *Letters* 76). This is a guiding theme of *The Silmarillion*. However, some critics find the message of *The Silmarillion* to be less optimistic. Brian Rosebury perceives the work to be bitter and tragic, preoccupied with ruminations on original sin (Rosebury 103). It is not a tract, but it is more overtly theological than any of Tolkien's other works. The work is not a novel, but a collection of stories on the early history of Middle-earth.

Tolkien goes *all* the way back in his chronicles of Middle-earth—characters that have a connection to the events of *The Hobbit* and *The Lord of the Rings* do not appear until well into the book. He starts with a variant of Genesis in which he "not only expands on, rewrites, and changes the Genesis story but he considers his myth a supplement to the Bible" (Sammons 155). This statement goes too far, but it does give a sense of the seriousness with which Tolkien treated this material. Tolkien's publisher immediately realized that *The Silmarillion* was too serious, and too difficult to read, to be popular. Stanley Unwin diplomatically rejected *The Silmarillion* in 1937 and nudged Tolkien toward the path that would result in his conception of *The Lord of the Rings*. Tolkien writes: "Unwin thinks 'The Silmarillion' contains plenty of wonderful material which might be mined to produce 'further books like the Hobbit rather than a book in itself'" (Scull 208). Unwin was right.

There are remarkable passages in *The Silmarillion*. The most striking is the creation of the world through divine music as "a sound arose of endless interchanging melodies woven in harmony that passed beyond hearing" (Tolkien *Silmarillion* 15). The archangels have each been given a part of a celestial theme to sing creation into existence. The most powerful archangel, Melkor (Satan by another name—and, in *The Lord of the Rings*, the old boss of Sauron), decides he wants to exalt his part over that of the others. The other angels sing the world into being, and Melkor destroys it with his song. The angels and Melkor sing back and forth, creating and destroying the world, until equilibrium is reached in a flawed creation and the world "was established at last in the Deeps of Time and amidst the innumerable stars" (22).

A more human moment describes an angelic artist in love with his creations. The archangels in *The Silmarillion* act like aloof versions of Greek gods and goddesses. The passage that describes Aule's plea to God is unusually emotional, perhaps because Tolkien identified with the supplicant.[6] The archangel Aule (associated with honest craft) secretly creates his own race to populate Middle-earth. God finds out about this unauthorized creation and confronts Aule. The smith answers, "I devised things other than I am, to love and to teach them.... For it seemed to me that there is great room in Arda for many things that might rejoice in it" (Tolkien *Silmarillion* 43). God has pity on the poor creations (only God can create independent life) and invests them with true life, stipulating only that they will not enter Middle-earth until his favored races (elves and humans) have populated the land.

The key story in *The Silmarillion* is the romance of Beren and Luthien. The Silmarils are three gems of immense power. They are not Hitchcock-like MacGuffins that have no meaning other than to drive the plot—but their nature is mysterious. It is not clear if they are quasi-sentient and malicious like the One Ring of *The Lord of the Rings,* but they are capable of great harm. Beren is a man and Luthien is an elf. He falls in love with Luthien on sight, and she falls in love with him (to her doom). Luthien's father has no interest in a mortal son-in-law so he sends the man on an impossible quest to steal a Silmaril from Melkor.

Luthien aids Beren, and they manage to steal a Silmaril. Beren loses his hand in the quest, as Frodo loses a finger in *The Lord of the Rings.* Luthien loses much more. Her father allows her marriage, but the archangels force upon her a choice—"the doom of Luthien" (Tolkien *Silmarillion* 167). She must either be parted from Beren or forsake her elven immortality. The archangels insist that Luthien make this choice because they have no right to interfere with God's command that, unlike elves, all humans must die. The archangels have no idea of the purpose or ultimate fate of humanity, while God has revealed to them the basic destiny of the elves. They (and, in *The Lord of the Rings,* the elves) are perplexed and wary of all things human.

Luthien chooses to live with Beren and die as a mortal. "This doom she chose, forsaking the Blessed Realm [so that] the fates of Beren and Luthien might be joined, and their paths lead together beyond the confines of the world" (Tolkien *Silmarillion* 167). The pairing of Beren and Luthien is the first of three couplings of human men with elven women. These unions determine the destiny of Middle-earth. The third interspecies couple in Middle-earth is Aragorn and Arwen in *The Lord of the Rings.* This couple is linked to the earlier joining of Beren and Luthien, but a reader of the novel who has not read *The Silmarillion* (all readers before 1977) is likely to miss the significance of this relationship. It always had significance for Tolkien. He had "Beren" carved after his name and "Luthien" after his wife's on their family tombstone.

The Hobbit (1937) is a lighter and better book than *The Silmarillion.* It is a novel written for children, though not necessarily young children. Tolkien noted that his then-thirteen-year-old son was interested in it, but his younger children were not (Tolkien *Letters* 21). Some critics find it more palatable than *The Lord of the Rings.* One noted that " ... for Tolkien's hostile critics, patting *The Hobbit* on the head has become something of a tradition ... before proceeding to ridicule the ambitious scale and implied adult readership of *The Lord of the Rings*" (Rosebury 113–14).

Tolkien would have his first experience with American readers with *The Hobbit.* The financial lure of the U.S. market was great, but Tolkien would have mixed feelings about working with Americans. This became clear when his publisher sent him a copy of the proposed cover for the American edition of *The Hobbit.* As Humphrey Carpenter described it, "Ballantine's cover picture seemed to have no relevance whatever to *The Hobbit,* for it showed a hill, two emus, and a curious tree bearing bulbous fruit. Tolkien exploded: 'What has it got to do with the story? Where is this place? Why emus? And what is the thing in the foreground with pink bulbs?' When the reply came that the artist hadn't time to read the book, and that the object with the pink bulbs was 'meant to suggest a Christmas tree,' Tolkien could only answer: 'I begin to feel I am shut in a madhouse'" (Carpenter 228).

He appreciated other aspects of the American response to *The Hobbit.* The *New York Herald Tribune* awarded him its $250 prize for the year's best book intended for younger children (Scull 215). He also shared a newspaper clipping about Shirley Temple's interest in the book with his publishers (220).

The Hobbit is a novel for children—although, perhaps, "children of all ages" is a better designation. Dwarves horrify the bourgeois hobbit Mr. Baggins in a charming early incident. They handle his prized tableware roughly as they sing, "Chip the glasses and crack the plates!" They repeat throughout the song, "That's what Bilbo Baggins hates!" (Tolkien

Hobbit 9). The novel deals with serious themes as well. The noble king of the dwarves is undone by greed. The hero, Bilbo Baggins, is a gentle soul. He is a remarkable specimen of the race of hobbits, a small-statured agrarian people. Hobbits are distant cousins of humanity. Bilbo loves and admires Thorin, the exiled dwarven king and leader of the expedition to reclaim the dwarves' birthright from a dragon. The wizard Gandalf arranges for the seemingly useless Bilbo to accompany the party of adventurers. At the climax of the novel, Thorin speaks to Bilbo (and to the readers) on his deathbed: "There is more in you of good than you know, child of the kindly West. Some courage and some wisdom, blended in measure. If more of us valued food and cheer and song above hoarded gold, it would be a merrier world" (Tolkien *Hobbit* 273).

The Hobbit is a bildungsroman for children. Bilbo starts as a child emotionally (if not in chronological age), as well as in stature, but he learns by the end of the book that he is a small part of a larger world, and that good intentions are not enough. He sits alone crying and reproaching himself after Thorin's death: "You made a great mess of that business with the stone; and there was a battle, in spite of all your efforts to buy peace and quiet, but I suppose you can hardly be blamed for that" (Tolkien *The Hobbit* 273).

Tolkien wrote of *The Hobbit:* "Mr. Baggins began as a comic tale among conventional and inconsistent Grimm's fairy-tale dwarves, and got drawn onto the edge of it—so that even Sauron the terrible peeped over the edge. And what more can hobbits do? They can be comic, but their comedy is suburban unless it is set against things more elemental" (Tolkien *Letters* 26).

II

The Lord of the Rings

Memory is not what the heart desires.—J.R.R. Tolkien

The great epic of *The Lord of the Rings* shows the influence of the children's novel *The Hobbit,* especially in the early chapters. The beginning of the books feels far less serious than its end. At one early point Frodo says, "I want to think!" and Pippin replies, "Good heavens! At breakfast?" (Tolkien *Lord* 86). The humor of this exchange has little to do with the existential struggle against Sauron or the One Ring.

One hundred pages into the novel the protagonists still have more than a hairy foot in the world of *The Hobbit.* Tolkien seems reluctant to release his merry hobbits into the darker environment of *The Lord of the Rings.* The characters themselves do not take their danger seriously even after being hounded across their bucolic Shire. The party even pauses from their desperate escape to take a nice, hot bath during which Pippin sings a cheerful ode to bathing: "Better than rain or rippling streams is Water Hot that smokes and steams" (Tolkien *Lord* 101). The tone of the novel shifts back and forth between high and low elements in the early chapters. These shifts make the first of the six books of *The Lord of the Rings* different from those that follow. Frodo will later be psychologically tortured for hundreds of pages, so it seems churlish to begrudge him food, friends, and levity early in the novel. The early chapters add depth to the book and emphasize the effect of the One Ring on the once-cheerful hobbit.

The early adventures of Frodo also make it clear that Tolkien had no interest in the neo–Aristotelian formulas that dominate much of the production of contemporary popular culture. Tolkien carefully constructs the plot of the novel, but does not attempt to go from build-up to climax in a neat arc. Nor does he attempt to create a consistent tone throughout his epic. The difference between *The Lord of the Rings* and many superficially similar fantasy novels that were written in its wake is most obvious in the early chapters: the digressions are more important than the plot or characters. Tolkien authority Tom Shippey writes that " ... the zest of the story goes not into the dangers but the recoveries—hot baths at Crickhollow, song and dancing at Bree, Goldberry's water that seems like wine, and Butterbur's 'small and cosy room' with its hot soup, cold meats, a blackberry tart, new loaves, slab of butter, and 'half a ripe cheese' ... Gildor Inglorion's pastoral elvish banquet and Farmer Maggot's 'mighty dish of bacon and mushrooms'!" (Shippey *Road* 104). The fantasy world of Middle-earth is not just a mise-en-scène that provides the background and tone for *The Lord of the Rings:* it is more important than any other aspect of the story.

Tolkien is still sporadically reassuring his audience a few hundred pages into the novel. An elf-lord speaks what could be one of the more mature speeches of *The Hobbit:* "The world is indeed full of peril, and in it there are many dark places; but still there is much that is fair, and though in all lands love is now mingled with grief, it grows perhaps the greater" (Tolkien *Lord* 348). The novel becomes less reassuring as it unfolds.

Tolkien does not feel that the present is inferior to an idealized past. The present has its griefs, but is no less precious. However, Tolkien does assert throughout his writings that the present is not inherently superior to the past—an attitude he detects in the modern world. In *The Lord of the Rings* he does not denigrate the present for not measuring up to some ancient standard.

The homeliness and humor of the hobbits returns to the novel occasionally even after the epic plot is in full swing. These passages remind the reader that high, heroic values are not the only source of virtue. They also lighten the mood a little. The lordly Faramir honors Frodo and Sam with this compliment: "Your land must be a realm of peace and content, and there must gardeners be in high honour" (Tolkien *Lord* 681). Seven hundred pages into the novel, when events have gotten serious, Sam remarks, "It can't be tea-time even, leastways not in decent places where there is tea-time" (700). The look back at the charming, parochial world of *The Hobbit* is brief. Gollum brings the narrative back to the grim plot: "We're not in decent places" (700).

Sam once thought that heroes in stories went out looking for adventures "because they were exciting and life was a bit dull." He and the other hobbits have to learn the difference between "what folk inside a story and not outside call a good end" (Tolkien *Lord* 711).

The impending disaster of the Second World War also influenced *The Lord of the Rings;* Tolkien began the novel's composition in 1938. He could not keep Middle-earth separate from contemporary Europe. While negotiating the translation of *The Hobbit* into German, he was asked by a Nazi censor to certify that he was not Jewish. He wrote on May 2, 1938, to his publisher, "I should be inclined to let to ... let a German translation go hang ... [I] should regret giving any colour to the notion that I subscribed to the wholly pernicious and unscientific race-doctrine" (Tolkien *Letters* 37). Warehouse stocks of English versions of *The Hobbit* were burned in a German air raid in 1942 (Croft *War* 155).

Tolkien wrote in February 1939 that he hoped to finish *The Lord of the Rings* that year (Tolkien *Letters* 42). He was about fifteen years off in his projection. He also declared that the book "is no bedtime story" (Tolkien *Letters* 41). His experience in the First World War made it unlikely that it would ever have been a bedtime story, but its composition during the Second World War—and its aftermath—ensured that it would not be.

Tolkien rued the connection between ancient Germanic culture and the Nazi regime. He had a grudge against "that ruddy little ignoramus Adolf Hitler." He wrote of his anger at Hitler in June of 1941: "Ruining, perverting, misapplying, and making for ever accursed, that noble Northern spirit, a supreme contribution to Europe, which I have ever loved, and tried to present in its true light" (Tolkien *Letters* 55).

The political environment of England during the Second World War disgusted him. He wrote in 1943, "My political opinions lean more and more to Anarchy (philosophically understood, meaning abolition of control not whiskered men with bombs).... If we could get back to personal names, it would do a lot of good.... If people were in the habit of referring to 'Winston and his gang,' it would go a long way to clearing thought" (Tolkien *Letters* 63).

Tolkien was no more sanguine about Americans during this period. He wrote to his son of a wartime encounter on a train with a young officer from New England. The officer was loudly bemoaning the legacy of feudalism on English class distinctions, and decrying the "pretentious" accent of people in Oxford. Tolkien wrote, "I stood the hot-air they let off so long as I could.... After I told him that his 'accent' sounded to me like English after being wiped over with a dirty sponge ... and ... together with American slouch, it indicted a slovenly and ill-disciplined people—well, we got quite friendly. We had some bad coffee" (Tolkien *Letters* 69–70).

Tolkien had no enthusiasm for the war even after it became clear that the Allies were going to win it. In particular, he had no stomach for the war against Japan. He wrote that "as I know nothing about British or American imperialism in the Far East that does not fill me with regret and disgust, I am afraid I am not supported by even a glimmer of patriotism in the remaining war" (Tolkien *Letters* 115).

He summed up his view of the war in a letter in January 1945: "Well the first War of the Machines seems to be drawing to its final inconclusive chapter—leaving, alas, everyone the poorer, many bereaved or maimed and millions dead, and only one thing triumphant: the Machines" (Tolkien *Letters* 111). He found the end of the war even worse. He wrote on August 9, 1945, "The news today about 'Atomic bombs' is so horrifying one is stunned. The utter folly of these lunatic physicists to consent to do such work for war-purposes: calmly plotting the destruction of the world! Such explosives in men's hands ... is about as useful as giving firearms to all the inmates of a gaol and then saying that you hope 'this will ensure peace'" (116).

One of the effects of Tolkien's inclusion of non-human races in *The Lord of the Rings* was that they enabled him to comment on the human condition from a position outside of it. A dwarf and an elf discuss humanity near the end of the War of the Ring. The dwarf is pessimistic—humans may start well, but fail to follow through on their nobler aspirations. "There is a frost in Spring, or a blight in Summer, and they fail their promise." The elf takes humanity's part and argues that, whatever its failings, humanity is resilient and will "spring up again in times and places unlooked-for. The deeds of men will outlast us." The dwarf responds that these new springs will only add up to "might have beens." The elf ends the argument: "To that the Elves know not the answer" (Tolkien *Lord* 873). Neither did Tolkien.

His career as a professor spanned decades. W. H. Auden, his most famous student, was an admirer. He defended *The Lord of the Rings* in print (Auden "End"). Diana Wynne Jones was also a student. She wrote the fantasy novel *Howl's Moving Castle* (1987), which was adapted as a successful 2004 film in Japan by Hayao Miyazaki. Her opinion was that, while C.S. Lewis was a charismatic speaker, Tolkien was difficult to understand. She wrote, "You couldn't hear him.... He worked at not letting you hear because he wanted to go away and finish writing *The Lord of the Rings*" (Butler 16). This is only the opinion of one student who had little direct contact with him, but Tolkien himself acknowledged his difficulties in being heard—attributing the problem to a rugby injury to his tongue from his youth (Carpenter 78). However, he was also known to give well-received dramatic readings. His biographer Humphrey Carpenter suggests that Tolkien had, not a speech impediment, but a selective lack of interest in being understood (Carpenter 78).

Professor Tolkien seems to have enjoyed interacting with advanced students and was an early advocate of women's pursuing advanced degrees and academic careers. He regularly tutored female students in his home, under the eye of his wife to maintain propriety (Carpenter 78). However, he seems to have been driven by his interest in philology rather than teaching, scholarly writing, or even his fantasy writing. In fact, much of his enthusiasm for *The Lord of the Rings* came from his passion for languages, not as an escape from them.

Critics who dislike *The Lord of the Rings* often imagine that it says something they disapprove of about race, sex, or (especially) class in postwar England. Critics may root out abortive evidence that Tolkien makes some unconscious comment on these issues in the novel, but he is concerned with other topics.

He rejects direct allegory and direct symbolic representation of real-world concerns. This rejection is unusual even in fantasy and science-fiction works of the twentieth century. It is particularly opposed to the dominant tradition of late twentieth-century and contemporary science fiction and fantasy: the drama of film and television. For example, the Vulcan Mr. Spock of the science-fiction *Star Trek* dramas is a fictional inhabitant of a fictional world, but the "logical thinking" of the Vulcans is a transparent representation of real-world, human rationalism. Alternately, screenwriters may use Mr. Spock to represent the ego of everyone's individual personality. The fantasy (clothed in science fiction) *Star Wars* franchise includes "alien" races like the Ewoks, which represent "primitive" peoples in the real world opposing technologically superior imperialists. Even the films based on *The Lord of the Rings* include scenes like that of Saruman addressing an immense crowd of villains gathering beneath him in *The Lord of the Rings: The Two Towers* (2002), which mimic the real-world propaganda of Leni Riefenstahl. Many critics seem to expect Tolkien to make or invite these sorts of analogies, but he does not. This is a key division between *The Lord of the Rings* and many dramas of contemporary popular culture that use fictional worlds.

The world of England in the Second World War (and early postwar England, since the novels were completed in the early 1950s) sneaks into the novel obliquely. Critic Judy Ann Ford believes that the setting of the city of Gondor, one of numerous locations in the book, suggests a historical analogue to a real-world civilization: "the fall of Rome with a happy ending: a decaying western empire which did not quite fall, which somehow withstood the onslaught of armies from the east, and which was restored to glory" (Ford 53).

The biggest contributions of the 1940s and early 1950s were not political events, but Tolkien's relationships with his children. Janet Brennan Croft identifies thirteen parent-child relationships (mostly between adult characters and father figures) in *The Lord of the Rings,* but finds none in *The Hobbit* (1937), which was written when Tolkien had no adult children[1] (Croft *War* 67–71). He was worried about his sons during the Second World War.

II. The Lord of the Rings

Hostile critics of *The Lord of the Rings* have many objections to it, but a surprising number of these are ill-considered. Tom Shippey comments on the "fierce and strong competition among literary critics for the honour of having made the least perceptive comment on Tolkien" (Shippey *Author* 156). Harold Bloom is a representative example of a dominant school of hostile criticism of the novel: "I am fond of The Hobbit, which is rarely pretentious; but LOTR seems to me inflated, over-written, tendentious, and moralistic in the extreme. Is it not a gigantic Period Piece?" (Bloom 1).

The Lord of the Rings is not pretentious because it is not pretending to be anything other than itself—a unique work with its own preoccupations. It is not inflated because it has no proper size. Much criticism of Tolkien damns him for not fitting the expectations of the critic. Bloom is offended by the novel's "moralistic" character, but it is Tolkien's adherence to orthodox Catholic values—rather than the gnostic philosophy Bloom prefers—that likely rankles him. Bloom fails to recognize that Tolkien does not impose these values on the reader.

Bloom continues by insulting Tolkien, his fans, and even Mormons: he implies that the writing of the novel is so bad that it is reminiscent of *The Book of Mormon* (Bloom 1). In fact, there are works of contemporary fantasy influenced by Mormonism, including Stephanie Meyers' popular series of young adult books, *Twilight* (2005–2008) and their film adaptations, as well as the 1980s *Dragonlance* fantasy series. There is nothing "Mormon" about *The Lord of the Rings* or its style. Bloom incorrectly asserts that a stylistic choice Tolkien makes in some later passages of the novel (to emulate the feel of the *Authorized Version* of the Bible in an attempt to elevate the tone of Aragorn's coronation) is typical of the style of the entire book (1).

Bloom prophesizes the disappearance of *The Lord of the Rings* not merely from the literary canon (to which he has not admitted the work), but from popular consciousness (Bloom 1). He theorizes that the novel may have fit some sort of atavistic need of the counter-culture of the 1960s, but that it has had its moment. In reality, *The Lord of the Rings* became more popular as the twentieth century came to a close. The 2001–2003 films raised the profile of the novel to an unprecedented level.

The popularity of *The Lord of the Rings* in the United States has also benefitted from the culture's greater appreciation of unironic works in the wake of the attacks of September 11, 2001.

Bloom is far from alone in his criticisms. Translator and poet Burton Raffel echoes Bloom when he writes that the poetry of *The Hobbit* is "much better (because less pretentious)" than that of Tolkien's novel for adults (Raffel 26). Criticizing the poetry imbedded in *The Lord of the Rings* is like criticizing a production of *Hamlet* for pedestrian fight choreography—it is possible, but it is a pointless exercise. The poetry in *The Lord of the Rings* is not meant to stand on its own. It can be enjoyed, despised, or ignored without significantly altering the experience of reading the text.

Critics have traditionally overemphasized the influence of medieval literature and mythology on *The Lord of the Rings*. This is easy to demonstrate by performing the simple experiment of reading *Beowulf* and then reading *The Lord of the Rings*. The two have little in common. Tolkien studied and wrote about *Beowulf*, but this does not mean that his works resemble the Old English poem. Tolkien's fantasy has little in common even with late medieval works written in Middle English such as *Sir Gawain and the Green Knight* and *The Pearl*. The novel has less in common with these medieval works than it does with Shakespeare, and although the Shakespearean influence on Tolkien is detectable, it is not great. Nor is the setting of Middle-earth itself medieval. Characters use swords in both Arthurian legend and *The Lord of the Rings*. However, characters drive cars in *To the Lighthouse* (1925) and *The Great Gatsby* (1925), and these works are not similar. Not only is Tolkien writing in a language different from that of the poet of *Beowulf*, but the writers are separated by more than a thousand years. *The Lord of the Rings* is one of the most original departures from the mainstream in the history of literature, but it is not a regression to medievalism. It is a modern book— not a modernist one. Nor does it primarily belong to the post-war era in which it was published. Tolkien does owe a debt to William Morris, but little to the host of influences many critics have proposed. It is a novel conceived in the 1930s which looks back to Tolkien's personal mythologized version of the world of his childhood.

II. The Lord of the Rings

Critic Jared Lobdell locates Tolkien at the spiritual wake of the Edwardian era, "the Edwardian inheritance between the storytellers and the world-recreators—between Edgar Rice Burroughs and Angela Thirkell, the pulp writers and the country-house novelists.... Tolkien brought the long-sundered branches of the Edwardian line back together again—for which reason he, more than P.G. Wodehouse, deserved the title of 'the last Edwardian'" (Lobdell *Defining* 121). Edgar Rice Burroughs's magazine serials create fantasy worlds like Middle-earth, although much less detailed and sophisticated. In particular, "A Princess of Mars" (1912) introduces Barsoom—a fantasy world that shares a little in common with Middle-earth—although it shares much more with the Hyborian Age of Robert E. Howard, Tolkien's fellow 1930s world-building fantasist.

Regarding Angela Thirkell, it might seem that Tolkien's fantasy novel would have nothing to do with the realistic books of the grand-daughter of pre–Raphaelite painter Edward Burne-Jones. However, a comparison between the beginnings of *The Lord of the Rings* (started in 1937) and Thirkell's *Three Houses* (1931) shows that this is not the case. Thirkell writes: "We walked along past early eighteenth-century houses, each in its own garden of elms and cedars and mulberries. The air was warm, the sun shone on the blossoming trees hanging over the brick walls, and so we came to the Grange" (Thirkell 1). Tolkien was not yet in Oxford during Thirkell's childhood, but he might have liked to be. He was born only two years after she, and was a professor at Oxford by the publication of *Three Houses* in 1931. An early passage from *The Lord of the Rings* reads, "The Hobbits named it the Shire ... a district of well-ordered business of living, and they heeded less and less the world outside where dark things moved until they came at last to think that peace and plenty were the right of all sensible folk" (*Tolkien* Lord 5).

Tolkien went back to the introduction of the Thirkellian hobbits in *The Hobbit* (1937) to revise it to fit more with the darker Middle-earth of *The Lord of the Rings*. He drafted a revision of *The Hobbit* in 1944, and published it in 1951 (Rateliff xxv). Tolkien did not need the grim events of the Second World War to "darken" his vision of Middle-earth—his experiences in the First World War were more than dark enough to influence his outlook. The revision was done primarily to turn the mysterious, but not evil, magic ring of the original edition of *The Hobbit* into a more menacing force.

The finder of that ring (and hero of *The Hobbit*), Bilbo, bequeaths the ring to his nephew Frodo at the start of *The Lord of the Rings*. John Rateliff notes that the name "Bilbo" is reminiscent of the names of characters in the books of P.G. Wodehouse like "Bingo (Richard) Miller and Pongo (Reginald) Twistleton" (Rateliff 47). Wodehouse (1881–1975) and Tolkien (1882–1973) were almost exact contemporaries. "Bingo" was actually Tolkien's original name for the character of "Frodo" in what Christopher Tolkien calls (in his multi-volume study of his father's manuscripts) the first version of the first phase of the drafts of *The Lord of Rings* (December 17–19 of 1937) (C. Tolkien 11). The author was still using the ridiculous name in the draft Christopher Tolkien designates as being part of the third phase of the drafts of *The Lord of the Rings* composed from October to December of 1938 (309).

C.S. Lewis and Tolkien's other close friends called him by the nickname "Tollers" (Bratman 243). It may have been easier for a middle-aged professor used to being called "Tollers" by other middle-aged professors to overlook that "Bingo" was a disastrous, novel-killing name for a hero of a novel published in the 1950s. The name had to resemble "Bilbo," who was the hero of a children's novel. However, "Bilbo" and "Frodo" are archaic names which, while superficially close to "Bingo," actually fit in the hobbit's linguistic corner of Middle-earth.

The Hobbit is childish, imaginative, humane, overlong, wise, and a bit sad. Its humor is charming and dated (and was dated even in 1937). It also links Tolkien to his prewar self, and his friends of the T.C.B.S. club. Tolkien passed through the First World War and survived. Half of the T.C.B.S.ers did not. Tolkien watched with dread the approach of a second World War that would threaten not only civilization but his sons. He found he could no longer send Bilbo's successor "Bingo" (by any name) off on another jolly children's adventure—even a thoughtful one like *The Hobbit*. Tolkien had to reconcile the levity of *The Hobbit* and his childhood friendships with the world he was living in, and the war he had endured.

II. The Lord of the Rings

Tolkien also had to reconcile his sequel to *The Hobbit* with the aspirations of *The Silmarillion*. This is because the only way he saw to make a sequel to *The Hobbit* suitable for adults was to set it in the private fantasy world he had been developing throughout his whole life. The members of the T.C.B.S. may have been young and whimsical, but they were also serious: they were sneaking tea in the library while talking about ancient literature, not getting drunk or chasing girls. Tolkien, in particular, was a serious young man. He had little money and no obvious alternative other than working hard at his studies. *The Silmarillion* is quasi-religious, difficult, intermittently tedious and beautiful. It is as serious as both the young and middle-aged Tolkien's need to preserve the spirit of the ancient traditions he loved.

The Lord of the Rings is the merging of the sensibilities of *The Hobbit* and the works that would posthumously be called *The Silmarillion*. The coming of the Second World War was the catalyst for its formation. The war machine and state-driven world he saw at the end of the Thirties returned him to the mission of his youth. The disregard for the individual, for the land, and the good things of a forgotten English tradition drove Tolkien to spend fifteen years writing *The Lord of the Rings* in the hours free from his academic and family responsibilities.

An undated scrap of paper from the era of the earliest drafts of *The Lord of the Rings* identifies the key object in the transition between the juvenile sequel to *The Hobbit* and what the novel would become: "*The Ring*: whence its origin … it exacts its penalty. You must either lose it, or *yourself*" (C. Tolkien 42). Bilbo Baggins faced mortal danger in *The Hobbit*, but not moral danger. He benefits from the adventure. The ring he finds causes him to become invisible. It is a useful tool that should not be relied upon too much, but there is nothing apparently evil about it. The rings fails to corrupt Bilbo, while invisibility corrupts H.G. Wells' villain in *The Invisible Man* (1897). Bilbo is a kindly, harmless fellow with no ambition. *The Lord of the Rings* reveals that these qualities save him and the world from annihilation. The invisibility granted by the ring (or "One Ring"—because there are many magic rings in Middle-earth) is a side effect. The One Ring does not align the "refractive index" of the subject to the "refractive index of air," as does the process of the mad "Invisible Man" (Wells 65). The One Ring takes the wearer right out of the world of sunlight and into the world of the Dark Lord, leaving only a ghostly consciousness (sooner or later bent to the Dark Lord's will). The free individual becomes a shadow of evil. The effect is spiritual, not scientific. This is an excellent example of the difference between science fiction and fantasy.

Tolkien jotted down a note about the One Ring on the back of his first surviving map of Middle-earth: "Ring must eventually go back to Maker, or draw you toward it" (C. Tolkien 42). Along with this note he wrote a brief list of the events that would form the core of the first book of *The Lord of the Rings*. Once the beginning is set, the theme of the journey of the One Ring either back to its place of forging for its destruction or to its demonic master (and the destruction of everything else) drives the plot through a novel of a thousand pages. At some later date, Tolkien wrote at the top of the reverse side of this map: "Genesis of the Lord of the Rings" (42).

Tolkien is not much interested in politics in *The Lord of the Rings*. Critic Stratford Caldecott recognizes this, but exaggerates it, saying that "the real danger is not that the free world might be defeated; it is that we might be corrupted, brutalized and degraded by the conflict itself, and in particular by the means employed to secure victory" (Caldecott 2). Sauron is attempting through the "politics by other means" of war to be the real danger of the book. Readers are not in danger from Sauron, so it might seem that Caldecott's idea is more appropriate—that the danger Tolkien is warning of is to the moral sense of the readers. However, with the partial exception of his consistent thematic and stylistic privileging of nature over machines (technological or political), Tolkien is not interested in providing a message for his readers. He may be moralistic (or, more accurately, a practicing Catholic of his place and time), but his important work is not.

Auden wrote in a book review of the final part of *The Lord of the Rings* for the January 22, 1956 issue of the *New York Times*, "Even the One Ring, the absolute physical and psychological weapon which must corrupt any who dares use it, is a perfectly plausible hypothesis from which, the political duty to destroy it which motivates Frodo's quest logically follows." Auden was attempting to make the book understandable for readers of the *New York Times*, to whom the novel must have seemed even more alien in 1956 than it still does for many people today. He was also lending his considerable literary prestige to a work that lacked any.

Author Peter Beagle wrote, "*The Lord of the Rings* is made with love and pride and a little madness. There never has been much fiction of any sort made in this manner, but on some midnights it does seem to me that my time is cheating itself of even this little" (Beagle xvii). Some readers may disagree that there is "madness" in the book, and others may find there is more than a little. The novel did obsess its author: he spent 18 years of his free time writing it.

Tolkien was not healthy during the critical period of the initial composition of *The Lord of the Rings*. In the last half of August 1938 he was "so depressed by trouble that he reache[d] the edge of a nervous breakdown." A doctor ordered bed rest and he kept to his bedroom for a week (Schull 220). The world around him was also on the edge of a nervous breakdown, which would officially begin in September of 1939 with Britain's entry into the Second World War.

Tolkien's description of Bilbo at the beginning of the novel must have resonated with the author's personal feelings and with the atmosphere in England during the build-up to the Second World War. The ring has, unbeknownst to Bilbo, placed him in an ominous stasis that has halted his natural aging process. This preservation has come at the cost of a weary nervousness: "I feel all thin, sort of stretched," he complains, "like butter that has been scraped over too much bread" (Tolkien *Lord* 32).

Gandalf directs Bilbo to leave the ring to his nephew Frodo. Bilbo is too old—the younger generation must now carry the burden of its elders. Gandalf summarizes the sorry history of the One Ring: "Always after a defeat and a respite, the Shadow takes another shape and grows again" (Tolkien *Lord* 51). This is an example of Tolkien's frequent use of the Augustinian metaphor of evil as a shadow—evil is not a power in itself, but a shadow cast when the light of God is blocked. However, this citation of that idea recalls the situation of a young generation in England forced to go to war to fight an evil that should have been put to rest before their time. Frodo asks, horrified, "Why, why wasn't it destroyed?" Gandalf continues with some more practical and historical information, but he has no answer.

An attitude of war-weariness is prominent throughout the book. The older characters, like the immortal elf Galadriel, are often depressed by the history they have lived through: "Together through ages of the world we have fought the long defeat" (Tolkien *Lord* 357). Frodo inherits this war-weariness. Much of the action of the last third of the novel is the psychological and moral warfare the ring is waging on Frodo: the One Ring seeks to convert his war-weariness into despair. Despair will enable its master Sauron (or, perhaps, the One Ring itself is the true master) to destroy the world.

The perspective of the mature characters on the War of the Ring reflects Tolkien's view of the Second World War. The depression-prone king of a people who must survive the onslaught of Sauron's armies laments, "The young perish and the old linger, withering" (Tolkien *Lord* 517). The king later decries the state of his world: "The world changes, and all that once was strong now proves unsure. How shall any tower withstand such numbers and such reckless hate?" (539).

The threat of Sauron works well as an echo of the threat of Hitler. Even the creature Gollum, driven feral by the absence of the One Ring, which he once possessed, knows what will happen if Sauron succeeds: "He'll eat us all, if He gets it, eat all the world" (Tolkien *Lord* 637). However, Tolkien's perception of an apocalyptic threat need not have derived from observation of the Nazis. Tolkien was a devoted heir to both the "Northern" tradition and medieval Christianity—of Ragnarok and Christian millennialism.

His dismay at the effects of the war on English society also enters *The Lord of the Rings* around its edges. The hobbits return to find their beloved Shire diminished by bureaucratic malice. They are told, "Everything except Rules get shorter and shorter" (Tolkien *Lord* 1012). There are aspects of this episode (which the now-empowered hobbits take care of through force, to the disgust of the wounded, pacifist Frodo) which seem to briefly comment on post-war England. However, the chapter of "The Scouring of the Shire" (998) is also a natural outgrowth of earlier events in the novel which—like the entire epic—are primarily concerned with fictional events of Middle-earth, not Tolkien's England.

Some critics find Tolkien's work too narrow—an odd genre-work displaying the limitations (as they perceive it) of fantasy and of science fiction.[2] To the extent that Middle-earth comments on Earth, the novel is an implicit argument for the widening of humanity's perspective. This theme is introduced early in the novel in a brief exchange between Frodo and an elf. Frodo is overwhelmed by his burden, and outraged that he is in danger even in the Shire. He complains to his unsympathetic companion. The hobbits have many virtues, but Tolkien also portrays them as dangerously (not just charmingly) parochial. The elves and Gandalf often lose patience with the hobbits and the exaggerated sense of these little people that they are special. The elf tells Frodo, "The wide world is all about you: you cannot for ever fence it out" (Tolkien *Lord* 83).

The hobbits must learn not simply to "grow up," but to widen their perspective. The hobbits repeatedly meet forces beyond their little world. An extreme example of this is their meeting with Tom Bombadil. Bombadil is a folksy, almost silly, presence. Yet he is also enigmatic and powerful. Like Gandalf, he is not human, even though he appears to be at first sight. He is odd because his actions are not based on hobbit (or human) values. He is an ancient remnant of a force that predates civilization, although not a straightforward personification of nature. The hobbits find themselves in a world that predates not just hobbits but speech itself. They find that it is easier to sing than to speak in Bombadil's presence (*Tolkien* Lord 125). They learn not just that theirs is not the only way of life in the world, but that the world does not run in accordance with their way of thinking: "As they listened they began to understand the lives of the Forest, apart from themselves, indeed to feel themselves strangers where all other things were at home" (Tolkien *Lord* 129).

The world of Middle-earth is not merely a battleground between good and evil. There are many forces within it that are not concerned with the fight between good and evil. Some of these figures, like Bombadil, are benign. Others are malevolent, but have nothing to do with Sauron or his plans. Aragorn (the companion of the hobbits who restores kingship to Middle-earth) is aware of this and tries to explain this concept to his companions, who are wrapped up in the struggle for survival against evil (Tolkien *Lord* 289). Aragorn becomes king through his wisdom. In the film version, he is an appealing and (unusually for an action hero) humble character. However, unlike the Aragorn of the novel, the film character has no sense of this wide perspective and wisdom because these qualities are absent from the film itself.

A striking passage in the novel is characteristic of Tolkien's perspective. The fellowship is exhausted and fleeing from an overwhelming force of orcs. Their leader has just been lost. In addition to the immediate danger, they need to get out of the open country—the longer they are out in the wilderness, the more likely the forces of Sauron will discover the location of the One Ring. The dwarf in the party realizes that they have just run near to the location of a famous natural landmark celebrated in the legend of his people. He accosts a grieving (and fleeing) Frodo and makes a passionate plea to the hobbit to follow him for a moment to see this wonder. Frodo wearily complies. There is no discussion of the wisdom of this sightseeing detour, although Aragorn does redundantly urge them to make their excursion a quick one. The passage reads: "They stooped over the dark water. At first they could see nothing. Then slowly they saw the forms of the encircling mountains mirrored in a profound blue, and the peaks were like plumes of white flame above them; beyond there was a space of sky. There like jewels sunk in the deep shone glinting stars, though sunlight was in the sky above" (Tolkien *Lord* 334).

This episode is like the heroes of a thriller driving through the desert to disarm an activated nuclear device ... and then deciding to pull to the side of the road to take in a scenic overlook. Yet the digression is less an implausibility than an illustration of Tolkien's priorities. There is a detailed, consistent plot in *The Lord of the Rings,* but the author makes clear in both subtle and obvious ways throughout the epic that the nature and history of the world are more important than the plot of the story. He never lets the attentive reader forget that there are other things in Middle-earth besides a desperate struggle between good and evil. The films skip these incidents because they focus upon the plot—

which is largely a desperate struggle between good and evil. Few popular novels, even in the fantasy genre, would include such an incident with little relevance to plot or character.

The ring psychologically tortures Frodo, page after page, chapter after chapter. The brutal slog of Frodo and Sam (stripped of their companions) through stark landscapes in enemy territory comprises a large part of the second half of the novel. A broken Frodo describes this desolation in terms of his inability to remember the natural environment of his home country: "No taste of food, no feel of water, no sound of wind, no memory of tree or grass or flower, no image of moon or star are left to me. I am naked in the dark" (Tolkien *Lord* 937).

Tolkien describes nature in a remarkable number of lines in *The Lord of the Rings*. These descriptions are not ornamentations to the story but a major concern of the novel. Nature is central to the book to a unique degree. Tolkien uses the freedom of the fantasy genre to illustrate this: for example, the heroes encounter sentient trees, both maleficent and noble. Treebeard (who, like many characters and places in the novel, has different names in different languages of Middle-earth) is an unusual creation. In the distant past (when events were more mythical in character than in the current age of Middle-earth) elves spoke to trees and awakened a buried intelligence in a few of them. These awakened trees constituted a new race of creatures, the Ents. Treebeard is the leader of a small colony of this diminished race. Middle-earth is coming to the end of a long process of transition from a "magical" landscape to the domain of human history during the events of the novel. Some trees still retain a kind of passive sentience, and these are watched over by the handful of remaining Ents—giant tree-like creatures who walk and talk. The corrupted wizard Saruman has encroached upon the domain of the ancient forest of the Ents, recklessly sending his orcs to destroy the forest to provide fuel for his proto-industrial operations. Treebeard laments this destruction: "Many of those trees were my friends, creatures I had known from nut and acorn; many had voices of their own that are lost for ever now" (Tolkien *Lord* 474). Treebeard leads his Ents to war and defeats a shocked Saruman. The wizard prematurely calculated that the natural world had lost all of its power. Treebeard supports the cause of Gandalf and the heroes against Sauron, but is not an enthusiastic participant in the war: "I am not altogether on anybody's *side,* because nobody is altogether on my *side,* if you understand me: nobody cares for the woods as I care for them, not even Elves nowadays" (472).

Tolkien's emphasis on the woods was not a personal idiosyncrasy. A contemporary English editorial argues that trees are central to the British imagination: "In Britain's conception of itself ... the myth of the wooded island looms large. William Shakespeare put fairies in the forests. It was forestry that sheltered Robin Hood from tyranny. Oak built our navies which sailed the globe" ("Can't"). However, even if Tolkien's interest in nature was not unique, the enormous amount of description of the natural world in *The Lord of the Rings* is impressive.

Tolkien makes his most striking (implied) case for the worth of the unspoiled natural world in his constant descriptions of it. He does not segregate descriptions of nature in pastoral asides, but places them in all conceivable parts of his novel—for instance, between lines of dialogue, and during battles. The author lovingly describes trees, flowers, mountains, streams, hills, and rivers—both fantastic and mundane: "The night was clear, cool, and starry, but smoke-like wisps of mist were creeping up the hill-side from the streams and deep meadows. Thin-clad birches, swaying on a light wind above their heads, made a black net against the pale sky" (Tolkien *Lord* 71). Again: "Nodding on slender stalks were other flowers, white and palest green: they glimmered as a mist amid the rich hue of the grass" (350). No one in the novel would merely gather firewood: "Leaving the road they went into the deep resin-scented darkness of the trees, and gathered dead sticks and cones to make a fire" (72). He tends to describe architectural features as if they were natural: for example, a house with "hall opening out of hall, dome after dome, stair beyond stair; and still the winding paths led on into the mountain's heart" (Tolkien *Lord* 547).

Sauron often defeats humans, elves, and dwarves; but despite razing the countryside and occupying all lands under his sway, he is never able to defeat Middle-earth itself. Frodo and Sam pause in their trek through enemy lands in a country that was once civilized but has long since been desolated by Sauron. Frodo is disheartened by the sight of a beheaded statue of a king from ancient times, but Sam notices that a string of flowers has curled around the statue's head like a crown (Tolkien *Lord* 702).

A befuddled warrior asks the more experienced Aragorn: "Do we walk in legends or on the green earth in the daylight?" Aragorn replies: "A man may do both. For not we but those we come after will make the legends of our time. The green earth, say you? That is a mighty matter of legend, though you tread it under the light of day!" (Tolkien *Lord* 434). This is the voice of Tolkien himself, betrayed by the professorial cast of the lines. It is an encapsulation of Tolkien's attitude toward nature.

Scholar Steve Walker explores the author's style, discussing Tolkien's use of pathetic fallacy and personification: "As hobbits break out from the confining maze of the Old Forest ... they notice the sun in reinforcing parallel pattern 'escaping from the breaking clouds' ... that sort of emblematic reiteration of narrative situation occurs persistently in the trilogy, in hobbits smoking while Isengard smolders ... in Bilbo before a 'small bright fire' very like himself" (Walker 134).

Tolkien is not a Romantic poet or Gothic novelist. The nature he describes is not part of this world—it is supernatural as much as natural. He does not use pathetic fallacy: the trees in Middle-earth have some degree of sentience. Human characteristics are not being metaphorically foisted upon objects of the natural world, because Tolkien is not writing about the natural world. As scholar Neil Isaacs writes: "Tolkien's world is, after all, and most of all, *not* our world" (Isaacs 5).

However, Tolkien means for the treatment of the "nature" of Middle-earth in *The Lord of the Rings* to have moral implications. He judges characters to be either good or evil by their actions toward the "natural" world in Middle-earth rather than by any application of Catholic dogma. Tolkien intertwines nature and morality. Nature is an animate object in Middle-earth. In some cases in Middle-earth objects can freely choose between good and evil, as Tolkien believes that people can. Evil creatures in *The Lord of the Rings* are those that treat everything except for themselves as having no meaning. In the novel, treating nature as intrinsically valueless material useful only to build machines leads to treating people as valueless machine-parts. This attitude also destroys those who employ it: there is no real victory possible for Sauron—only defeat for everyone else. Even if the demon could conquer everything outside of himself, he would only succeed in self-destruction.

Tolkien was not alone in England in decrying the ethics of a society based on machines and power. Poet Richard Aldington (1892–1962) was born in the same year as Tolkien. Aldington was also a veteran of the First World War. He expressed his attitude towards contemporary values in his poem "Whitechapel" (1916). The third of five stanzas reads:

> Soot; mud;
> A nation maddened with labour;
> Interminable collision of energies—
> Iron beating upon iron;
> Smoke whirling upwards,
> Speechless, impotent.

He ends the poem: "Noise, iron, smoke; Iron, iron, iron" (Aldington 524).

Director Peter Jackson mostly ignores or deemphasizes the ethics of the novel in his films based on Tolkien's work (2001-present). The main theme of the films seems to be that humans, elves, hobbits, dwarves, and walking trees have to stick together and persevere in the face of overwhelming odds. Tolkien's son and literary executor, Christopher, was disgusted with Jackson's changes to the themes of the novel: "The chasm between the beauty and seriousness of the work, and what it has become, has overwhelmed me. The commercialization has reduced the aesthetic and philosophical impact of the creation to nothing" (Rérolle, section Action Movies, paragraph 4).

However, in place of thematic depth, the films offer more depth of character. Jackson and the screenwriters reinterpret the characters to fit in the modern dramatic tradition of film. For example, Aragorn is played as the anti–George W. Bush—humble and full of self-doubt. This reference to President Bush is not frivolous—the films were clearly influenced by the early years of the "war on terror." Some examples of this are obvious: one scene in *The Lord of the Rings: The Two Towers* (2002) has an orc acting as a suicide bomber! However, there are subtler signs of the times in the films. The most important of these is the overriding theme that the good (Western) people have to stick together and must not allow their differences to cause them to be estranged from each other in the face of Sauron (terrorism). The character of Aragorn in the novel has nothing to do with either President Bush or humility. Tolkien has Aragorn speak in a stilted and archaic manner: he is meant to be noble and heroic, but not in any sense like the reader. Tolkien seems to admire Aragorn in the novel, as he admired Beowulf, but he intends for the modern reader to identify with the hobbits.

Underneath the overwhelming focus on entertainment, the films seem to suggest that the story of *The Lord of the Rings* is a sort of plea for the United States, Britain, France, and Australia to hang together against Islamic terrorism. The films are notable for their impressive production design, music, and the unusually strong performances of the actors for a big-budget movie. The cast shot three films simultaneously, and developed into something closer to a theater company than, for instance, the cast of a *Star Wars* movie. The final film, *The Lord of the Rings: The Return of the King,* received the Academy Award for Best Picture in 2003. All such awards are subjective, but supporters of the movie can make a strong case that it was at least as good a film as the others nominated for Best Picture that year—such as *Seabiscuit* and *Lost in Translation.* Few fantasy films are comparable in quality to Peter Jackson's trilogy.

Early attempts at adapting the novel into a film highlight just how much of an improvement in quality were the 2001–2003 films. The first proposal for a film based on the novel was made in 1957. It was meant to be a three-hour film, perhaps a low-budget competitor to the biblical epics of the day (Croft "Three" 8). However, the movie was not likely to be a strong competitor against well-financed films like *The Ten Commandments* (1956): the proposed mixture of animation, live action, and miniatures with 1950s technology would have been a disaster.

Tolkien eventually sold the film rights of both *The Hobbit* and *The Lord of the Rings* to United Artists in 1969 for just over £104,000 (Croft "Three" 10). This was the equivalent of about $250,000 in 1969 (*Historical Rates* n.p.). This was no small sum—it is equivalent to the 2013 buying power of about $1.5 million (*CPI* n.p.).[3]

The United Artists film was supposed to be made by John Boorman, who had recently directed Lee Marvin in *Point Blank* (1967) and would go on to have a long career directing such well-received films as *Deliverance* (1972) and *Hope and Glory* (1987). The film was (mercifully) never made. A draft scenario by Boorman survives. A sample passage: "Gandalf ... leads Gimli through a primitive rebirthing ritual, making him dig a hole and crawl into it, covering him with a cloak and violently beating and verbally abusing him, until he springs forth with recovered memories of his forgotten ancestral language and speaks [the password]" (Croft "Three" 11). Despite Harold Bloom and other claimants to the contrary, *The Lord of the Rings* and the spirit of the late 1960s were never a good match.

Ralph Bakshi made an animated version of the novel in 1978. Bakshi was never given enough money to complete a version of the full story of *The Lord of the Rings,* so the action stops abruptly in the middle of the story. It is an odd adaptation that includes a memorable musical number featuring frog-like orcs bemoaning their fate as innocent pawns: "We don't wanna go to war today, but the lord of the lash says: 'Nay, nay, nay!' We're gonna march all day, all day, all day! Where there's a whip there's a way!" The film made almost eight times its budget, which suggests that by 1978 there was demand for any sort of adaptation of *The Lord of the Rings* ("Lord" IMDB).

The impressive production values and the strong performance of the cast of Peter Jackson's films make them notable popular films of the early twenty-first century. They miss most of the thematic depth of the novel, but probably no more than most film adaptations of Shakespeare or Jane Austen miss the larger meanings of their sources. Jackson has continued his Middle-earth adaptations with three films based on *The Hobbit.* The first of the films, *The Hobbit: An Unexpected Journey* (2012), is a bloated disaster—as might be expected when one children's book is stretched into three long movies.

The journey of J. R. R. Tolkien through the turbulent twentieth century was a long one: from the prologue of the Boer War era in southern Africa, to the early chapters of being rescued by Catholic priests and a love of languages, to the horror of young manhood during the World War, to a career at Oxford, to a wife and four children, to a climax of unexpected literary fame. The journey of the fellowship of heroes in *The Lord of the Rings* is also long. After a thousand pages of great deeds, it ends quietly. Sam Gamgee leaves his damaged friend Frodo with the elves. Frodo has been too wounded by the war to live in hobbit society. He will spend his final days peacefully with the elves. Sam makes his way back to the small rural village of his home—Tolkien's idealization of the rural England of his youth. Sam is weary. His wife puts his young daughter in his arms, welcoming him home. The last line of the book: "Well, I'm back" (Tolkien *Lord* 1031).

III

Robert E. Howard
(1906–1936)

I never could understand why anybody should ever have begun
to live at Dillsborough, or why the population there should have
been at any time recruited by new comers. That a man with a
family should cling to the house in which he has once established
himself is intelligible. The butcher who supplied Dillsborough, or
the baker, or the ironmonger, though he might not drive what is
called a roaring trade, nevertheless found himself probably able
to live, and might well hesitate before he would encounter the
dangers of a more energetic locality. But how it came to pass that
he first got himself to Dillsborough, or his father, or his grandfa-
ther before him, has always been a mystery to me. The town has
no attractions, and never had any.
—*Anthony Trollope, The American Senator*

Country doctor Isaac Mordecai Howard moved his family to Cross
Plains, Texas, in 1919 (Finn 43). No one knows why. Perhaps he hoped
that oil, the greatest of all twentieth-century American attractions, would
come to town and bring "civilization." He may have hoped that prosperous clients would allow his practice to thrive and support his wife Hester
Ervin Howard and their thirteen-year-old son, Robert Ervin Howard.
Whatever Dr. Howard's motivation, civilization gained a life-long enemy
in Robert E. Howard.

Howard was a proud Texan, but he did not romanticize the country
he lived in. He fictionalized the landscape around Cross Plains in a story,
writing, "The sky was lurid, gloomy and repellent, of the blue of tar-
nished steel, streaked with dully crimson banners. Against the muddled
red smear lowered the low hills that are the peaks of that barren upland

which is a dreary expanse of sand drifts and post-oak thickets, checkered with sterile fields where tenant farmers toil out their hideously barren lives in fruitless labor and bitter want" (Finn 160).

Howard writes in a letter that the countryside around Cross Plains looked "not unpleasing to the sight" in the summer. The view was different in the winter: "a weary brown—brown earth, brittle brown trees—even the sky seems brownish." He captures the look of his town in one line: "The town presents an appearance about like the thousand other small West Texas towns—one wide main street, unpaved back alleys, oil derricks rising up here and there all over the business and residential sections" (Howard *Letters* 2: 521).

He continues his description with a wearying catalogue, typical of similar passages in many of his letters, of the precise racial and ethnic strains of various groups in Cross Plains. He writes, "There are no negroes in the county, and but a very few Mexicans" (Howard *Letters* 2: 523). He is concerned with more than just non-whites. He details the vaguely sinister presence of "Teutonic and Scandinavian strains" of recent oil-boom settlers (Howard *Letters* 2: 522). These aliens come from such foreign lands as Pennsylvania and Kansas. This concern is odd because he explains a few paragraphs before this passage that the entire area was originally settled by Germans. Whatever the ethnic shortcomings of the Teutonic and Nordic interlopers, he writes that at least these people "assimilate," unlike the "dark-skinned breeds" of Italians and American Indians.

Howard is also interested in the history of Cross Plains: "Some twenty years ago the coming of the rail-road caused the whole town to be moved perhaps half a mile to the east, to its present location. That's a peculiarity of many Texas towns; the first settlers were inclined to build as near the banks of creeks and streams as possible; later the towns were moved up on higher grounds, because of various reasons—or sometimes for no apparent reason" (Howard *Letters* 2: 521). He lived in a town that had to uproot its buildings to make way for the economic interests of the East. He resented it.

He felt that the history of Texas was a history of subjugation. All the achievements of the Lone Star state could not make up for losing the Civil War. Howard still felt this shame seventy years after the end of the war. He also resented his personal history. He had worked hard at making something of himself as a writer, but received no praise from his community. He felt like an outsider in his own town surrounded by locals who could not relate to his work. This web of resentments shrouded him until he shot himself at thirty.

Robert E. Howard needed a fantasy world. So he made one with his stories:

> Know, oh prince, that between the years when the ocean drank Atlantis and the gleaming cities, and the years of the rise of the Sons of Aryas, there was an Age undreamed of, when shining kingdoms lay spread across the world like blue mantles beneath the stars—Nemedia, Ophir, Brythunia, Hyperborea, Zamora with its dark-haired women and towers of spider-haunted mystery, Zingara with its chivalry, Koth that bordered on the pastoral lands of Shem, Stygia with its shadow-guarded tombs, Hyrkania whose riders wore steel and silk and gold. But the proudest kingdom of the world was Aquilonia, reigning supreme in the dreaming west. Hither came Conan, the Cimmerian, black-haired, sullen-eyed, sword in hand, a thief, a reaver, a slayer, with gigantic melancholies and gigantic mirth, to tread the jeweled thrones of the Earth under his sandaled feet.—The Nemedian Chronicles ["Phoenix" ch. 1].

These are the first words of the first Conan story. The passage is unique and beautiful. Fantasists before and since have tried to accomplish the same setting of scene, but none has succeeded in painting a world in a paragraph. Many have tried and failed to accomplish the same feat in a series of books. These lines have hooked boys on fantasy for life like so many adolescent, adventure-craving fish.

Howard worked in genres, but his writing is anything but generic. Where did his style come from? It is hard to compare him to another literary figure. It is also hard to imagine a mainstream market in the 1930s that would have published his Conan stories.

There is a sense of wonder and innocence in the passage above not typical of his personal letters. The tone of his letters is not universally morose. He writes of his passion for boxing and the joy he felt traveling through Texas and the Southwest. He writes of his zest for homemade ice cream and his greater zest for prohibited bottles of beer. He writes

III. *Robert E. Howard (1906–1936)*

many poems in his letters, and expresses a great interest in history. However, there are many passages bristling with resentment and racism and despair. The Great Depression and the catastrophic political events of the 1930s leading to the Second World War did not brighten his outlook. He writes about what did bring wonder into his life:

> Magazines were even more scarce than books. It was after I moved into "town" (speaking comparatively) that I began to buy magazines. I well remember the first I ever bought. I was fifteen years old. I bought it one summer night when a wild restlessness in me would not let me keep still, and I had exhausted all the reading material on the place. I'll never forget the thrill it gave me. Somehow it never occurred to me that I could buy a magazine. It was an *Adventure*. I still have the copy [Howard *Letters* 3: 87].

Pulp magazines were a unique part of Howard's adolescence. He could not go to the town library for books because there was no public library in Cross Plains until 1978 (Finn 49). He had built up a personal library by the time of his death. Some of these books must have been given to him during his youth, as some of the titles are boys' adventure books and Horatio Alger novels (Burke). Books were not common in the area: according to a June 1931 survey of five central Texas counties the Bible was the only book in one-third of the households. The survey also reported that half of the respondents heated and cooked their households with wood, and biographer L. Sprague de Camp claims that "90 percent of women boiled their clothes in a big iron pot in the yard" (de Camp 134).

Radio might have offered a link to life outside his hometown, but it was not available in his youth. A *Cross Plains Review* article includes the sixteen year-old Howard in a list of locals working to install "radio wires" at the Cozy Drug store (Finn 44). He writes of going to a theater to hear a radio broadcast of The Jack Dempsey–Jack Sharkey heavyweight match when he was twenty-one, "Dempsey finished Sharkey with a terrible smash to the jaw that came clearly over the air like the sound of a woodsman's axe cleaving a tree-trunk"[1] (Howard *Letters* 2: 473). He listened to the international situation deteriorate in his last years. He writes of a speech by Mussolini in 1935 justifying an invasion of what is now Ethiopia, calling it a "sickening and nauseating outspewing of blustering hypocrisy ... though I found equally revolting the brainless cheers of the thousands of poor idiots he is leading to the shambles" (Howard *Letters* 3: 370). He could and did see movies in his youth. The main street in Cross Plains was unpaved until 1928, but there were already two movie theaters on it (de Camp 129–30). Still, he could not re-read a movie or watch it in his bed at night. *Adventure* was a unique part of his life.

Reading *Adventure* wasn't like reading *Life* or *Time*. It was an invitation to a brotherhood. The issue of *Adventure* published on July 3, 1921, is from the year he bought his first magazine. It is an impressive issue whose 192 densely-packed pages (largely uninterrupted by advertising) promised readers like the fifteen year-old Howard entry to a miraculous sort of adulthood. The *Adventure* man was manly, but not boorish; adult, but not boring.

The "Lost Trails" column for locating former comrades bound *Adventure* readers together. Robert L. Ziller of Austin, Texas, sought lost friend Charles Hamilton, describing him as "British aviator in late war. Occasionally called 'The Grasshopper.'" Charles J. ("Mac") Macguire wrote to members of a French artillery battalion, "Any men of this outfit will learn something to their advantage." This notice seems to promise an adventure of its own for any man of "Battery B" brave enough to respond. Some trails, like that of a Scottish carpenter last seen in Cleveland forty-eight years before, seem sadly unlikely ever to be picked up again. The editors attempted to prevent the column's being used for romantic reunions, informing contributors that except for family, "inquiries from one sex to the other are barred." They may not have been successful. Paul Rosenblum wrote that he was looking for "A.T. Daly [who was] ... in Medical Corps at General Hospital, P.I. 1916. Was associated with me in Philippine Carnival in a show called 'Darktown Cabaret'[2] (*Adventure* 191).

The magazine did not merely include a letters column, but ran an impressive answering service. "Ask Adventure" offered a panel of experts in forty different fields with carefully detailed specialties to answer questions for the price of postage (*Adventure* 187). Curious about the produce of Portuguese East Africa? Write to R.W. Waring of

Ontario, Canada. Wondering about the historical use of pikes? Lewis Appleton Barker of Brookline, Massachusetts was your man. Several questions and their answers were published each month. In this issue readers learned many fascinating facts: that "ladies alone can travel with perfect safety ... from Japan through Indo-China and the Straits Settlements to Burma and India"; that a Cree-English dictionary written several years before by a Canadian archbishop named McKay could be obtained from the Manitoba Synod (188), that it was quite possible to learn to throw a knife. Trees, household pets, and little brothers across America may have had reason to complain about the magazine's somewhat reckless distribution of knife lore: it told its readers to "take blade by tip and cast it vigorously, with the tiniest of turning motions" (*Adventure* 189). This was the kind of school that could encourage Howard's intellectual curiosity far away from the "confinement" and "clock-regularity of everything" that he hated in his mundane school. He found *Adventure* full of wonder, but free of teachers who presumed they had the right "to question my actions and interfere with my thoughts" (Howard *Letters* 3: 31).

The king of "Various Practical Services Free to Any Reader" was the *Adventure* identification card. A reader received a free card by sending his or her address and the address of his or her next-of-kin. The card was printed with a serial number and the following inscription written in several languages: "In case of death or serious emergency to bearer, address serial number of this card, care of Adventure, New York, stating full particulars, and friends will be notified." Waylaid in a wadi? An encounter with a cutthroat in Cathay didn't go your way? Card-bearers had peace of mind. A solicitous native would find your *Adventure* card and return it to the magazine's New York offices—ideally with a letter describing your demise. Language was no barrier because the staff was full of linguists. The magazine would match the serial number on the card with the next-of-kin information on file and cheerfully send out both notification and explanation of the adventurer's doom. The stamped metal version cost a quarter, but promised superior survivability. This may be the most impressive membership card of all time. The editors of the magazine were justly proud of their product, and proclaimed, "A moment's thought will show the value of this system of card-identification for any one, whether in civilization or out of it" (*Adventure* 183).

Robert E. Howard was not a fan of civilization, but with features like those it is not surprising he was a fan of the magazine. He was not alone. Celebrities like Theodore Roosevelt were also fans, and *Adventure* had an impressive peak circulation of 300,000 a month (Belk, paragraph 5). The features of the magazine were appealing, but the bulk of the magazine contained adventure stories of all kinds.

The July 3, 1921, issue included an installment of a serial by the Italian-born British historical novelist Rafael Sabatini. Gentleman pirate Peter Blood lived the kind of adventure just not available in Cross Plains[3]: "In old Tortuga, that nest of piracy, the captain took his ease, what time his eight-score reckless followers gamed and drank and squandered in excess the gold they had brought back from their last raid upon the sea-going subjects of the King of Spain" (*Adventure* 71).

Sabatini had been a successful author for over a decade, but his debut in *Adventure* introduced him to the American audience and made his fortune (DeForest 38). Sabatini was only the ninth author billed on the July 3 cover, but the serial in *Adventure* would lead the author to treasure. The serial starred gentleman pirate Peter Blood and was published as *Captain Blood: His Odyssey* the next year. The novel led to the silent film *Captain Blood* (1924). Warner Brothers remade the movie in 1935. The film launched the career of Errol Flynn. Sabatini received $30,000 for the sale of movie rights—the equivalent of over $400,000 in 2013 dollars (CPI).

"The Grand Cham" by Harold Lamb is another notable story in the July 3, 1921, issue. Lamb was a favorite of the readership (Jones 6). *Adventure* published more than forty of his stories over two decades. Lamb and Howard share a sensibility.

"The Grand Cham" opens with evocative and intentionally pompous language: "The sun was a glimmering ball of red, peering through a haze of dust at the caravan of Bayezid the Great, surnamed the Thunderbolt, Sultan of the Osmanli and Seljuke Turks, master of the Caliphate and overlord of the Mamelukes of Egypt" (Lamb 111). The ornamental language has a purpose beyond exoticism. Lamb builds up the oppressive and overweening authority of Bayezid until it crashes into the defiance of the hero. Michael Bearn, another hero with an Irish mother, finds himself a Turkish prisoner in "the year of Our Lord 1394." The Irish mariner is not only out of place in the Anatolian desert, but in horrible danger from the egomaniacal sultan and his obsequious followers.

The unrestrained authority of the Eastern tyrant against the Western individual is a literary conflict as old as Herodotus. Bearn is ordered by the sultan to abase himself. He replies, "I hear ... I will not obey" (Lamb 112). This line is more reminiscent of Howard's work than Sabatini's. Errol Flynn could have delivered the line, but in one of his films the sultan would have admired his courage and freed him. The sultan in this story is less impressed with Bearn's derring-do. He uses an instrument of torture that breaks Bearn's arm and grinds the ends of the break together.

Bearn survives and launches an epic quest for vengeance that is absorbed by a larger world. He moves from the slaughter of a Crusader army to intrigue at the Maritime Council of Venice to a quest to Cathay to find "the Great Cham" and, ultimately, into the presence of the conqueror Tamerlane. The mood of the piece is adventurous but dark. In an aside, Bearn speculates that only those who have never seen war could believe in God (Lamb 171). The "Grand Cham" of the title is a sham. Bearn uses the mythical figure to bilk his Venetian backers into financing his quest for vengeance. Bearn's sidekick (a fool in the medieval sense) takes his share of the spoils at the end of the novel and establishes a castle in the realm awarded to Bearn by Tamerlane. By the end of the novel the Great Cham, mysterious ruler of the East, is not only sought by fools; he is a fool. Lamb expresses skepticism about human nature and religion in the guise of a historical romance.

Adventure favorite Talbot Mundy did not have a story in the July 3 issue, but was a favorite of Howard's (Burke). Mundy is the perfect fulfillment of the myth that writers of adventure are rogues who live adventurous lives themselves. He started life as William Lancaster Gribble in

London before becoming a man of the world. Pulp historian Tim DeForest writes that "Mundy ... had been an ivory poacher and a con artist, who seemed to have had one or two more wives than is strictly allowed by Western law" (DeForest 40–41).

Howard would later attempt to portray himself as, if not a rogue, then a man of the world in his letters to colleagues and publishers. This was difficult for a man who lived his life within feet of his parents' bedroom. He may have been trying to live up to an ideal formed reading *Adventure* in his youth. The most famous twentieth-century author with an "adventurous" image was Ernest Hemingway. He was only seven years older than Howard. They may have been exposed to similar ideas about what an American writer should be.

Fourteen years after Mundy was first published in *Adventure*, he introduced a series that has been called his most memorable and perhaps the best series ever published in *Adventure* (DeForest 41). The conflict between its hero, Tros of Samothrace, and the devious Julius Caesar during Caesar's campaigns against Britain incited a passionate debate in the letter column of *Adventure*. Some readers defended the Roman Empire against Mundy. Howard continued this debate years later with his great forensic opponent H. P. Lovecraft. For Howard, this was a debate between barbarism (good, Celtic, Western, himself) and civilization (evil, anglophile, Eastern, Lovecraft).

Howard tries to maintain a decorous tone in his debates, but in the end Lovecraft aggravates him too much to maintain this facade: "I was deeply interested in your remarks concerning the Roman occupation of Britain.... If I thought I had a drop of Roman blood in my veins, I'd be glad to take a knife and let it out. My pride in my distant ancestors is not based on the fact that they were conquered by the Romans, but on the fact that they whipped the socks off those big-shot racketeers of antiquity" (Howard *Letters* 3: 232). He is responding to Lovecraft's pompous championing of imperialism. However, he is not just opposing imperialism. He dismisses Romans as a bunch of Al Capones in togas. Ancient Rome was the urban and cosmopolitan head of a multiethnic empire. He disapproves of all of these concepts. Rome may also have had too much in common with his least favorite powers of history: the

British Empire, oppressors of the Irish; and the Union during the Civil War, oppressors of the South.

Adventure set the tone for Howard's life. There are three major biographies of that life: a psychoanalytical biography by Conan's popularizer L. Sprague de Camp, a more recent biography focusing on his Texas roots by Mark Finn, and Howard's own autobiographical writings. Howard included biographical information in his letters, and wrote an autobiographical novel while he was still a young man, years before he created Conan.

Post Oaks and Sand Roughs is both an autobiography and an attempt at a modern novel. It was not published until 1982. He mentions the project in a letter written in 1928 (Howard *Letters* 1: 291). This was about four years after the publication of his first story in *Weird Tales* and about four years before the publication of his first Conan story. He was twenty-two and shows little distance from his protagonist, "Steve Costigan." He uses his personal letters as notes for the book, at times transcribing whole passages into the novel. His lack of perspective cripples the book as art. He never attempted anything like it again.

The novel opens with Steve at a football game, thinking, "Tear their god damn guts out! Kill the bastards! Let the other rooters urge for a touchdown, which only symbolized their desire for blood!" (Howard *Post* 11). Steve takes everything, especially himself, too seriously. His rage starts out as normal, but he fears he is in the grip of overly dark impulses. He is caught in a cycle of expressing his rage, feeling guilty about expressing his rage, and defensively overstating his next claim because he is angry about feeling guilty.

Howard writes, "At any rate, no matter what the contest might be, he always found himself taking sides with violent partisanship" (*Post* 11). This is the most important insight into Howard's psychology. His "violent partisanship" gave him the ability to write with tremendous energy and immediacy in his Conan stories. Howard cares if an opponent's sword strikes Conan or whether Conan pivots and shatters the ribs of his foe. An attack on Conan is an attack on Howard and everything he believes in. Howard is a partisan, not a chronicler.

This partisanship makes his prose special, but it also leads him astray. It is one thing for him to feel so passionate about a football game that he screams for his team to tear "their god damn guts out." It is another for him to "cheer" with the same passion for his "teams" in history, such as the Confederacy.

History serves Howard as an endless procession of racial conflicts from which he can choose sides. These identifications can be ridiculous. He writes that he is impressed with a priest he has met, "a scholar of the highest order, and a purely Nordic type" (Howard *Letters* 2: 299). This is apparently a surprise to him: "I always had a prejudice against Hessians, dating from Revolutionary days." This is an almost unbelievable prejudice. He is using biases he may have developed from reading a boys' history of the Revolutionary War to dictate his reactions to the world. His historical grudges can be both obscure and eternal. Washington's crossing of the Delaware and defeat of the German mercenaries had not cleaned the slate for him.

Howard held onto so many historical animosities that even he could not keep them straight. His "horror and rage" (Howard *Letters* 2: 412) at the torture and execution of William Wallace led to a tangle of competing resentments: "a savage satisfaction at the memories of King's Mountain and New Orleans, with the British soldiers falling like ripe grain before the American rifles—yet I deplore the Scottish groups that fell there."[4] There is a sense in his letters that he must go through a calculus of historical grievances to determine his reaction to any given ethnic group or nationality.

Racial prejudice is a fearsomely broad field for Howard. He warns of a sinister racial threat in a personal letter: "This race has swarmed into Texas in large numbers, following the oil fields, and most of them are easily recognized by their large noses and dark, almost—and sometimes—swarthy skins. Was that their original complexion, or have they mixed with some Latin or Slavic invader since coming to America?" (Howard *Letters* 2: 288) He again mentions these "primitive hill people" (2: 302) in a later letter. Who are these malefactors? "Pennsylvania Dutch"—the Amish. It is not clear what threat these Plain People roustabouts pose. Perhaps they are going to perform some demonic barn-raising and sacrifice of Anglo-Irish Texans?[5] There is no racial or national group or subgroup too obscure to escape his prejudice. Howard's racism illustrates that he had already constructed a fantasy world long before he wrote the first Conan story.

He was aware of his prejudice. He writes about his novel *Post Oaks and Sand Roughs*, "I wouldn't take it myself if I were a publisher.... I've cursed out every known cult, creed and nationality in it" (Howard *Letters* 1: 290). Actually, *Post Oaks and Sand Roughs* contains no significant reference to race or ethnicity. He writes of personal pain and rage, not generalized prejudice.

Much of the novel deals with his struggle to write. Steve meets Lars, a writer in the realist tradition. The meeting focuses Steve's attention on his own artistic and economic inferiority. He thinks, "Doubtless his stuff was worthless and trashy ... his wild fantasies were only moon mist and shadow, dark children of his own brain, while Lars wrote solid cross sections of life dealing with flesh and blood. This was, surely, superior to fantasy—and moreover Lars received two cents a word, while he, Steve, got only half a cent" (Howard *Post* 37). Steve struggles with the need both to express and conceal himself. "He felt that his stories blazoned in the sight of the world all the imperfections and mistakes of his character and his life" (41). Steve does not have the experience to know that these feelings are normal.

Steve's decision to be a writer isolates him. He feels guilty that he has not pursued a career more acceptable to Cross Plains society. "He could have easily got a job in the oilfields as roustabout or roughneck, that is: unskilled labor; but his mother did not want him to, dreaded the heavy work and objected to the company in which he would be thrown; and Steve used her objections as an excuse. The real fact was he was too lazy, even if his weak heart could have stood the heavy work" (Howard *Post* 70).

Howard was not lazy. He wrote thousands of pages without any assurance that they would be published or that he would be paid. However, his mother may have influenced his choice of career. The writing profession had a unique advantage for Robert and his mother: it kept them within feet of each other in the family home during working hours.

Post Oaks and Sand Roughs shows that all of Steve's attempts to work outside the home end badly. He is conned by his boss the postmaster, "a lanky dolt with a predilection for petty graft" (68). The postmaster pays Steve a minuscule "training wage" for a month, but promises to pay a good wage once he is established. He blithely rescinds his promise, earning a place on Steve's "enemies list."

Howard cannot capitalize on the inherent humor of many of the situations described in the book because the pain and embarrassment of his early career is too recent. Steve moves directly from embarrassment to resentment. The problem of the novel is that Howard moves with him. One scene in the book could have been pure comedy. Steve had previously flirted with a girl accompanying his best friend. He holds on to an exaggerated sense of guilt from this transgression. One day Steve and his friend are in the school library together. Steve sees the girl walk into the room. He jumps out of a window without thinking: "An open window was near and he took advantage of it" (Howard *Post* 71). Instead of focusing on the absurdity and comic possibilities of this overreaction, Howard follows Steve's resentful musings: "The librarian came running, anxious, womanlike, to poke her nose into something that does not concern her" (72).

Steve portrays himself as someone largely ignorant of many types of poetry. He "had not the slightest idea of what a sonnet might be, had always preferred ballads and narrative poems, and had read only such of the moderns as he had come upon in magazines" (Howard *Post* 87). He is about twenty at this time. Nevertheless, he has a favorite poet. He and a friend debate whether Rudyard Kipling or Robert W. Service is the greatest poet of all-time: "Steve leaned toward Kipling, because, as he said, Service wrote a few rotten poems, but Kipling never did" (74).

Steve seeks to learn more about poetry on his own and opens himself up to a wider world (although there is no evidence he ever cottoned to sonnetry). He "discovered Wilde, Swinburne.... New vistas opened to him. He thrilled and expanded as he read. He sought poetry and more poetry" (Howard *Post* 87). These poets are mentioned in Howard's letters, along with Omar Khayyam; but their poetry is never discussed in detail. However, Howard's own poetry is a constant feature of his early letters. The primary purpose of many of them seems to be to send poems to his friends.

The narrative covers an exciting event in Howard's early writing career—his first personalized rejection letter from *Venturer's Magazine* (a thinly disguised version of his beloved *Adventure*). Steve is thrilled and grateful for more than a form-letter rejection. However, this gratitude brings fear. "He stopped sending stories there, for fear that, as he put it, 'the editor would get such a rotten opinion of him that he would buy anything, anytime.' Which was about as logical as most of [his] conclusions, and symbolized his fear of offending or disappointing someone, even someone he had never seen" (Howard *Post* 76). Howard did submit more material to *Adventure* later in his career, but this episode shows an intense fear of rejection that he usually covered with bluster in his letters.

The best passage in the novel is a short dialogue that he also used in a letter to a friend (Howard *Letters* 1: 72). He parodies the message he hears from his society: "Jerk out of it dreamer! This century is no time for visions; go root with the rest of the herd. Money, that's the stuff. Boost, don't knock. Be a hustlin' he-man, a go-getter, grab the business. That's the stuff. Give 'em a square deal, but be sure an beat 'em" (79).

This passage is part of a long tradition that doesn't end with Howard. Compare the passage to this tirade from the 1960 *Twilight Zone* episode "A Stop at Willoughby": "This is a push business, Williams.... Push and drive! ... It's push-push-push, all the way, all the time, right on down the line!" (Serling). The jargon and mindless repetition of American business enraged writers of different eras.

Twentieth-century America had no monopoly on these sentiments. A famous author wrote something similar in *Our Mutual Friend* (1865): "Where does he come from? Shares. Where is he going to? Shares. What are his tastes? Shares. Has he any principles? Shares ... Perhaps he never of himself achieved success in anything, never originated anything, never produced anything? Sufficient answer to all; Shares. O mighty Shares!" (Dickens n.p.).

Howard knew Dickens, but was not much of a fan.[6] He could not abide the "spineless cringing crawling characters he portrays. I don't doubt he was drawing them true to life, but that realization makes the matter more damnable. Nicholas Nickleby was about the only one of his characters that had any guts at all. Why good gad, his characters submitted to indignities and insults and outrages that made me grind my teeth merely to read about. And I'm a peaceable man" (Howard *Letters* 2: 470). He felt he had to submit to enough indignities, insults, and outrages in his own life.

Food service was a particularly poor career choice for Steve. Unfortunately for his sanity, he chooses to work as a soda jerk. Howard characterizes the soda fountain as a rough-and-tumble dive bar. This episode does take place during Prohibition; a soda fountain patronized by exhausted oil workers might feel somewhat like a bar. However, Howard exaggerates the iniquity of what is a drug store serving up ice-cream sodas.

He writes, "Steve hated his job worse than he had ever hated any task, and contempt and apprehension which he felt toward the mass of oil field workers grew to a fear and venomous hatred of dangerous and abnormal size" (Howard *Post* 93). This passage is rare in Howard's work because it identifies fear as a source of Howard's intense personality. This fear would prove to be a source of strength in his best stories, but it must also have made dealing with people painful.

The long hours and raw fear involved in facing the public unbalance Steve: "If he worked very much longer at this hellish job, he would in a moment of semi-insanity, either kill or be killed. As for killing, he had no scruples; in the hate he felt for all connected with the oil game, he would have shot down or stabbed any of them with as little compunction as he would have killed a snake, and with much more real enjoyment" (Howard *Post* 99).

Steve tries another job, but ends up exploding at his boss when the authority figure dares to confront him about being twenty minutes late for his first day of work. "'I understand you are a poet'" the employer says. "'You may now explain your being late by saying that you stopped to write a sonnet about a little flower you saw on the way, Mr. Costigan' … The man laughed hatefully. He was putting this sullen young barbarian in his place." The boss' triumph does not last long. Steve beats him senseless: "The youth grinned savagely and smashed his right fist into the flabby, bloody face, again and again" (Howard *Post* 145). Steve has done what Howard wanted Dickens's characters to do. Howard is not interested in "Please sir, I want some more." He wants, "Bastard, have some more of my fist!"

Most of *Post Oaks and Sand Roughs* is based on Howard's personal letters. He doesn't seem to know where to take the narrative after this apocalyptic assault. An interesting late passage has Steve writing the book that the reader is reading. He gives a review of the book in which he is a character: "It was too vague, too disconnected, too full of unexplained and trivial incidents—too much like life in a word" (Howard *Post* 141). This comment is not an apt description of the novel, but it is a revealing insight into how Howard felt about life.

Steve rides off into the sunset in a bus leaving, as Howard never would, for a life beyond his corner of Texas. Even so, Steve's state of mind is not triumphant: "Bewildered and baffled by life, full of savagery he could not control and knew not where to direct, hurling his ferocity at random against what seemed to him to be obstacles, battered and beaten, never winning, never admitting defeat, doomed to go down that rough road forever. Was that Steve Costigan's fate?" (Howard *Post* 158). Was that Robert Howard's fate?

He would not go down that rough road forever. Steve advises a writer friend in the novel, "You'll succeed if you don't die or kill yourself in a moment of depression" (Howard *Post* 156). Howard would admit defeat with his suicide ten years later. In that decade he clawed out a career from nothing. *Post Oaks and Sand Roughs* is not just the obscure juvenilia of a pulp author. Along with his personal letters' it shows the raw material of a fantasy world that has already survived eighty years longer than its maker. The Hyborian Age is not just far-off lands that never were, but a creation of Howard's emotions. Conan is not a mindless brute, nor are his stories simple power fantasies. The barbarian transmuted the pain in Howard's life into heroism by artistic alchemy.

Fans of Robert E. Howard have preserved an impressive amount of autobiographical writing considering his obscurity during his lifetime. However, there are few first-person accounts of Howard. Biographer L.

Sprague de Camp places a lot of emphasis on comments by E. Hoffman Price, a pulp writer who detoured to Cross Plains with his apparently patient new bride on a cross-country honeymoon trip. Price gives a pedestrian account of the visit that tells little about Howard except that he was a large, soft-spoken man. His summary of the brief visit is oddly sensational, calling the writer "a strange character: gracious, likeable, congenial—and nutty as an almond bar" (de Camp 250). Price does not give much information to justify his conclusion. He spent only a few hours with Howard. Price was a pulp fiction writer whose work was forgotten during his lifetime. He may have resented Howard's fame.

Fortunately, there is one person who knew Howard and wrote extensively about him. Novalyn Price dated him in the Thirties. She was an aspiring writer in her late twenties when she came to Cross Plains to teach high school. She left town for graduate school before his suicide. She wrote a memoir of their relationship fifty years later. By this time Conan was famous and de Camp had been painting a dismissive, Freudian portrait of Howard for years. Price tries both to tell the story of the Bob Howard she knew and to insert her own uncelebrated life story.

One Who Walked Alone by Novalyn Price Ellis (1986) is the story of two young people who were deeply interested in the profession of writing, but lived in an environment hostile to it. Price was better-read and better-educated than Howard, but carried the burden of being a woman in small-town Texas in the 1930s. Even though she was two years younger than Howard, she felt pressure to settle down. Price was a teacher because it was the only socially acceptable literary career open to her, but she dreamed of writing. She was first interested in him because he was a professional writer, but she started to fall in love with him when he took her literary aspirations seriously. This was not an anomaly. Howard shows empathy and respect for women throughout his letters and stories.

She believed in his writing, particularly in his stylistic abilities. She argued with colleagues in her English department that attention should be paid to Howard's poetic language rather than the pulp subject-matter. She attempted to get them to see him as a writer like Poe—a man with perhaps objectionable taste, but with a vibrant, poetic style. She gives up with a Parthian shot: "Someday, some English teacher will be telling kids to write like Bob" (Ellis 84). The teachers were skeptical. However, many bestselling authors and screenwriters today could learn from his style. He uses adjectives and action to replace extensive narrative exposition and avoids the bloated page-counts of many contemporary writers.

This advocacy does not mean that Price enjoyed or understood the Conan stories she read. She was fascinated more by the question of why he wrote the stories than by the stories themselves. She asked him again and again to explain what he was trying to accomplish with his Conan stories. She sensed that they were not disposable. Howard gamely attempted to answer her questions in many different ways.

His early attempts to explain his writing used clichés. For example, "The people who read my stuff want to get away from this modern, complicated world with its hypocrisy, its cruelty, its dog-eat-dog life. They want to go back to the origin of the human race. The civilization we live in is a hell of a lot more sinister than the time I write about. In those days, girl, men were men and women were women. They struggled to stay alive, but the struggle was worth it" (Ellis 63). She was not satisfied by explanations like these.

She wrote, "Who cares about barbarians.... It's real people—real live people—I want to write about" (Ellis 20). She told him, "I want to know what kind of comment you make about life in your Conan stories." He answered more honestly as he grew to trust her and "began to talk of good and evil in life. He said that life was always a struggle between good and evil, and people like to read about that struggle.... He said he wasn't about to write those psychological yarns that sophisticated, half-educated people went for" (Ellis 151).

He tried to explain the appeal of his Conan stories. He talked about the nature of evil in his stories, and revealed a lot about himself in the guise of explaining the needs of his market: "He wrote for readers who wanted evil to be something big, horrible, but still something a barbarian like Conan could overcome. Evil could be found in another person who was about to kill you, or it could be found in a different race of people, a witch, a ghost, or some manifestation of the supernatural" (Ellis 151).

Their debates about literature reveal conflicting world views. She was literal-minded and sought to find her place in a society that constricted her, while he was prone to fantastic thinking and could barely control his anger at even the thought that he might have to conform to society. She wrote, "He says its better to take life the way Conan does … he can shake off involvement and go on to new fights and new adventures without worrying about *why* things were as they were. I said that sometimes bad things were just below the surface and that they might determine life or death … as it sometimes does in a Henry James novel. Bob said, 'To hell with Henry James'" (Ellis 83).

Henry James is mentioned several times in the memoir. The pair discussed the novella *Daisy Miller* during a drive in the country. The story concerns the conflicting mores of an American society girl and European aristocrats' which leads to her tragic death. Price believed that Daisy was "too dumb or too selfish" to follow the conventions of European society, thus leading to death rather than the wealth and happiness she might have had (Ellis 152). Howard was so angered by this interpretation that he ran off the road. He was shocked at the assertion that an individual should ever stop doing what is right to appease society. Price mused for the rest of the drive, "I was still bothered by an idea that was mixed up with Bob and Henry James, though two more unlike writers had never before inhabited the earth. But it seemed to me that they had a philosophy in common" (Ellis 153).

An obvious reason why Howard did not read a lot of Modernist literature is that he did not go to college or to a high school that was likely to assign it. He may have felt alienated from Modernism because of class and regional resentments: James may not have been Howard's opposite, but upper-class English modernists like Virginia Woolf were.[7] Howard wrote, "I prefer jazz to classical music.… A. Conan Doyle to Balzac, Bob Service's verse to Santayana's writing, a prize fight to a lecture on art" (Howard *Letters* 3: 66). His animosity toward modernism also had a more personal aspect: "These damn pseudo-scientific writers of today who try to explore a man's inner mind ain't worth a damn. Evil, they say, lurks inside a man. I hate those damn bastards who write stuff like that, because every decent impulse a man has is given a dirty meaning.... A man loves his poor old sick mother, and those damn bastards call it the 'Oedipus complex.' A doctor goes to see an attractive sick woman, and it's portrayed as lust" (Ellis 151–52).

This shows that Howard was aware of the charge that he had Oedipal feelings for his mother, perhaps even making it himself and displacing the blame to "pseudo-scientific writers." This is the exact charge made by his biographer de Camp, and resisted by contemporary Howard fans such as his biographer Mark Finn. Howard's father may have been accused of infidelity. Gossip along these lines is understandable because his mother was sick with tuberculosis for many years and his father was often away from home. If this charge had been made, Howard would have resented it fiercely. The linkage of personal resentments to a broader concept, be it civilization or Modernist literature, was in keeping with his personality.

Novalyn and Robert could not easily communicate with each other. Dates were made by post. Mrs. Howard could sometimes fend off contact between them since Robert worked as a writer inside the family home. She was a formidable obstacle for Novalyn. Price wrote, "She had convinced Bob of two things: first, that a wife handicaps a man; and, second, and more important, that I was an Indian woman.... I was part of a mongrel race, not a pure 'Irish-Gaelic' race!" (Ellis 149). Novalyn had confided to Robert that a grandparent might have had some "Indian blood" in her, and that her father had suffered discrimination because he was accused of being a sort of recusant American Indian. Novalyn believed that Mrs. Howard had tried to convince Robert that while Novalyn might look sufficiently white, they would be in danger of having a "throwback" child who looked like a American Indian.

The fact that Robert had any sort of relationship with Novalyn suggests that he did not always listen to his mother. He countered his mother's deep prejudice against American Indians with opposing prejudices: "Well, goddam, there's nothing wrong with being an Indian. I— Hell, there were some damn good Indians. Trouble is they got mixed up with the Spanish and French who came over here" (Ellis 157). He practically shakes with internal tension in this statement. It was a brave thing for him to say.

He said many less brave things about race to Price. He was horrified when he saw her greet a mulatto man in public (Ellis 92). He later warned Novalyn never to repeat what she had told him about her belief that half-white children were just as good as their white fathers. He explained that, while he didn't care, townsfolk would tar and feather her if they heard of her dangerous views (Ellis 100). Their roles were reversed in matters of race: the defiant Howard was afraid of the community, and Price the conformist believed it important for her to speak her mind.

The memoir suggests that Howard may have had a more realistic view of their community than Price, but not of romantic relationships. He did not know how to talk to her when not telling a story. She writes, "Then he began to ask those impossible questions such as did I believe a woman now-a-days could love a man the way women in prehistoric times did—enough to take her sword and stand by her man in battle and fight beside him. You can't answer a question like that" (Ellis 120).

He once told Novalyn that he had been reincarnated, and that in a past life his best friend had stolen his girl. She replied that if he was as hesitant in making a commitment in his past life, his friend did not steal the girl—he gave her to him (Ellis 130). It was exchanges like these that led to the memoir's being turned into a film by one of Price's high school students. *The Whole Wide World* (1997) is a well-acted, low budget film that was a box office failure. The most significant impact of the film was that Renee Zellweger's performance as Novalyn Price started her Academy Award–winning career.

The dramatic problem of the film and the memoir is that Robert Howard and Novalyn Price did not have sex. It is unclear if he wanted or was capable of a romantic relationship. She was in love with him at times. He does not mention her much in his surviving letters. She wanted him to court her. There is no record of him using his primary talent to do so. He sent her poems, but of the wrong kind. Instead of speaking of love, he wrote of "blood from stumps of severed wrists" (Howard *Letters* 3: 28). He could be polite and entertaining in his correspondence, but he would also periodically write something he knew would offend the recipient. This proved sustainable with male writers who lived in other parts of the country, but was never going to work with an insecure young woman looking for something more.

Price was always fascinated with his verbal ability: "I've never dated a man before who can talk on so many different subjects nor one who uses words so beautifully. Let him describe a scene from history, or a cowboy riding the Texas hills in search of adventure, and I hear English spoken at its best" (Ellis 121). She wanted to be a writer, and Howard's life was writing. He was also a supportive and perceptive critic of her efforts. This attention to her writing probably kept her around long after she might have left.

Howard gave her good writing advice: "Your yarns never have any real conflict. Your girl comes from a good home; everybody loves her; everything's pleasant. She is happy, and, if she wants something, she gets it.... What about you, the unwanted child.... Why don't you write about girls with problems like that?" Price responded, "I can't. It hurts too bad" (Ellis 289).

A pleasant life is far more fantastic than prehistoric swordplay for Howard. The conflict in his stories was often an external manifestation of his internal emotions, so it makes sense that he would urge Price to tap into her emotions to improve her writing. He told her that everyone suffers. Yet he also seemed to believe that it was not useful to urge someone to deal with her own personal pain. He offers another writing suggestion based on an inspiration for his own writing: his view of history as an eternal pageant of violence and suffering. Looking at her house in the Texas countryside, he said, "Life out here wasn't all sweetness and light. Gunman roamed the countryside. The weather. Every damn thing you can think of happened to them. But it's the blood and guts life itself is made of" (Ellis 289).

Price tried hard to learn about writing from Howard and he attempted to help her despite the vast difference in the literary traditions each had adopted. The relationship ended when Howard gave up trying to make her a better writer. She seemed to go beyond not being interested in fantasy to having no understanding of the concept that fictional people might act in ways different from real people because they exist within a fictional environment.

She did grab onto something in his writing technique that electrified her. She believed that his fantasy world-building was the answer to her struggles with writing. He suggested that she write backgrounds for the characters in her stories to give them more weight. She believed this was what he had done in creating a background for the Conan stories, a fantasy world made up of different countries and races based on his view of history. It was not at all the same, but he did not or could not explain this to her. He used his fantasy world to serve as a background that made inherently unreal stories seem real, to create a setting in which his worldview and violent fantasies were sane and appropriate, and to save the countless hours needed to research the historical background for each low-paying pulp story he wrote. He probably made his suggestion about character backgrounds to her because he did not want to tell her directly that her characters were flat. Howard shows in his many personal letters to writers that he never criticized the writing of people he knew.

Price did not understand. She felt that she had made a breakthrough both in her writing and their relationship. This proved to her that they had something in common, that he wanted to and could help her with her writing, and that they could both be equals as writers. She told him that she had kept a journal with descriptions of people and situations that she named "Vanity Fair" and that she could now use to write successfully, like Howard. She wrote, "At this moment, I was in love with him again, ready to go over and run the nurses off and take care of his mother myself in order to spare him the troubles he had" (Ellis 293).

His response was devastating to her. "I can't say much for Thackeray's *Vanity Fair*," he said shortly. "It's not worth a damn. I don't think you've got the idea at all. I know I'm a damn fool for making any suggestions about your writing or anybody else's.... Just forget what I said. I'll keep my mouth shut in the future" (Ellis 293). She had no more reason to see him.

Price left Cross Plains for graduate school and was on campus when word of Howard's suicide reached her. Her dissatisfaction with accounts of his suicide seems to have been the primary motivation for writing the memoir in her old age. De Camp interviewed her for his biography and she seems to have given him access to the diary on which she later based her memoirs. She opposed his conclusions: "It was not just because he was so tied to his mother's apron strings that he could not live without her. I would never believe that.... Bob could not live in the world as he found it. I had vaguely recognized it, but it was not clear to me until now. He had told me many times when he said, 'Life is not worth living in this rotting civilization.' He made himself believe it" (Ellis 315).

Novalyn Price reduced her view to an even purer form in a brief dialogue with a college girl she had told about the suicide. The girl was insensitive and blurted out that "most writers are crazy." She replied, "He was not ... he just didn't want to live" (Ellis 307).

Howard's suicide has exerted a powerful influence on biographers, critics, and fans trying to make sense of his life. L. Sprague de Camp's *Dark Valley Destiny* (1980) reads in many places like a mystery story attempting to argue the motives for Howard's suicide—except that here the mystery is revealed in every chapter. This book is important because it provided a view of Howard that lasted until his scholar-fans had the critical mass to take control of the image of their hero in the twenty-first century. It is fascinating because de Camp is no disinterested biographer: he is Salieri to Howard's Mozart. He had a respectable career writing stories in the Golden Age of Science Fiction of the 30s and 40s. He knew Isaac Asimov, Ray Bradbury, and Robert Heinlein and his stories appeared in print alongside their much more famous works. He also wrote fantasy stories and had a life and career that ran five decades longer than Howard's. However, he is best known today not for his own works, but for bringing the Conan stories to a mass audience. De Camp's biography crackles with psychological tension—he knows that even as he psychoanalyzes Howard he is dependent on him.

De Camp's case is simple: Robert E. Howard was a Freudian train wreck. In an earlier attempt at biography, he wrote, "Posthumous psychoanalysis is ... at best a jejune form of speculation" (*Miscast* 21). He had radically changed his mind by the time he wrote *Dark Valley Destiny*. Howard is described as the Oedipus of Cross Plains. First, his father is profiled in language whose style suggests poor pulp fiction writing: "Conan resembles Robert's father. Dr. Howard has been described by those who remember him in his youth as an imposing figure, a tall, dark-haired, choleric man whose bright-blue eyes made a lasting impression on all who saw him and whose air of authority, worn casually like a cloak, moved people to admire and obey him" (de Camp *Dark* 13).

Dr. Howard bears little resemblance to Conan, but this portrayal fits de Camp's model. De Camp declares that Mrs. Howard dominated her son. He feels that Howard's "dominant and eventually fatal personality trait" was his over-attachment to his mother (de Camp *Dark* 79). The main evidence for this is that Howard killed himself after he learned of her impending death. His personal letters do not support this. He rarely mentions his mother or father in years of correspondence. If Howard was obsessed with his mother, it is reasonable to assume he might have mentioned her more frequently in his letters. Also, there is no sign in the letters of the resentment toward his father that someone with a raging oedipal complex would be expected to have.

De Camp is successful in detailing the impact of Hester Howard's health on her son. He drove her over 100 miles on country roads to sanitariums more than once, but the medical science of the era could do little for her. Her medical treatments caused additional suffering (de Camp *Dark* 329–30). She endured "pneumothorax aspirations" in which a doctor jammed a long needle between her ribs and collapsed a lung while blowing air into her pleural cavity. This was a progressive treatment for the time, and was more effective than the traditional warehousing of tuberculosis patients in sanatoriums (Herzog 11). However, it was not effective for Mrs. Howard.

The last days of his mother must have been nightmarish. De Camp interviewed survivors and describes a harrowing scene. Howard did not sleep or eat for three days. He drank cup after cup of coffee as he watched his mother suffer (de Camp *Dark* 346). Their small home was filled with nurses and onlookers. It was summer in West Texas in the Dust Bowl year of 1936. The heat and smell must have been oppressive. These conditions could have triggered his suicide without any contribution from oedipal difficulties.

III. Robert E. Howard (1906–1936)

De Camp also offends fans by his judgment of Howard's worth as a writer: "Had not Conan stood at Howard's shoulder and dictated stories for his scribe to set down, Robert Howard would be forgotten today" (de Camp *Dark* 334). An entire movement of scholar-fans has spent decades refuting this charge. Howard wrote hundreds of stories, but only a score of Conan tales. De Camp annoys the scholar-fans because he dismisses most of Howard's non–Conan stories. Worse than this, he implies that Howard's fame is a result of his own popularization of the Conan stories. These contentions provoke responses from Howard scholars like his biographer Mark Finn: "In truth, Conan was little more than just another speed bump in Robert's varied career" (Finn 165).

The Conan stories are Howard's most important works—hardly speed bumps. The statement is informed by the history of exploitation of his work. Lyon Sprague de Camp is the perfect villain for the Texas sensibility of the scholar-fans: he is pretentious, irreverent, Eastern, and grasping.

The Conan stories trekked a tortured path. Howard left them behind in a trunk holding all of his writing. Dr. Howard was already an old man at the time, and he withered in his grief. He became unable to support himself. He had no pension and little money. He obtained board for his old age by giving all his possessions, including the rights to his son's writings, to a doctor for whom he also worked part-time. This Dickensian arrangement left the rights to Conan to an obscure, small-town doctor. The doctor left the rights to his daughter when he died in 1958 (Nielson 45). In 1965 Texan Glenn Lord was appointed as literary executor for Howard and served as the greatest advocate for Howard's writings until his death in 2011.

De Camp recalled in his autobiography that he had almost become familiar with Howard as early as 1930 (*Time* 216). He reported that he stopped reading the first Howard story he encountered after the first sentence because, though it was set in Roman Britain, it disturbingly mentioned a stirrup, and he knew even as a young college graduate that stirrups had not been invented in Roman times.[8] This put him off Howard for two decades. A man who would both want to read a story in a magazine called *Weird Tales* and be upset by a passing historical anachronism seems to be spectacularly unsuited to be trusted with the works of Robert E. Howard. It is difficult to imagine a writer more hostile to de Camp's positivist world view than Howard, or a scholar less suited to interpret Howard than de Camp.

After Howard's death the Conan stories should have been fading memories like thousands of other pulp stories, but fans kept them alive. This interest eventually led a science fiction publisher to the trove of Howard stories. Since the character of Conan had never been a main-stream success like Tarzan, or even Captain Blood, the rights to his stories could be had cheaply. The Conan stories were ordered chronologically, based on speculations about the course of Conan's career, to present a saga of Conan from young thief to middle-aged king in a series of books in the early fifties. De Camp was called in to rewrite three unpublished Conan stories and add them to the series (de Camp *Time* 230). De Camp did not treat the work of the obscure, uneducated, unscientific Howard with respect. He admits to editing with "a heavy hand." He went so far as to change even the names of Howard's characters.

The appetite for Conan material exceeded the supply. The publisher asked de Camp to search through Howard's writings for stories that could be rewritten as Conan stories. De Camp took stories with settings such as twentieth-century Afghanistan and transported them to a fantasy setting. He eliminated references to modern technology and added unconvincing "fantasy elements." In his mind this was appropriate because Howard's heroes were mostly "mighty loners with dour and dangerous dispositions" (de Camp *Time* 231). This shows de Camp's lack of understanding of even the Conan character. The barbarian is dangerous, but hardly dour. He is independent, but not particularly solitary. The character of Conan as written by Howard is the opposite of generic. The watered-down character of the Conan of popular imagination is the result of decades of adulteration, which started with de Camp.

However, those wishing to exploit Conan did not truly hit literary bottom until de Camp got a call from the publisher Martin Greenberg in 1957. De Camp describes the event: "Greenberg received in the mail the manuscript of a novel, *The Return of Conan*, by Lieutenant Bjorn Nyberg of the Swedish Air Force. Nyberg had written the story to prac-

tice his English, and would Mr. Greenberg care to publish it?" (de Camp
Time 231). He did. In contrast to his feelings about Howard's style, de
Camp praises Nyberg's English. He does note regretfully that it contained
"many non-English constructions." De Camp collected a check for this
job, but the publisher lost money. He blamed the commercial failure of
this novel on the poor cover art and paper. It is more likely to have failed
because it was written by a man practicing his English.

The evolution of the post–Howard Conan saga led to de Camp's
collecting all of the rights to the Conan stories and publishing a paperback series in the 60s which expanded to twelve books. The use of
Howard's original stories caused no legal problems for de Camp, but he
was sued by the bankrupt publisher of his first Conan pastiches when
he proposed the new Conan series. He was sued for violating the copyright of his own editing of Howard's stories.

De Camp wrote his own completely original Conan stories at the
urging of his new publisher "to strengthen our legal position" and "pad
out" the series (de Camp *Time* 305). He enlisted Linwood Vrooman
Carter, an advertising copy writer active in the science fiction community, to help write new stories and to complete some stories left unfin-
ished by Howard. De Camp (and his wife and writing partner, Catherine
Crook de Camp) eventually settled out of court and gained the right to
publish his new Conan series. This series included de Camp's versions
of all of Howard's finished stories, his and Carter's pastiches, and even
the Swedish novel. The books were packaged with spectacular painted
covers by fantasy artist Frank Frazetta and launched what de Camp calls
"the Conan boom" (de Camp *Time* 308).

The rights to Conan traveled a winding path from this point.
Another lawsuit ended with the creation of Conan Properties, which
essentially gave the de Camps control of the character until L. Sprague's
death in 2000 (Nielson 46). During this time Conan was treated as a
property and comic book, film, and merchandising rights were sold.
The successful de Camp paperback series was privileged over the original stories. The stories as Howard wrote them were unavailable and
their re-publication was blocked.

After 2000, the rights were first sold to comic-book legend Stan

Lee, who sold them to Paradox Entertainment, a Swedish media company. Today, Paradox claims the rights to "Conan, associated characters and the Hyborian Age as created by Robert E. Howard and expanded upon by acclaimed authors and artists for decades." It is important to note that the fantasy world itself, the Hyborian Age, is explicitly treated as an intellectual property.

De Camp's paperback series is responsible for Conan's great popularity beyond the limited circle of true Howard fans, and the media properties like the films and comics licensed by de Camp are responsible for much of the rest of the character's fame. However, this popular version of the character is not Howard's version. To add insult to injury, de Camp's biography portrayed Howard as pathetic and insane.

Many Howard fans take criticism of their hero personally because he represents more to them than a beloved author. Mark Finn's dedication of his biography gives a sense of this admiration: "This book is dedicated to anyone who ever drove to Cross Plains, Texas, stood in the doorway of Robert E. Howard's room and felt a perceptible chill at the thought of being so close to where he created his blood and thunder."[9]

For many people, Texas is not just a state, but a state of mind. Texan Mark Finn emphasizes Howard's identity as a Texan throughout his biography. The civic organization Project Pride of Cross Plains, Texas, has made the Howard home a museum. It has also held an annual two-day gathering in celebration of the author since 1986. An advertisement for the 2012 festival read, "Come to Cross Plains to celebrate Conan's Birthday. There will be cake!" (Cavalier n.p.).

Howard felt that to be a Texan was to be exploited: "The city of Cross Plains can't even dam up Bee Branch, because it runs into Turkey Creek, which turns into Pecan Bayou, which is a tributary of the Colorado River—because Mr. Beloved Insull owns the Colorado and all tributaries.[10] As a result, citizens of the town have to use water out of wells that would ruin the system of a brass monkey" (Howard *Letters* 2: 413). It seemed to him that even the water he drank was held captive by Eastern interests.

He grew up with a personal resentment of the depredations of the oil industry in his town, but he felt the exploitation reached across the vast territory of Texas. He wrote, "The Texas people have been as ruthlessly exploited as if they were painted savages. And what grates me, is, they've put up with it …. The people of this section, especially the country people, are so inured to suffering and hardship that it would take a veritable cataclysm to cause them to rise. Their capacity for enduring hardship is incredible—more, it is appalling." (Howard *Letters* 2: 445).

He did not feel the suffering of Texans was a recent development. He conflated the trials of Texans with the wider catastrophe of the South's defeat in the Civil War. Resentments of the past combined with resentments of the present. For him the past was never dead, and the Civil War was not even past.

William Faulkner and Robert E. Howard were contemporaries—Faulkner's *Light in August* (1932) was published at time of Conan's first appearance. Cross Plains is a long way from Yoknapatawpha County, but the two authors shared a common history. Faulkner writes in *Light in August* of "the phantom of the old spilled blood and the old horror and anger and fear" (Faulkner 22). It is hard to think of a phrase that better captures the heart of Howard's life and works.

Howard often provided historical primers on Texas for friends from other parts of the country with whom he corresponded. This is what he wrote about Reconstruction in his state: "Texas was in the grasp of the carpet-bag vultures…. Free niggers—more primitive and ferocious than anywhere else on this continent—were swaggering over the countryside, plundering, murdering and burning. The niggers and the carpet-bagger had Federal soldiers behind them. Resistance against oppression resulted in outlawry" (Howard *Letters* 3: 75). He feels that civilization resulted in the suffering of white Texans after the defeat of the Confederacy. He gives the impression that he can almost smell the burning homesteads and hear the cries of violated white woman.

Howard writes, "There is no hell more abominable than living in a defeated land under the arrogant heel of the winners" (*Letters* 3: 294). He does not only mean that the time after the Civil War was bitter for Texans. He also means that he is still living in a defeated land in the 1930s.

He feels varying degrees of personal anger and resentment toward figures who opposed the South decades before his birth. In "Abe Lincoln," a poem rhetorically addressed to the late President, he suggests "What a damnable pity it is \ That you were not drowned in a handy rain barrel" (Howard *Letters* 2: 344). The poem also shows some sympathy for Lincoln. It is a hymn of praise compared to a poem he wrote to John Brown. The poem describes the sound of Brown's neck being snapped (Howard *Letters* 2: 344).

The greatest lesson of the Civil War, and of all history for Howard, is that civilization leads to oppression. There is some complexity in Howard's theme of the conflict between civilization and barbarism that runs through the Conan stories and much of his other work. However, the issue is at its core a simple one and goes back to his interpretation of Reconstruction: "Those who are strong enough to loot the others are the 'civilized' and the conquered are the barbarians" (Howard *Letters* 2: 443).

Howard's ideal era was not his Hyborian Age, but a historical epoch just as fantastical: "I have often wished strongly that I had lived on the ancestral plantations of the Deep South, in the days before the Civil War!" (Howard *Letters* 2: 91). It is not clear what Howard thought was going on in the ancestral plantations of the Deep South. He knew life could be horrible for slaves, but in general, he felt that the mistreatment of slaves had been exaggerated. He was confident that whatever abuses did take place, none were perpetrated by his family. "Thank God the slaves on my ancestors' plantations were never so misused" (76).

His mother was probably an important source for these attitudes. She turned away from a bleak present as a sick, struggling woman to a mythical past of wealthy and righteous plantation owners. Even this past was not delusional enough as she aged and sickened. She started affecting an Irish brogue in middle age (Finn 107). This was only fitting for one who claimed she and her boy had the blood of Irish kings flowing through their veins.

Howard's biographer Finn writes, "At the age of eighteen, Robert E. Howard was as racist as he was ever going to be" (79). However, in 1930—six years after his suggested age of maximum racial prejudice—Howard wrote the following about joining an athletic club: "When I looked around at the wops, spicks, Chinees and niggers who were among my club brothers it gave me a big laugh" (Howard *Letters* 2: 44). The same year in several letters he writes of his rage at a court case in Hawaii. The prosecutor had charged whites for shooting a man of Hawaiian ancestry after failing to beat a confession out of him. The man had been tried but not convicted of raping a white woman (329n). Howard raged over this offense against justice and the white race in three separate letters. He composed a poem on the subject in which he wrote that he hoped the prosecutor would be nailed into a barrel full of razor blades and rolled "down a hill into hell" (345).

Howard's racism and paranoia led him to ridiculous places as well as dark ones. He wrote a letter in 1932 about rumors of "the mysterious presence and vaguely sinister activities of a hundred thousand Japanese in the interior of Mexico. It is well known that in several cases of banditry, the Mexican outlaws were led by Japanese. Possibly these Orientals were mere renegades—possibly not" (Howard *Letters* 2: 303). He may have been so unhinged by the combination of Japanese and Mexicans banding together against white America that he not only did not immediately reject this preposterous rumor, but passed it on as news to one of his correspondents on the East Coast.

He boils down his position on race: "Texas, whatever its virtues or faults, is a white man's State, and that fact is reflected in the manner of the non-white races. They know their place" (Howard *Letters* 2: 357). He rarely writes of interaction with non-whites in his letters. According to the 1930 census, everyone in Cross Plains was white (*1930 Texas Population* n.p.). When Howard was writing he would often see only his parents. He thought the Old South might not have been morally right in all things, but he believed it placed people like himself on top. He wanted to go to such a place.

Howard fans do not—they have no sympathy with the author's racial attitudes or the racism of his time and place. They need not even have a special interest in the Texas found on maps. The "Texas" that is appealing is the idea of a place whose people have suffered and been exploited, but who have violently and heroically fought against this suffering and exploitation. The Hyborian Age of the Conan stories, in particular, is a fantasy world largely free of the corrosive racism of Howard and his environment. One of his greatest achievements is his transmutation of the anxieties and resentments of his life, including his racism, into a fantasy world that transcends them.

Weird Tales is the last piece of the puzzle of Howard's fantasy world we need before examining the Conan stories themselves. *Adventure* was a vital inspiration for the writer as a boy and shaped his imagination, but there would have been no Conan or Hyborian Age without the magazine *Weird Tales*. The Conan stories published in Howard's lifetime were published in this unique venue.

Frank Munsey, financier of Theodore Roosevelt's Progressive Party, created pulp fiction magazines for both commercial and ideological reasons. His sales pitch was, "The story is more important than the paper it is printed on" (Haining 9). He felt large numbers of Americans were not reading because to them three-decker novels were "unreadable and the 'slicks' uninteresting and too expensive." The slicks were the standard magazines of the time—printed on expensive "slick" paper, and marketed to the prosperous readers who could afford them. Munsey was able to use cheap paper made from inexpensively processed coarse wood pulp to create a new mass market of magazine readers (Haining 9). Pulp magazines contained a variety of fiction, from detective stories to adventure stories to sports stories. Munsey could not have anticipated the types of stories contained in *Weird Tales*.

"Weird" is not a synonym for fantasy or horror, though it is related to these. The word does not seem to have had quite the same connotation for the writers and publishers of *Weird Tales* in the 1920s and 1930s as it does for people today. Maybe the founder of the magazine used the word as Tolkien might have: layering the meaning of an archaic form of the word such as "wyrd" from *Beowulf,* which meant fate, with the contemporary meaning of the word (*weird*). The use of "weird" as a description of a genre may have been meant to recall the "weyard sisters" (witches) of *Macbeth* (*weird*). Perhaps the subject matter just felt "red hot," as a movie Howard saw in 1928 felt to him (Howard *Letters* 1: 214). The silent film *The Wizard* (1927) is presumed lost. It was a remake of a 1913 film with the unpromising title of *Balaoo, the Demon Baboon*.

Both films were based on a novel by Gaston Leroux, who also wrote the more famous *The Phantom of the Opera* (1909). The atmosphere and mood of *The Wizard* are more important than the title or the plot. A lobby card for the film survives (*The Wizard*). The beautiful expressionist-influenced painting depicts a couple huddled together in terror. Behind them their shadows are swallowed by two reversed shadows of supernatural size. Presumably these are the shadows of the mad genius and his ape-man creation come to doom the hapless couple. The pair cower in a huge chamber that looks like a sitting-room in the House of Usher painted by Edvard Munch.

Weird Tales sought to mix various pulp genres with odd supernatural melodrama. The stories also reached for an intense emotional atmosphere—not exactly of the uncanny, but still sublime. Some of the stories were straight horror stories such as "The Man Who Returned" by popular contributor Edmund Hamilton. The subtitle explains that the tale is "the story of a man who was laid away in his coffin, and the unexpected reception he got when he returned to his friends" (Haining 21). Leigh Brackett, Hamilton's wife, also wrote for *Weird Tales*. However, her film projects are far more famous. Her first screenwriting job was working with William Faulkner on *The Big Sleep* (1940). She called him "courteous" in an interview, but Faulkner was not much for chit-chat (Truesdale n.p.). He told her which chapters he would write, which she would write, and then walked into his office. She said, "I never saw him again, except to say good morning." Brackett went on to do scripts for other Howard Hawks films such as *Rio Bravo* (1959). She turned in the first draft of what would become *The Empire Strikes Back* (1980) shortly before her death. She thus linked *Weird Tales* with the Star Wars movies by way of Faulkner, Humphrey Bogart and John Wayne.

The "weird" genre was difficult to explain when the magazine started in 1923. An editorial in 1924 attempted to give the magazine's manifesto. It decried modern stories as mechanical: "The soul of the story is crushed—suffocated between the weight of technique. True art—the expression of the soul—is lacking" (Weinberg 16). The broadside asserts that Poe could never get his stories published in 1924. The editorial then presents a potted history of the fantastic, focusing on the

English tradition from the Gothic to early twentieth-century writers. A sort of alternative literary canon is listed, pairing authors who are rarely considered together: H. Rider Haggard, Jules Verne, Algernon Blackwood, and Joseph Conrad. The message of the editorial is that *Weird Tales* offers an outlet for imaginative personal expression in a clockwork world.

The magazine was founded by Clark Henneberger. His great business success was to collect stories from college humor magazines and publish them together in *College Humor* (Haining 10). This was a sort of *Reader's Digest* for the flapper set. The college magazines carried the air of the safely risqué and modern. Henneberger went on to found the *Magazine of Fun, Detective Tales,* and *Weird Tales.*

Henneberger sold the successful *Detective Tales* and poured the money into the failing *Weird Tales*. This act of devotion set the pattern for the magazine's three-decade run. The owner had chosen to publish a magazine that would always struggle to stay afloat. He may have expected everyone else to sacrifice because he was sacrificing for the good of the genre his plucky magazine represented. The magazine was supposed to pay its authors upon publication (a poor arrangement for writers at the best of times), but only paid them at its convenience. Rates started at a half-cent a word. This would prove devastating for Howard. The magazine's lack of cash also meant that the editor had to pay close attention to the slush pile of unsolicited submissions rather than paying famous authors to submit stories likely to draw readers. In other words, the stories had to be good because the magazine could not rely on the drawing power of famous names—but also cheap because it had no money. The magazine would not have survived without an editor with an eye for finding literary talent from obscure places—like Cross Plains, Texas.

Farnsworth Wright edited the magazine during Howard's era and was responsible for its remarkable survival. He was a baby-faced bald man with a strong nose (Weinberg n.p.). He looked like a tough-but-fair assistant principal from any year in the middle part of the twentieth century. He served in France during the First World War and returned to the United States diagnosed with a case of "sleeping sickness" (Haining

4). He was sick for the rest of his life, and was eventually diagnosed with Parkinson's disease. He shook so badly by the time he was publishing Howard that he could not sign his name. He had to be carried into his office every day. He died in 1940, shortly after retiring, from an unsuccessful operation to relieve the pain of his condition. Henneberger recruited Wright when he was working as a music critic for the Hearst paper the *Chicago Herald and Examiner* (Haining 4).

Wright had an eye for talent. In August of 1928 he was the first to publish a sixteen year-old boy named Thomas Lanier Williams. Tennessee Williams wrote a story based on one of many anecdotes in Herodotus describing the outrages barbarian (non–Greek) women get up to when given power—usually unauthorized sex or killing men (Herodotus 2.100). "The Vengeance of Nitocris" has little plot because it adheres closely to the brief original anecdote. It fulfills the mission statement for *Weird Tales* magnificently: it expresses the author's soul.

Williams uses the word "sacrilege" eight times in the early part of the story to describe the horror of the community at the behavior of the pharaoh. The pharaoh appears in the story only long enough for his physique to be admired: "Superbly tall and muscular, his bare arms and limbs glittering like burnished copper in the light of the brilliant sun, his body erect..." (Williams "Vengeance"). This paragon ignores the crowd that the jealous priests of Egypt incite, and is slain by the mob.

Queen Nitocris (pharaoh's sister) pretends to bow before the priests, and invites everyone to a huge banquet in a tomb beneath a pyramid. She then floods the tomb by opening a secret door to the Nile: "a room of orgy and feasting suddenly converted into a room of terror and horror, human beings one moment drunken and lustful, the next screaming in the seizure of sudden and awful death" (Williams "Vengeance"). The people discover the mass murder and slay Nitocris. The last line of the story is "Only her beautiful dead body remained for the hands of the mob."

It does not take a Tennessee Williams scholar to recognize ideas and obsessions in "The Vengeance of Nitocris" to Williams would return throughout his career. The author discussed the story three decades later in a *New York Times* piece about the origins of his need to write. He starts the essay by examining his earliest impulses to write: "I discovered writing as an escape from a world of reality in which I felt acutely uncomfortable. It immediately became my place of retreat, my cave, my refuge. From what? From being called a sissy by the neighborhood kids, and Miss Nancy by my father ..." (Williams "Wells" 1).

He then recounts in detail his experience writing the story. Thirty-one years later he still expresses satisfaction at his first heroine's vengeance, "drowning her guests like so many drowned rats." His assessment of his *Weird Tales* story: "If you're well acquainted with my writings since then, I don't have to tell you that it set the keystone for most of the work that has followed" (Williams "Wells" 3).

"The Vengeance of Nitocris" is not an important pulp story; Howard wrote better ones. He had the cover story in that August 1928 issue with his first Solomon Kane story, "Red Shadows." The story illustrates an important point about the stories in *Weird Tales:* the good pulp authors used the stories to express their deepest emotions and thoughts. They could do nothing else. Tennessee Williams could not have kept himself from writing about sexuality, gender, love and violence if he had been writing a cookbook. The "weird story" was not a formulaic straitjacket for Williams, but a medium so well-suited to self-expression that he could use it at the age of sixteen to escape from the abuse of neighborhood kids and his father. Similarly, a picture-book by Howard would have had to contain elements of exploitation, resentment, violence, civilization, barbarism, and heroism. Not only was passionate and intelligent self-expression possible in *Weird Tales,* but the format encouraged it. Supernatural forces, violence, and adoring women can be clichés when used by writers who are too lazy or unskilled to do anything else. However, they can also be manifestations of the shared hopes, fears, loves, and hates of the author and the audience. The great pulp and fantasy writers allow willing readers to operate on this deep emotional level at a younger age than the great authors of other forms of literature. For fans this dialogue can continue from youth to old age.

This does not mean that *Weird Tales* was not full of formulaic stories with little happening in them on either an emotional or intellectual level. Seabury Quinn was the most popular writer in the magazine during

III. Robert E. Howard (1906–1936)

Howard's era (Haining 15). His prolific character Jules de Grandin is a psychic detective who appeared in ninety-three adventures in *Weird Tales*. The character is like a denatured Sherlock Holmes who manages to run into a lot of half-clothed women being whipped. If de Grandin had starred in *The Hound of the Baskervilles* (1902) instead of Holmes, the hound would have been an actual hound from hell—also, a young woman would have been stripped and whipped on the moors. Quinn's regular job was editing *Casket & Sunnyside,* a trade journal for morticians (Haining 15). Perhaps his stories *were* his way of escaping and expressing his deepest emotions.

Howard's Conan yarns (as he called them) were unique among *Weird Tales* stories: barbarian heroes adventuring in a fantasy world were not a sub-genre of the weird tale until Howard created them. He may have distinguished himself in his *Weird Tales* career in another way. *Weird Tales* represented an opportunity to get published for writers like Tennessee Williams and Ray Bradbury who would later move on to better paying markets. Many writers for *Weird Tales* probably had day jobs like Seabury Quinn's. Howard depended heavily on *Weird Tales* for his living, perhaps more heavily than the magazine could bear given its own financial situation.

Howard published in many magazines other than *Weird Tales: Action Stories, Argosy, Cowboy Stories, Fight Stories, Oriental Stories, The Magic Carpet Magazine, Spicy-Adventure Stories, Strange Tales,* and *Top Notch* (Nielsen 11). However, many of these markets were ephemeral. He never broke his dependence on *Weird Tales*. As he wrote to Farnsworth Wright, "Of course, I sell to other magazines from time to time, but these sales are uncertain ... for several years most of my time and effort has been devoted to stories written for *Weird Tales* ... it is as much a part of my life as are my hands" (Howard *Letters* 3: 307). This financial dependence had serious consequences for Howard.

Economic distress was nothing new for him. The entire Conan series was written in the Great Depression, but just as damaging to his prospects was the gulf between writing a story and getting paid for it. *Weird Tales* was not paying Howard promptly even at the beginning of the series. He wrote nine Conan stories before *Weird Tales* published the first one! This meant he spent months of effort before being paid since the magazine paid only upon publication even when it did pay promptly.

By May of 1935 his mother's health was failing and *Weird Tales* had become erratic at paying. He wrote to Farnsworth Wright of his "dire" need for money, and noted that the magazine's practice of paying half of what it owed him had degenerated into paying nothing at all until months after publication. He tried to gain Wright's sympathy: "To a poor man the money he makes is his life's blood, and of late when I write of Conan's adventures I have to struggle against the disheartening reflection that if the story is accepted, it may be years before I get paid for it." He wrote to the agent he hired in an attempt to place his stories in better-paying markets, "*Weird Tales* owes me over $800, some of it for stories published six months ago. I'm pinching pennies and wearing rags, while my stories are being published, used and exploited (Howard *Letters* 3: 308). This was not a trivial sum: the amount Howard felt Wright owed him comes to almost $14,500 in 2013 dollars (CPI n.p.).

By February of 1936 he had given up on *Weird Tales,* Conan, and fantasy: "Slowness of payment in the fantastic field forces me into other lines against my will" (Howard *Letters* 3: 414). He was still writing and selling stories to other markets, but the end of his most important market and character must have been a blow. He gave up on life that June.

IV

Conan

In civilized countries I believe there are no witches left; nor wizards, nor sorcerers, nor magicians. But, you see, the Land of Oz has never been civilized, for we still have witches and wizards among us.

—Baum, *The Wonderful Wizard of Oz*

Howard's character Conan never gave up. The vitality of Conan came from the hopes, fears and rages of Howard. He built a fantasy world, the Hyborian Age, which created an environment in which Howard's emotions were clean, sane and appropriate. Howard wrote many stories, but the Conan stories are the heart of Howard's writing.

Anti-authoritarianism is a pervasive theme of the Conan stories. Even when Conan is a king his authority is being usurped and he is fighting greater forces of the status quo. Howard has Conan fight more than monsters: he often fights corrupt justice systems and cleaves the forces of oppressive ruling classes.

The Conan stories show Howard's class resentment at its strongest when the barbarian encounters the criminal-justice system. This theme is not a natural fit for stories set in ancient or medieval settings, but the Conan stories don't take place in real ancient or medieval settings. Howard makes the Hyborian Age more than a bare set for Conan to stride through. He creates a setting for his ideas and feelings to be expressed without the restraint of historical or contemporary reality.

In the posthumously published "The God in the Bowl" (1975) Conan encounters Demetrio, a character with similarities to Sherlock Holmes.[1] Conan is a young thief and has been hired to steal an artifact from a dealer in curiosities. The dealer is found dead and Conan is discovered on the premises. Demetrio leads the thuggish officers and men of the watch. The proto-detective is portrayed with some sympathy. He does not bluster like his comrades, who are enraged that Conan is not bowing down to their authority. However, Demetrio is exposed as another civilized hypocrite when he offers to ignore Conan's offense as a favor to the callow aristocrat who hired him.

This would be a practical and merciful decision in a Sherlock Holmes story set in a civilized world. In Howard's world the decision is hypocritical and cowardly. Howard gives the impression that the standard procedure of the watch in a case like this with a lower-class thief would be to arrest him, torture him, and then send him off to ten years of hard labor—even if he were found to be innocent of the murder. Demetrio only holds his sadistic guardsmen back because of his fear of Conan. Demetrio is flummoxed as Howard may have thought Holmes would have been in the Hyborian Age. He cannot solve the case in time because there is a supernatural answer to the mystery.

Conan is not going to go meekly to a Hyborian Age chain gang. He explodes and slices his way through the guards. Howard "punishes" Demetrio with a sword through his thigh. Demetrio is a wan Sherlock Holmes figure. In Howard's view, whatever the virtues of Sherlock Holmes, he is also an authority figure. Howard consistently associates authority with hypocrisy and corruption. In addition, Holmes represents the British Empire, which Howard hated. Demetrio represents an authority that is undeniably corrupt—though reasonable compared to the other representatives of civilization in the story. He is lucky to survive an encounter with Conan. Neither Conan nor Howard recognizes the concept of the state's monopoly of force.

Watchmen, in particular, have a short life expectancy in Conan stories. Conan slays them and the author insults them: "If he had thought, he would have known that that door had been opened since the watchman passed; but thinking was not his trade" (Howard "Hour" ch. 9). Conan dispatches a jailer in a particularly memorable way in "Rogues in the House" (1934). The jailer spots Conan feasting in his cell. Conan is waiting to be released from the jail by a noble who has also provided him with a good meal. The noble has bribed a turnkey to allow Conan to escape in exchange for doing a job for him, but this man has been seized for an unrelated act of corruption. The replacement jailer is outraged to see a prisoner being treated well. He foolishly opens Conan's cell to upbraid him. The barbarian knows how to deal with officious bureaucrats: "Conan brained him with the beef bone, took his poniard and keys, and made a leisurely departure" (Howard "Rogues" ch. 2). Howard expects representatives of civilized justice to be venal, but sanctimony is punishable by death.

Conan is brought to trial in "Queen of the Black Coast" (1935). The court wants him to inform on a friend who has killed a city guardsman. The guardsman accosted the man's girlfriend. Conan feels that the guardsman got what he deserved, and refuses to betray his friend. The judge responds by lecturing him about "duty to the state, and society, and other things I did not understand." He loses his patience with this civilized nonsense. "The judge squalled that I had shown contempt for the court, and that I should be hurled into a dungeon to rot until I betrayed my friend. So then, seeing that they were all mad, I drew my sword and cleft the judge's skull; then I cut my way out of court" (Howard "Queen" ch. 1).

Conan becomes a king of the most powerful Western kingdom in the Hyborian Age in a coup later in his career. He addresses legitimacy when he is mocked by a rival king for being a usurper in "The Scarlet Citadel" (1933): "What you inherited without lifting a finger—except to poison a few brothers—I fought for" (Howard "Scarlet" ch. 2). Howard is not arguing for the rule of a strong man over democracy. There are no democracies in the Hyborian Age. Within the Hyborian Age, he prefers a kingdom ruled by a non-hereditary king than an empire. (The king Conan deposes has a Roman name and resembles Nero.) However, his main point is to strike out against oppressive forces who threaten the individual, whether spoiled hereditary kings, sorcerer-priests, or Eastern business interests.

Howard dislikes not only the civilized ruling class, but also the commoners they dupe. He writes in the only Conan novel, *The Hour of the Dragon* (1935), "Such a wave of enthusiasm and rejoicing as swept the land is frequently the signal for a war of conquest" (Howard *Hour* ch. 2). In "A Witch Shall Be Born" (1934) Conan tells a civilized villain, "Your fortitude consists mainly in inflicting torment, not in enduring it" (Howard "Witch" ch. 6).

There are some villains in the stories who are not just functionaries in an oppressive social hierarchy. One of the appeals of Conan is his ability to destroy some maniacal foes. The character's violence is a rational response to the kind of enemies who cannot be bargained with, avoided or handled by the state. Howard has created a world in which the states (generally monarchies or despotisms) function only to oppress the common people. Conan must kill or be killed.

If the villains in the stories were mere stock moustache-twirlers, then Conan's dismembering of them would be a disproportionate response. This is not the case. His villains are such maniacs that the only sane response is to annihilate them. For example, a sorcerous assassin dispatched to kill Conan is more than just dedicated to his work. He is asked how much farther he is going to chase his prey after tracking Conan across the world. He replies, "To the ends of the world, perhaps … or to the molten seas of hell that lie beyond the sunrise" (*Hour* ch. 14). This fiend is not going to be stopped by a restraining order. There is no escape from figures like the witch who accosts a queen in her chambers. The queen threatens to call for guards. The witch invites her to "scream until the roof-beams crack" (Howard "Witch" ch. 1). No one is going to save her—this is the Hyborian Age.

The consequences are dire when the villains have more ambition. The battle cry of an ancient sorcerer resurrected to defeat Conan is, "By the lore of the dead we shall enslave the living!" (Howard *Hour* ch. 19). Howard uses sorcery to represent advanced learning and other forms of culture used to prop up the elite and keep the ordinary people down. The ancient sorcerer here goes beyond domination to threaten widespread slaughter, and perhaps genocide. He does not just talk of ruling the world bloodlessly as if it were an eccentric hobby. Howard's villain plans to "enslave the world, and with a deluge of blood wash away the present and restore the past!" (Howard *Hour* ch. 22). This rhetoric is more Goebbels than Goldfinger.

Such absolute evil demands absolute destruction. Conan does not just kill his foes: he tears apart their bodies. A bloodless sword thrust is insufficient for the kind of opposition he faces. The sorcerer out to devastate the world requires an even more spectacular death than Conan's sword can deliver. He is struck down by a "jetting beam of blinding blue light" and "before he touched the ground" his body is turned into a "shriveled mummy, a brown, dry, unrecognizable carcass" (Howard *Hour* ch. 2)." This is similar to what happens to the Nazis trying to subvert the Ark of the Covenant in *Raiders of the Lost Ark* (1981). This film may be the most popular "weird story" of all time. Co-creators Steven Spielberg and George Lucas make their villains Nazis. This choice gives them license to dispatch their villains with gusto. Howard dispatched *all* of his villains with gusto.

Combat in the stories is fast and bloody. Conan is never sadistic, unlike many modern-action heroes and anti-heroes. He never tortures. He fights like a barbarian. This means to Howard that he is a natural fighter who shows neither mercy nor cruelty in combat. His attacks are representations of Howard's rage, justified and made clean by the environment of the Hyborian Age. Rage is fast: "Conan wheeled and thrust murderously for Demetrio's groin ... [he] barely deflected the point which sank into his thigh.... The bill which Dionus flung up saved the prefect's skull from the whistling blade which turned slightly as it cut through the shaft, and sheared his ear cleanly from his head" (Howard "God" 56).

Battles with Conan, like this one from "Red Nails" (1936), do not last long: "Realizing that the warrior was hopelessly insane, the Cimmerian side-stepped, and as the maniac went past, he swung a cut that severed the shoulder-bone and breast and dropped the man dead" (Howard "Red" 263). Sometimes the violence is more stylized and he seems to move into the realm of Beowulf: "Conan gripped his wrist with a wrench that tore the arm clean out of the socket" (Howard *Hour* 199). More frequently, Howard's interest in boxing keeps the action grounded. He invites readers not to glory in hacked-up bodies, but to invest in each thrust and whirl, as he does.

The stories are not full of unrelieved violence. Howard has a poetic flair. He writes, "Dawn ran like a prairie fire across the grasslands"

(Howard *Hour* ch. 7). In one line we are transported from the Hyborian Age to a West Texas Iliad. In "Queen of the Black Coast" (1934) he writes that "autumn paints the leaves with somber fire" (Howard "Queen" ch. 1). His early letters are filled with poems, and he writes more poetry than prose in *Post Oaks and Sand Roughs*. Blood and guts provide a pulse for the Conan stories that have thrilled adolescents of all ages and genders, but they would not have been enough to take the tales beyond the ephemeral pages of *Weird Tales* in the 1930s.

Conan is mentally healthier and far more hopeful than Howard. In a fascinating passage, the barbarian debates a figure who sounds much like Howard as revealed in many of his personal letters. A priest drones on about the impending end of civilization. Conan ignores the doom and gloom. He repeatedly interrupts the depressed prelate with the short demand: "What do you mean?" He persists until the priest realizes that there is a way to save the day. Conan saves it (Howard *Hour* ch. 10).

Conan is famous even within the stories. People often recognize his name, which is no mean feat in kingdoms without mass communications. In "The Scarlet Citadel," we learn that his journey on the road to kingship is the subject of "a whole cycle of hero-tales" (Howard "Scarlet" ch. 1). A woman in "The Black Stranger" feels that meeting Conan is "like encountering a legendary character in the flesh.... A score of ballads celebrated his ferocious and adventurous exploits" (Howard "Black" 143).

This discussion of aspects of the barbarian and his stories has so far omitted quotes from the two best Conan stories: "The Tower of the Elephant" (1933) and "Beyond the Black River" (1935). The Conan stories are not interchangeable, nor are they of similar quality. Any discussion of the writings of Robert E. Howard should include careful consideration of his greatest stories. They represent more than high points of the Conan saga. "The Tower of the Elephant" was one of the first Conan stories written, while "Beyond the Black River" was one of the last. The character is a reckless youth in "The Tower of the Elephant." He is an experienced soldier in the second. Howard is different, too.

He sets the scene in two sentences better than most of his peers could manage in a chapter: "Torches flared murkily on the revels in the

Maul, where the thieves of the east held carnival by night. In the Maul they could carouse and roar as they liked, for honest people shunned the quarters, and watchmen, well paid with stained coins, did not interfere with their sport" (Howard "Tower" ch. 1). The story moves into a den of thieves, which is part Prohibition-era speakeasy and part Mexican cantina. Howard was acquainted with both. The paragraph moves like a camera from an exterior establishing shot to a tracking shot into the bar to close-ups of each of the denizens of the establishment. We meet "dark-skinned, dark-eyed Zamorians, with daggers at their girdles and guile in their hearts," "a giant Hyperborean renegade," "a Shemitish counterfeiter," " a bold-eyed Brythunian wench," "a tawny-haired Gunderman … a deserter from some defeated army," and a "fat gross rogue" from "distant Koth." This is not the world we know, but the names resonate with half-familiar names from history and myth.

Patrice Louinet suggests that Howard meant the place names to be fantasy precursors to historical tribes and nations (Louinet *Coming* xxii). This is in opposition to the tradition exemplified by his correspondent H. P. Lovecraft, who often used names to separate his stories from reality or to suggest the alien lurking outside the porous borders of mundane life: Ulthar, Sarnath, the Unknown Kadath.[2] Howard's names suggest places from half-forgotten history lessons—exotic, but somehow connected to the real world. He uses names to create the Hyborian Age as Tolkien used language to develop Middle-earth.

The Hyborian Age is a mythical epoch that lies between the fall of Atlantis and historical times. It is the time of heroes. Gods and monsters still exist, but they no longer dominate the world. The mundane forces of human history exist, but they do not yet rule. In this way the Hyborian Age resembles the setting of the *Iliad* and the *Odyssey*.

Howard wrote a history of his imaginative epoch and drew maps of his fantasy earth. His essay on the Hyborian Age is about eight thousand words. He wrote four drafts of it (Louinet *Genesis* 443). He spent a lot of time and effort on this material, considering that no Conan stories had yet been published.

He claimed that the essay made it easier to make Conan "a real flesh-and-blood character rather than a ready-made product" (Louinet

Genesis 381). The essay accomplishes these goals, but it goes much further. If the essay were just providing background, it would not need to be so extensive. Instead he could have written a few notes for himself, since he never planned to publish his history. This would have made more sense for a writer who had to produce a lot of stories to scrape out a living from low-paying magazines. In addition, much of the essay tells what happens to the kingdoms of the Hyborian Age after Conan's death. It continues thousands of years up to the dawn of recorded history. He could have stopped his fictional history when it reached the time of Conan if he were only concerned with background.

He presents history as a constant clash of races punctuating the ebb and flow of civilization. Civilization is smashed by barbarism. It recovers, and is smashed again. The essay drones hypnotically with an endless procession of races clashing against races. He does not mean this to be a reflection of the racial situation of his time. Howard writes that the Hyborians of the Hyborian Age are precursors to "Aryans." However, the Hyborians of the Hyborian Age are not a master race. Their race falls and rises like all the other races. Conan is not even a Hyborian himself: he a proto–Celt—a much better identity in Howard's eyes. Race in the Hyborian Age is not primarily a basis for superiority or inferiority, but the animating force of history.

Howard did not create this outlook. He owned H. G. Wells' four-volume history of humanity (Burke n.p.). Wells' view of ancient history is the history that Howard was returning to in his Hyborian Age. For example, "The Aztecs seem to have been a conquering, less civilized people, dominating a more civilized community, as the Aryans dominated Greece and North India. Their religion was a primitive, complex, and cruel system, in which human sacrifices and cannibalism played a large part" (Wells 746). This is a time when barbarians could conquer more civilized people. The mythical distant past of the Hyborian Age avoids the recent centuries of barbarians being slaughtered and colonized by more civilized and technologically advanced foes.

Howard also used the background materials of other pulp writers as source material for his mythical history. He was not the first to include Atlanteans or Lemurians or Hyperborians in his works, but neither were his pulp colleagues. All of these terms are discussed and represented as true occult knowledge in Madame Blavatsky's *The Secret Doctrine* (1888)—written about thirty years before the founding of *Weird Tales*. Edgar Cayce's Association for Research and Enlightenment is still aggressively searching for Atlantis in the twenty-first century. Researchers from the association announced in August 2011 that they had found underwater remains whose carbon dating readings match Cayce's predictions for the location of the Atlantean "Hall of Records." Cayce, the most famous psychic of the twentieth century, was a contemporary of Howard who lived in Texas for four years trying to strike oil during Howard's early years in Cross Plains ("Pre-Ice" n.p.).

Howard is not concerned in his essay with racial supremacy, but he does laud "racial purity," asserting, "Only in the province of Gunderland, where the people keep no slaves, is the pure Hyborian stock found unblemished" (Louinet *Hyborian* 386). Conan's bloodlines are safe because "the barbarians have kept their bloodstream pure; the Cimmerians are tall and powerful, with dark hair and blue or grey eyes" (387). He is not obsessed with blood purity in the stories. However, he notes the race of almost every character in the Conan stories. This is partly because he treats race and nation as synonymous. In his scheme, almost any description of a character automatically includes race even in situations where he is not interested in describing race.

He tries to make the history of the Hyborian Age consistent with his view of history. However, he has no interest in scientific plausibility for his fictional era. When a race falls into barbarism, it can fall all the way out of the human race into "apedom" (and back again). There are evil non-human races like the serpent people. Howard does not have Nazis to use as shorthand for evil—so he uses snake-worshipping priests.[3] The priests are a perfect metaphor for his view of civilization: they lurk in urban temples casting spells, kill each other for power, and feed the odd commoner to pet giant snakes. The reader immediately knows the character of the priests of Set—who else but evil maniacs would worship a giant snake? They are remnants of non-human races that once ruled the world. The record of their rule and how they formed each nation of Conan's time sets the stage for Conan's adventures. The medium of the essay is pseudo-history rather than pseudo-mythology. However, the concept of an ancient age of the world ruled by monsters has similarities with ancient Greek mythological concepts like the rule of the titans and the giants.

The chronicle continues long after Conan's time. Howard seems to get more invested in the narrative as it moves from a background to Conan's world to a record of its collapse. He stops the historical narrative to tell a parable: "Arus was the product of an innately artistic race, refined by centuries of civilization; Gorm had behind him a heritage of a hundred thousand years of screaming savagery" (Louinet *Hyborian* 389). Arus is a missionary who teaches a savage ruler about civilized values and technology. The barbarians keep the technology and reject the values. The missionary ends up dead, and the chief uses technology to wipe out Hyborian civilization. This world had weakened itself by imperial wars. Conan's kingdom, once "reigning supreme in the dreaming west" (Howard "Phoenix" ch. 1), saps its own strength by belittling and alienating the Texan-like frontiersmen who guard its borders. The civilized world collapses, as it always does. Eventually humanity recovers enough to spawn the historical ancient civilizations.

The Hyborian Age has similarities with Tolkien's Third Age of Middle-earth. There is sadness at the end of *The Lord of the Rings* because a whole world of wonder, with elves and unbroken forests, is passing. However, good news is coming for Tolkien: Jesus and everything of value in human history, such as the languages and literature he spent a life appreciating. Howard has no such faith. For him the world is not redeemed, but endlessly built up and burnt down. Worse, he feels that he is stuck at the end of a civilized era in which culture has long since outlived its early promise and become a prison for the individual. He wrote in January of 1934 of "Europe seething like a volcano" and "a madman running wild in 'civilized' Germany" (Howard *Letters* 3: 180). He sees the world setting itself on fire, and is not interested in seeing the ashes.

Howard focuses on the individual while Tolkien is more concerned with an entire civilization with its own languages and histories. All the forces of civilization are arrayed against Conan, but he fights on. Howard felt he could not fight the forces inside and outside himself like shame, civilization, and the sickness of his mother. Tolkien honors and mourns the passing of his fictional past, but he does not mean to go there. Howard wants to go to the Hyborian Age. He does not want to be Conan but seeks a world where it is appropriate for him to slay his enemies or die trying.

In addition to the essay, he also built the Hyborian Age by drawing maps. These maps started as tracings of the outlines of Western Europe (Louinet *Coming* 423). Another building block in the Hyborian Age is a letter Howard wrote responding to fans who constructed a chronology of Conan's career. The letter was used by de Camp to fill out his series of Conan books. He wrote or commissioned pastiches built on the Conan adventures Howard mentions in this letter but never wrote. This association upsets many modern Conan scholars who have struggled for years to propagate Howard's artistic vision unsullied by de Camp. Patrice Louinet finds even the idea of having a biography of a fictional character ideologically sinister: "Conan's adventurous life becomes a 'manifest destiny.'" He implies that framing the Conan stories as "a cohesive saga with a beginning, middle, and an end, a kind of Tolkienesque quest," is an injustice (Louinet *Conquering* xvii).

Other critics have tried to disassociate Conan from Tolkien. George Knight writes that Howard should be compared to Dashiell Hammett instead (Knight 127). Don Herron calls "the imaginative world tradition, unimportant to Howard—quite important to Tolkien" (Herron 155). De Camp started the process that linked Tolkien and Howard. De Camp tried to make his Conan paperback series appear to be as much like Tolkien's fiction as possible because he was trying to cash in on the phenomenal popularity of the American paperback editions of *The Lord of the Rings*. The Conan stories are unique—weird in many senses of the word. They don't obviously resemble either *The Maltese Falcon* (1930) or *The Lord of the Rings*. The valid link with Tolkien is the use of an imaginary world, not commercial imperatives or textual similarities. The imaginative-world tradition may not have been important to Howard, but the imaginary world of the Hyborian Age is vital to the Conan stories. It is not just a labor-saving device to spare

Howard from excessive historical research or tedious editing for anachronisms.

Howard sets "The Tower of the Elephant" in Zamora. This is not just an exotic place. It is a land on the eastern edge of the Hyborian (proto–European) countries. Its culture is older than that of the Hyborian kingdoms. It lies west of the steppes that lead to the Turanian Empire (proto–Turks). Its dark-skinned inhabitants are the best thieves in the world. Similarly, when Howard writes of the Picts in "Beyond the Black River" he knows that their country borders Aquilonia and the Ocean. He also knows their precise racial history, which goes back to the sinking of Atlantis and the consequences of this history—that the Picts and the Cimmerians have hated each other for millennia. Their "blood" remembers the hatred.

Without the background of the Hyborian Age, the place-names are silly. Robert Bloch wrote a critical letter on this point to *Weird Tales* as a teenager before he started a long career as a writer. (Bloch's novel *Psycho* [1959] was filmed by Alfred Hitchcock.) The teen wrote, "From the realms of the Kushites to the lands of Aquilonia, from the shores of the Shemites to the palaces of Dyme-Novelle-Bolonia, I cry: 'Enough of this brute ... may he be sent to Valhalla to cut out paper dolls" (Bloom 60). Bloch wrote that he liked Howard's writing in other instances, but not the Conan stories. He misunderstood their setting. Without at least an unconscious appreciation of the Hyborian Age, the setting indeed becomes a Dyme-Novelle-Bolonia like the mise-en-scène of a Conan film.

Howard introduces Conan in "The Tower of the Elephant" after surveying the den of thieves. He is skittish. He does not understand how to deal with civilized abuse. He is as out of place among these urban ruffians as young Robert Howard was among the roughnecks of the soda fountain in Cross Plains. A bully ridicules Conan at length for asking why no one has stolen from the great tower in the center of the city. Howard muses, "Civilized men are more discourteous than savages because they know they can be impolite without having their skulls split, as a general thing" (Howard "Tower" ch. 1). Young Conan does not know how to respond: he is "bewildered and chagrined, and doubtless would have slunk away." Robert probably would have slunk away in a similar situation in real life. However, in fantasy the bully pushes his luck by pushing Conan. The barbarian knows how to deal with this kind of threat. The sole candle in the room is knocked over, and when the room is relit the bully is dead and Conan is gone.

This is a perfect cinematic opening scene: Howard establishes the setting, develops the character of the protagonist, and unobtrusively handles the necessary exposition about the Elephant Tower. He introduces the mystery of a fabled gem at the top of a tower that has swallowed many generations of intrepid thieves. He tells of an evil priest whose power is said to come from the gem, "The Elephant's Heart." He establishes the theme of the story with the sudden death of a bully who had been laughing moments earlier. He accomplishes all this in less than four pages. Many contemporary screenwriters could learn from this opening. Unfortunately, there is nothing even approaching the quality of this opening in any of the Conan films. The opening also suggests the sensibility of a Depression-era Warner Brothers movie.

The Conan of the stories is not a brute. He muses that he has "squatted for hours in the courtyards of the philosophers, listening to the arguments of theologians and teachers" (Howard "Tower" 64). He is interested in the spiritual and intellectual discourse of civilized men, but not impressed by it. He concludes that philosophers and priests are "touched in the head."

Howard uses the surroundings to comment on religion by discussing Conan's religious beliefs. The god of Conan's people (the Cimmerians) is Crom—one of the more useless deities in fiction. Crom neither helps you if obey him nor hurts you if you shun him. He provides no guidance of any kind. He is gloomy and savage, and hates weaklings. The Cimmerians believe he gives the gift of courage and hatred of one's enemies to them at their birth. Conan believes this is "all any god should be expected to do" (ch. 2). Howard was probably not comfortable embracing atheism or agnosticism because he associated these philosophies with sophisticates. However, the worship of Crom is closer to atheism or agnosticism than to Christianity. Howard preferred to see a world run by a gloomy, savage god who hates weaklings (perhaps including himself) rather than one run by a civilized, Christian God worshipped by hypocrites.

Conan walks to the Elephant Tower to prove himself. He means to steal the fabled Jewel of the Elephant. He does not know what it is supposed to look like. He does not even know what an elephant looks like.

Both Howard and Tolkien use the concept of an elephant's being a legendary beast to the heroes of their stories. Sam wants to see the fabled "oliphaunt" in *The Lord of the Rings*. He recites a naïve Shire nursery rhyme about a beast that is "Grey as a mouse / Big as a house" (Tolkien *Lord* 646). He gets his wish, and the real creature fills him with "astonishment and terror, and lasting delight" (661). Sam finds the wonders of far-off lands dangerous as well as wondrous. The creature looks to him more like "a grey-clad moving hill" than a house.

Both Howard and Tolkien use the concept in a melancholy way. Conan will find something far sadder than a fantastic beast. Sam sees the oliphaunt at his first sight of a human battle. Tolkien tempers Sam's excitement at seeing what is to him a mythical creature with his first sight of an enemy corpse: "He wondered what the man's name was and where he came from; and if he was really evil of heart, or what lies or threats had led him on the long march from his home; and if he would not really rather have stayed there in peace" (Tolkien *Lord* 661). It is appropriate that a First World War veteran wrote this passage.

Howard was not a soldier. However, despite the violence in his works, he also abhorred modern war. He saw the war of his times not as barbaric but as the offspring of a rotting civilization. It was "sadistic and degenerate," exemplified by "flying over a city and dropping bombs that will rip the brains out of children, disembowel old men and dismember women" (Howard *Letters* 3: 442). Howard felt that civilized men were far worse than any barbarian. "The butchery of a city becomes: 'the cleaning up of a given area' and so ceases to be bloody murder, and becomes a beautiful mathematical problem to be worked out by placid scientists and scholarly intellectuals at a safe distance, who would never, never think of getting their hands in the blood and fecal matter" (442–43).

"The Tower of the Elephant" seems to be concerned with thievery, not war. It is actually concerned with mortality while still managing to be a cinematic adventure story. It is also a coming-of-age story starring a young Conan inexperienced with the civilized world. The master of the tower is so feared by the king of Zamora that he "kept himself drunk all the time because that fear was more than he could endure sober" (Howard "Tower" ch. 2). Legend claims that Yara, the evil priest who resides in the tower, will live forever because of his possession of a fantastic jewel: the Heart of the Elephant. Conan detects a guard outside the tower. Moments later he finds the guard dead. A shadowy figure addresses him.

Conan has met the master thief Taurus. The man is huge—as tall as Conan, but "big-bellied and fat." Howard quickly establishes the character as charismatic and likable. His size is contrasted with his feats of agility—the bull as thief. He shows a single-minded dedication to his thievery. He proudly tells Conan that he has completed a great exploit just to gain a tool to rob the tower: "I stole it out of a caravan bound for Stygia [Hyborian Age Egypt], and I lifted it, in its cloth-of-gold bag, out of the coils of the great serpent which guarded it, without waking him" (Howard "Tower" ch. 2). He genially allows Conan to share in the adventure for which he has so assiduously prepared, but he was ready to strangle Conan until he saw the youth's ready sword. Also, it is not clear how the pair would share the treasure. There is only one Jewel of the Elephant.

A garden in the tower is guarded by lions that do not roar. The thieves kill them silently with the cloud of poisonous powder that Taurus stole from the caravan. Taurus himself is suddenly and soundlessly killed a couple of pages later: "Death had come to the prince of thieves as swiftly and mysteriously as he had dealt doom to the lions in the gardens below." A giant spider killed Taurus. Howard was not alone in using this trope in a fantasy story. Tolkien used giant spiders in *The Hobbit, The Lord of the Rings,* and *The Silmarillion.* He used giant spiders as Howard used giant snakes. Howard uses the spider here to connote more than an obstacle. Conan faces the monster in a treasure-room filled with gems. The spider itself, with its many-faceted eyes, is symbolically a living gem. Taurus is killed by an arachnid manifestation of greed. Conan desperately heaves a chest of gems at the giant spider and destroys it with a "muffled sickening crunch." The spider lies "among the flaming riot of jewels that spilled over it ... the dying eyes glittered redly among the twinkling gems" (Howard *Tower* ch. 2). Howard returns to this image in the final line of the story.

Conan still has not found the Heart of the Elephant, and presses on to his climactic encounter with the "elephant" of the title. He meets the creature, but there is no battle. Conan freezes in fear, hardly an indomitable warrior. As he looks more closely he sees the creature is a wretch who has been blinded and tortured. "And suddenly all fear and repulsion went from him, to be replaced by a great pity. What this monster was, Conan could not know, but the evidences of its sufferings were so terrible and pathetic that a strange aching sadness came over the Cimmerian, he knew not why" (Howard "Tower" ch. 3).

The creature reveals that he is an exiled alien who came to Earth and was stranded before the dawn of man. Howard puts paragraphs from his essay on the Hyborian Age into the alien's mouth about different races of man growing from apes, and civilizations being built and then destroyed. After all, the long-lived alien was an eyewitness! Its interstellar wings atrophied on Earth, so it was stuck watching the sorry pageant of human history. It made the best of a bad situation by posing as a god in a quiet corner of the world inhabited by "kindly jungle-folk" where "offerings of fruit and wine heaped my broken altars" (Howard "Tower" ch. 3). Unfortunately, the evil priest Yara posed as a student, enslaved it, and brought the creature back to Zamora. Yara forced it to construct the Elephant Tower and do his evil bidding.

This is the "weird" territory of H. P. Lovecraft.[4] Howard admired Lovecraft and established an intense correspondence with him. Lovecraft was supportive of Howard's writing and tolerant of his argumentative letters. Howard praised him as "one of the greatest writers of our time" to Novalyn Price, but she refused to read Lovecraft and purposely misspoke his name out of pique (Price 151). She would not have found Lovecraft's nihilistic tone a good influence on her potential boyfriend. He was a mainstay at *Weird Tales* before Howard. He had even been offered the editorship of the magazine in 1924 after he was the standout contributor of the magazine's first year (DeForest 44). Lovecraft did not accept because he was as bound to New England as Howard was to Texas. He is best known for stories of cosmic horror in which the hopes and dreams of humanity are exposed as inconsequential compared to the interstellar forces of the true powers of the universe. These beyond-good-and-evil titans drive mad the unfortunates who encounter them by revealing the complete irrelevancy of human existence. These forces often came from places like the home of Howard's creature, the "green planet Yag, which circles for ever in the outer fringe of this universe" (Howard "Tower" ch. 3). Howard uses Lovecraft's language, but not his themes.

Howard writes of pity, which would be a pointless human emotion in Lovecraft's fantasy world. The creature urges Conan to take its heart to end its suffering and to defeat Yara. It does not resemble one of Lovecraft's alien abstractions of cosmic indifference: it symbolically resembles Mrs. Howard. The suffering of the eternally captive creature suggests the suffering of his mother endlessly dying of tuberculosis. Conan's pity is a reflection of Robert's pity for his mother.

Conan follows the instructions of the creature. He takes the object of his quest, the jewel called the Heart of the Elephant, and covers it with blood from the real heart of the "elephant." The jewel destroys Yara, and Conan flees the tower. The jewel proves a false heart. It symbolizes greed, death, and suffering: the bully killed in Conan's quest for reputation, the guard and lions killed by Taurus, Taurus killed by the spider, the spider killed by Conan's hurled chest of jewels, the exiled alien tortured by Yara, races of humans rising and collapsing in the history of the Hyborian Age as witnessed by the alien, the alien's death, and Yara killed by the power he used to kill so many others. The real strength did not come from a jewel, but from the living heart of the creature.

Conan survives because he has pity, not because he has big muscles. He escapes from the tower of the dead to "the cool fragrance of luxuriant growths." He looks back to see "the gleaming tower sway against the crimson dawn, its jewel-crusted rim sparkling in the growing light, and crash into shining shards" (Howard *Tower* ch. 3).

"Beyond the Black River" lies near the other end of Conan's—and

Howard's—career. An early piece of criticism from 1959 lauds it as the story in which "Conan and his creator get acquainted" (Scithers 54). Conan shares the story with Balthus, a settler from a section of Aquilonia called the Tauran. This region still has some contact with the wild, although it is no longer wilderness. George Scithers identifies Balthus with Howard and the Tauran with Texas.

It is remarkable that there is any sort of criticism of what could have been a forgotten pulp story from the 1930s. A few hardback editions of Conan stories had been published by a small press, and de Camp had started his involvement with the character. However, the mass-market paperback series that made Conan famous was not published until the late 1960s and 1970s. Fans kept Conan alive. Scithers published the fanzine *Amra* from 1959 to 1982. This amateur journal, named after one of Conan's aliases, featured contributions from fantasy writers about Conan and related topics. The devotion of fans of Conan has been a constant phenomenon since the 1930s, but it is most striking in this early period before the character appeared in paperbacks, comic books, or film.

"Beyond the Black River" features Conan as "the other." Most of the story is told through young Balthus's point of view. Howard intends for the reader to admire Conan in this story, but not to identify with him. He emphasizes that Conan is a barbarian. For Howard, this is not a life-style choice or an occupation, but an intrinsic identity.

Howard may have identified with Balthus, but the character's main function is as a surrogate for the reader. Howard, a master of unobtrusive exposition, has Conan explain to Balthus the dire situation of the frontier. The settler and the reader find themselves in the middle of an intense and bloody Western in the weird environment of the Hyborian Age. Conan plays the role of the veteran filling in Balthus the greenhorn. The tone of the story is strikingly similar to that of movie Westerns produced decades later, such as *The Searchers* (1957) and *The Outlaw Josey Wales* (1977). "Beyond the Black River" is set firmly in the Hyborian Age, but the most significant difference between the story and the Western films is that of the main characters. John Wayne's Ethan Edwards and Clint Eastwood's Josey Wales may be alienated and immoral, but they are not barbarians. The distinction between the barbarian and the civilized is the heart of "Beyond the Black River."

Conan tells Balthus that the kingdom of Aquilonia has pushed too far into the territory of the barbarian tribes of the Picts. The Picts play the roles of American Indians ... if American Indians were maniacs who summoned demonic forces and liked to run around screaming and slaughtering people. This view of American Indians seems more compatible with the racism of Mrs. Howard than that of the author himself, especially since at the time he was seeing Novalyn Price, who had American Indian ancestors. The background of the story is derived from the American frontier. However, it is no more concerned with historical American Indians than "The Tower of the Elephant" is an allegory of a gypsy or medieval underworld. Howard is adding depth to his theory of barbarism. In other Conan stories he presents barbarism as superior to civilization, largely by praising the barbaric qualities of Conan, who is superior to everyone he meets. "Beyond the Black River" shows that barbarians can be savage and bloody, as are the Picts, and that even our barbarian is far from a civilized hero.

Conan explains to Balthus that because of "your idiotic king" and his refusal to understand frontier conditions, the fort and settlers in the area are in danger of being wiped out. Conan calmly diagnoses the problem—imperialism—and suggests a surprising solution: land reform. "This colonization business is mad, anyway. There's plenty of good land east of the Bossonian marches. If the Aquilonians would cut up some of the big estates of their barons, and plant wheat where now only deer are hunted, they wouldn't have to cross the border and take the land of the Picts away from them" (Howard "Beyond" ch. 1). This is a fascinating conflation of ideas from medieval and American history. Conan's essential point was made throughout American history by colonists from Pennsylvania to Texas.

Conan talking politics is jarring, but it makes sense considering Howard's political feelings. He supported populist Texas governors Ma and Pa Ferguson. "Farmer Jim" Ferguson served most of two terms as governor. He was against Prohibition and courted tenant farmers. He was impeached in his second term in a complex trial after which he complained, "Is it a crime for a man to borrow $156,000?" The impeachment barred him from serving in political office, so he had his wife run for office. She won running as an anti–Klu Klux Klan candidate. Her campaign's slogan was "Me for Ma—and I Ain't Got a Dern Thing Against Pa" (Gallagher n.p.). Ma and Pa served two more terms as governor of Texas. A Ferguson candidate defeated Lyndon Baines Johnson in his first attempt to reach the Senate, but Johnson was not bitter and gave this tribute to the Fergusons in 1955, when he was Senate majority leader: "Maybe they weren't always right, but they tried to be right, and you can ask no more of anyone."

Howard had a different perspective in 1932: "It's not Sterling against Ferguson; the issue is deeper. It's the common people, mainly the country people, against the corporations and the richer classes" (Howard *Letters* 2: 414). Nationally, he was a "staunch supporter" of Franklin Roosevelt, whom he wrote was "taking the only course by which the country can be saved from utter chaos.... Whether he can prop up a system rotten from the foundations is a question, but he deserves plenty of credit for trying" (Howard *Letters* 3: 163). Howard was concerned when the Supreme Court threatened the New Deal by ruling the National Recovery Administration unconstitutional. He was particularly irritated by "the spectacle of Republicans squawking about State's Rights" (326). He saw Republicans as one of many malign representatives of civilization. He felt that the same industrial interests that had smashed the rights of the Southern states were claiming to uphold the principle of states' rights for their own financial advantage.

Howard felt that one of the worst aspects of civilization was that it was used to justify "looting, butchering and plundering by claiming that these things were done in the interests of art, progress and culture" (*Letters* 3: 376). He rhetorically asks which recent war had defended civilization:

> Was it the Mexican War in which a Latin culture was simply replaced, in some regions, by an Anglo-Saxon culture? Was it the Civil War, in which an agricultural oligarchy was crushed by an industrial oligarchy? Was it the Spanish-American War in which our capitalists grabbed an island for its sugar? Or was it the world war in which the Germans butchered to expand Kultur, and the allies fought to 'make the world safe for democracy'? (And incidentally to protect Wall Street's European investments). (Howard *Letters* 3:376)

IV. Conan

Howard had Conan oppose imperialism. King Conan ignores advice to invade neighboring kingdoms: "Let others dream imperial dreams." He has overthrown an oppressive aristocrat to gain his throne, but he has no wish "to subjugate a foreign realm and rule it by fear" (Howard "Hour" ch. 11).

Near the end of his life Howard lost his faith that Conan could avoid imperial adventures. In March of 1936 he wrote a brief biography of his character in a letter to a fan. De Camp used this letter to construct his paperback series. Howard wrote, "At first [Conan] fought on the defensive, but I am of the opinion that at last he was forced into wars of aggression as a matter of self-preservation. Whether he succeeded in conquering a world-wide empire, or perished in the attempt, I do not know" (Howard *Letter* 3: 430). Howard's fantasy world could not escape his view of reality.

His essay on the Hyborian Age does not mention the reign of Conan. If Conan did conquer a world-wide empire, it did not save civilization. The essay is in accord with "Beyond the Black River" in its forecast of the doom of Aquilonia and the other Hyborian kingdoms: the end of the civilized world will come through imperial wars, and because the civilized elite will neglect the buffering (Texan-like) frontiersman who protect the cities from the barbarians. Above all, doom for civilization comes about through the barbarians.

In "Beyond the Black River" Balthus is shocked to find that the veteran briefing him is no less a barbarian than one of the savage Picts. Conan and Balthus discuss a barbarian victory on a different frontier years earlier. Balthus tells the tale told him by his uncle, who survived the attack: "The barbarians swept out of the hills in a ravening horde, without warning, and stormed Venarium with such fury none could stand before them. Men, women and children were butchered." Conan replies, "I was one of the horde ... I hadn't yet seen fifteen snows, but already my name was repeated about the council fires" (Howard "Beyond" ch. 1). Balthus is unnerved that the man next to him slaughtered men, women and children. He realizes his life is in the hands of one of those "blood-mad devils" who infamously ended Aquilonia's last colonial adventure.

Another barbarian gets the plot moving. A drunk Pict is caught attempting to steal. He is a shaman who is later revealed to have more political and magical power than the authorities realize. Conan advises that the shaman be executed or bought off, because he knows that in the culture of the Picts imprisonment is taboo. The civilized governor ignores his advice. This arrogance will lead to the annihilation of the garrison. Zogar Sag, the shaman, bears both a name and powers that seem to come from one of Lovecraft's stories, and may have had echoes in Mrs. Howard's fantasies of demonic American Indians. Zogar Sag declares that the five people involved in his dishonor will have their heads cut off. He accomplishes this goal by summoning various demonic creatures and monstrous animals who still heed the call of a primordial god. This is the weird element of the story, necessary for the *Weird Tales* market. The main thrust of the plot is not supernatural. Conan is sent on a mission into the deep wilderness with a group of picked frontiersmen to kill or capture Zogar Sag, in order to pacify the natives. Balthus volunteers to come along. Most of the story is told from his viewpoint.

The mission is a complete disaster. Conan's men paddle directly into a full-scale Pictish invasion of the frontier. Zogar Sag had been so enraged by his mistreatment that he used the prestige afforded by his magic to forge an unprecedented alliance of fractious tribes to wipe out the Aquilonians. The shaman mistakes Conan for just another civilized invader. This misjudgment leads to his death. However, first Zogar Sag destroys the fort and kills nearly all of the settlers on the frontier. The fort will not be rebuilt. Balthus must sacrifice his life to save the settlers. The empire is pushed back.

Conan moves on to his next role. The other stories and Howard's biographical letter imply that he soon tires of civilized incompetence and returns to Aquilonia to usurp the crown. Barbarians will rule not just the wilderness and the frontier, but the whole civilized kingdom.

Twentieth-century fantasy worlds often end in disaster. Conan may invigorate his kingdom for a while, but after his reign the barbarians will sweep over all of civilization and end the Hyborian Age. The fellowship of the free peoples in *The Lord of the Rings*—which in the film version even has its own fanfare—is lauded and launched on a grand quest. However, Tolkien emphasizes that its quest fails, and its fellowship breaks. The Third Age of Middle-earth does not end in total darkness, but it ends with its promise unfulfilled. The novel is a twentieth-century fantasy. Like "Beyond the Black River," it has no happy ending.

The canoes, fort, and frontier of "Beyond the Black River" resemble similar elements in the 1936 film version of *The Last of the Mohicans.* The 1992 version starring Daniel Day-Lewis is based more on the earlier film than the original 1826 novel by James Fenimore Cooper. Howard died shortly before the premiere of the 1936 film. However, he may have seen the 1924 film serial *Leatherstocking,* which was done by the same director who made the 1936 film. He may have read some of the original Leatherstocking Tales. At least, he would have been familiar with some of the many Western films and stories influenced by Cooper's classics. The Western genre influenced "Beyond the Black River."

No matter how different the various versions of *The Last of the Mohicans* may be, they all must include the last of the Mohicans—the death of the final member of an entire people. The essential plot detail of *The Last of the Mohicans* matches historical reality: there were many tribes in North America that were wiped out by European settlement. In "Beyond the Black River," the barbarians (Picts) destroy fictionalized versions of Europeans (Aquilonians)—even if they are not up to defeating the superior barbarian (Conan). Not only do the Picts (proto–American Indians) defeat the imperial proto–Europeans, but they are going to completely wipe out their entire civilization. This is the opposite of historical reality. If *The Last of the Mohicans* ended like "Beyond the Black River," then the American Indians would band together to defeat the French and British, and (even if the hero, Hawkeye, survived just as Conan did) it would be foretold that the Europeans were going to be driven into the sea in the future by American Indians. This story would fail because its audience lives in a world in which Europeans took over North America, and thrived. However, the defeat of imperialists in "Beyond the Black River" is consistent with the world of the Hyborian Age—the story is realistic because it does not take place in the real world.

World-building fantasy gives authors the freedom to express sentiments that could not be expressed in other genres. Howard can have barbarians beat imperialists. Tolkien can write a novel with the fate of the world in the balance in which the heroes refuse to use a devastatingly powerful weapon against a horrible evil. *The Lord of the Rings* could not be a thriller: if the "good guys" in any reflection of our world possessed a terrible weapon that could defeat a world-threatening evil, they would use the weapon. In *The Lord of the Rings* the weapon is not used, but destroyed. This goes against the history and logic of our real world in which nuclear weapons were developed and used. This course of action is possible (if not easy) in Middle-earth because it has a different history and operates under different laws than our world. The power of a work of art set in a fantasy world is that it allows the reader or viewer to escape the history, the assumptions, "the way things are." This can lead to questioning "the way things are." This is the true escapism that fantasy worlds can provide.

Fantasy stories are not as removed from mainstream culture as is often assumed. "Beyond the Black River" also has surprising similarities to the iconic film *Apocalypse Now* (1979). The film may not have overt supernatural elements, but Marlon Brando's performance fills the same function as a "weird" element in the film that Zogar Sag's magic does in the story. Both works have bloody river journeys into a jungle in an atmosphere of savagery and empire. The film is not that far removed from the fantasy tradition. It was famously supposed to have been directed by George Lucas. *Star Wars* (1977) might never have been made had this happened. Also, the first credited writer of the screenplay for *Apocalypse Now* was not Joseph Conrad or director Francis Ford Coppola, but John Milius. He went on to direct *Conan the Barbarian* (1982).

Howard wrote "Beyond the Black River" only thirty-six years after Conrad wrote "Heart of Darkness" (1899). Both stories were serialized in magazines. However, "Beyond the Black River" is more like *Apocalypse Now*. They share an anti-imperialist theme, as well as an American sensibility—notably the approach to violence. They are influenced by American history, while Conrad is not. At the end of "Beyond the Black River" imperialism (civilization) is defeated by barbarism. It is also forecast (and we know from the Hyborian Age essay that the forecast will come true) that imperialism is destined to fail and civilization is going to be wiped out by the barbarians (natives). Marlow may not be victorious at the end of "Heart of Darkness," but imperialism has not been defeated. The novella is not a story of civilization *versus* barbarism.

Howard's story has more resonance than *Apocalypse Now* because it does not pretend to be set in the real world. His feelings about imperialism and civilization are derived from his life and the environment of the 1930s. He can credibly talk about civilization and barbarism in a universal way because the action takes place in a specially designed fantasy world. Barbarians in the real world did not fare well against imperialists with guns. There are no guns in the Hyborian Age. The population of the Picts has not been devastated by disease before the Aquilonians confront them. The Hyborian Age is counter-factual to allow Howard to have his worldview seem both appropriate and triumphant.

The title of the story is important. Howard narrates the history of the region: "Back to Thunder River, and still back, beyond Black River, the aborigines had been pushed, with slaughter and massacre. But the dark-skinned people did not forget that once Conajohara had been theirs" (Howard "Beyond" ch. 2). The victims of civilization lie "Beyond the Black River." The Aquilonians committed atrocities against the Picts for the benefit of a corrupt aristocracy residing far from the frontier. The aristocracy will not immediately suffer. The white settlers are the people in danger of being wiped out.

These barbarians are not noble savages. "Beyond the river the primitive still reigned in shadowy forests, brush-thatched huts where hung the grinning skulls of men, and mud-walled enclosures where fires flickered and drums rumbled, and spears were whetted in the hands of dark, silent men with tangled black hair and the eyes of serpents" (Howard "Beyond" ch. 2). From Balthus's perspective, this means that beyond the river there are hordes of savages ready to kill him for the sins of his race.

The emotional charge of this clash of peoples comes more from the history of Texas and the American South than Aquilonia and Pictland. The Picts may be more than stand-ins for American Indians. They may also partially represent the minorities and immigrants Howard feared in the real world.

However, the story (like all of the Conan stories) is not a racial allegory. Howard interrupts the action of the story to correct Conan in a narrative aside. Conan implies that the Picts are non-white. Howard corrects him: "The Picts were a white race, though swarthy, but the border men never spoke of them as such" (Howard "Beyond" ch. 1). Howard does this because he set the racial and historical origins of every people in the Hyborian Age in his mind and in his essay on the age. He does not want the reader to be confused into thinking the story is a clash of whites and non-whites, although he allows that, from the perspective of Conan and the frontiersmen, this is what takes place. He wants the core issue to be the clash of civilization against barbarism, not race. He cannot separate his racism from his core ideas in his letters, and it is often hard for him to do this in his other stories. The Hyborian Age gave him the opportunity to put only as much racism and historical grievance into his Conan stories as he chose. He knows with certainty that the controlling forces in Conan's world are civilization and barbarism because he created that world.

The regions beyond the river also symbolize a more personal conflict. The governor intones, "Our knowledge extends just so far—to the western bank of that ancient river! Who knows what shapes earthly and unearthly may lurk beyond the dim circle of light our knowledge has cast?" (Howard "Beyond" ch. 2). This statement may show the influence of H. P. Lovecraft, but Howard's philosophizing is grounded by blood-and-guts passion and struggle. This struggle is expressed physically, but its origin is in Howard's unconscious mind—in other words, from beyond the Black River.

Conan in this story is not the young thief of "The Tower of the Elephant." He is not a mere barbarian, but practically a demigod of barbarians. He is above the atavistic struggle between civilization and barbarism taking place on the frontier. He tells Balthus of all the places he has been and all the roles he has played in his adventurous life, taking a tour of both his biography and the geography of his world. No number of savage Picts (or summoned demons and prehistoric animals) are going to stop his life's journey. At this point in his life he is smarter than everyone else in the story. He is not quite human here, but an Achilles full of divine wrath, using steel instead of bronze.

However, Howard does not discard reality. The main advantage Conan has over the other frontiersman is practical, not divine. He does not perform impossible feats of strength. He is merely strong enough and experienced enough to move silently through the jungle wearing oiled chainmail. The semi-barbaric frontiersmen dress like Davy Crockett in buckskin, and get slaughtered by the natives. Indian fighters on the American frontier might have fared no better had they lacked firearms.

Conan is in his prime. He may not have guns or germs, but he has steel and uses it. In one combat, a Pict leaps at Conan swinging an axe in one hand and stabbing with a knife in the other. "The knife broke on the Cimmerian's mail.… Conan's fingers locked like iron on the descending arm. A bone snapped loudly.… The next instant [the attacker] was swept off his feet, lifted high above the Cimmerian's head—he writhed in mid-air for an instant, kicking and thrashing, and then was dashed headlong to the earth with such force that he rebounded" (Howard "Beyond" ch. 5).

Conan is "the other" in this story. He is an exciting abstraction. Howard notes in some stories ways in which the barbarian is different from civilized men, but in these cases Conan is presented as superior. He describes Conan in "Beyond the Black River" as being less, as well as more, than a civilized man: "The warm intimacies of small, kindly things, the sentiments and delicious trivialities that make up so much of civilized men's lives were meaningless to him.… Bloodshed and violence and savagery were the natural elements of the life Conan knew; he could not, and would never, understand the little things that are so dear to civilized men and women" (Howard "Beyond" ch. 5).

The civilized Balthus does his best, but skills gained in the "open groves and sun-dappled meadows" of his home are not going to be enough to keep him alive (Howard "Beyond" ch. 5). He reaches out to a badly scarred dog whose owner has been slain by Picts: "Balthus smiled and laid his hand caressingly on the dog's head.… The frontier was no less hard for beasts than for men. This dog had almost forgotten the meaning of kindness and friendliness" (Howard "Beyond" ch. 6). The pair bond and fall together fighting the Picts. Scithers suggests the dog is modeled after Patches, the beloved pet of Howard's youth (Scithers 54). If so, Robert and Patches symbolically save the women and children of Cross Plains.

Conan had left Balthus to rescue the men of the settlements who had improbably decided to go en masse to the salt licks right before the Pictish invasion. Balthus cannot survive in this barbaric world without Conan to protect him. Conan finds the bodies of the man and his dog. He vows to take the heads of ten Picts in memory of Balthus and seven for the dog (no mere scalping for him).

Howard's prose is cinematic. Many lines from the story could be directions from a screenplay. For example, his description of an amphibious assault made by Picts in canoes on the stockade reads, "Stones and logs whirled through the air and splintered and sank half a dozen canoes, killing their occupants, and the other boats drew back out of range" (Howard "Beyond" ch. 6). This would look spectacular on film. Unfortunately, none of the films made about Conan has any scenes even remotely like this. None seems to take anything from "Beyond the Black River" or much from "The Tower of the Elephant." In fact, out of three Conan films, it is remarkable that little from any of the Howard stories has made it to the screen—not the personality of the character, not themes, not even plots. The films that have brought Conan to the widest audience have perversely managed to have little of Conan in them.

Arnold Schwarzenegger's starring role in *Conan the Barbarian* (1982) launched his career as a movie star. Oliver Stone, the writer of the first draft of the screenplay, went on to direct his own films. However, the vision of John Milius dominates the film. He wrote screenplays for films featuring the biggest stars of the 1970s, including Robert Redford in *Jeremiah Johnson* (1972), Paul Newman in *The Life and Times of Judge Roy Bean* (1972), and Clint Eastwood in *Magnum Force* (1973). He was part of the generation of successful filmmakers who went to film school at USC and UCLA in the 1960s, including Francis Ford Coppola, George Lucas, and Steven Spielberg. He was well-known by other filmmakers at the time and called in to do uncredited work on the scripts for such hits as *Dirty Harry* (1971) and *Jaws* (1976). He is the first writer credited for the screenplay of *Apocalypse Now* (1979), and had also directed ("John Milius" n.p.). He tried to use the Conan film to express serious ideas, even though his peers might have seen directing a film starring a body-builder as beneath him.

The first frame of the film telegraphs that the inspiration for the film is not the works of Robert E. Howard. A title card reads, "That which does not kill us makes us stronger—Nietzsche." This quotation is an English paraphrase of a passage from *Twilight of the Idols* (1889), which is translated as: "Out of life's school of war: What does not destroy me, makes me stronger" (Nietzsche n.p.). This is both the world's easiest philosophical maxim to disprove and an odd beginning for a Conan film. Albert Whitaker suggests that this version of the quotation comes from infamous Nixon aide G. Gordon Liddy, who used it prominently in the autobiography he published around the time of the film. He doubts that Milius read Nietzsche (Whitaker n.p.). A viewing of *Conan the Barbarian* shows that Milius did.

The themes of the film are taken from *Twilight of the Idols*. Nietzsche completed this work late in his career—only months before having a mental breakdown. It includes phrases such as "To pose questions with a hammer, and sometimes to hear as a reply that famous hollow sound that can only come from bloated entrails—what a delight ..." This may or may not sound more sane in German; regardless, it captures the violent texture of the film perfectly. A series of philosophical one-liners ("maxims and arrows") follows the introduction. Along with the quote from the title card (maxim #8) are many maxims that capture the spirit of the film (and even its plot). For example, maxim #6 contends, "In our own wild nature we find the best recreation from our un-nature, from our spirituality." Maxim #14 states, "What? You search? You would multiply yourself by ten, by a hundred? You seek followers? Seek zeros!" (Nietzsche n.p.).

These proverbs may seem too obscure to provide the spine of an action movie, but much of the film itself is obscure. In one scene, a child actor playing a young Conan is enslaved after his village is wiped out.

The boy is taken out into the middle of the Spanish desert. The desert is supposed to be in one of the icy northern countries in the Hyborian Age, but the fake snow used in the previous scene is gone. The terrain is recognizable to a cinephile as the Spanish location for spaghetti Westerns of the 1960s such as *The Good, the Bad and the Ugly* (1966). It is recognizable to everyone else as a place with no snow. Milius ignores Howard's geography and the essential fact that the character comes from a developed fantasy world.

Conan and several boys are chained to a giant wheel. They must push this sadistic merry-go-round endlessly while being whipped by an attendant. There are no other structures of any kind visible on the horizon. The device is dubbed "The Wheel of Pain." It may be an inefficient threshing device, but it is not clear where grain might come from in this waste land. There is a montage showing Conan growing older and stronger by tirelessly pushing the wheel. All the other boys have disappeared by the time Conan is old enough to be played by Schwarzenegger—perhaps some of these boys were intelligent enough to escape sometime in the decade young Conan has been pushing the wheel.

The "Wheel of Pain" is a representation of the film's motto: it did not kill Conan, but made him stronger. Unfortunately, it did not make him smarter. Howard transforms the tensions of his life and times into the violence of the Hyborian Age. He does not ossify his ideas into allegorical objects. His Conan is intelligent. He has to be to survive a lifetime of adventures and become a king. Milius and Schwarzenegger may have intended their Conan to seem intelligent, but they failed. The Conan of the film gives the impression that he does not know much of anything—not surprising, since he spent his formative years pushing a wheel in a circle. The second half of the film fully reveals its theme. Milius throws out every Howard plot and replaces it with an almost unbelievably bizarre story for a Conan film: the barbarian is sent by a king to retrieve his brainwashed, Patty Hearst–like daughter from a cult compound. The temple is sort of like the "Hotel California" with a giant snake. Instead of Jim Jones, the film gives us James Earl Jones playing an evil cult leader surrounded by counter-culture idiots in flowing white robes.

Milius had railed against privileged poseurs since his student film

Marcello, I'm Bored (1966), which featured party-goers acting as if they were sophisticated characters from a Fellini film. His screenplays celebrate individuals cutting through the dangerous herds of conformists. Conan makes the cutting literal. Milius uses a scene in a film from the 1930s to explain his philosophy.

Lost Horizon (1937) is Frank Capra's strangest film. It is a non-violent "weird tale." A title card attempts to excuse this strangeness and explains the rationale of the film: "In these days of wars and rumors of war—haven't you ever dreamed of a place where there was peace and security, where living was not a struggle but a lasting delight?" (*Lost Horizon*). Capra brought in Robert Riskin to adapt the 1933 novel by James Hilton. Capra and Riskin had paired successfully on films such as *It Happened One Night* (1934) and *Mr. Deeds Goes to Town* (1936), but they had not attempted to work with material like this before.

Both the novel and the film deal with anxiety about the imminent destruction of civilization. This relates to Howard's vision of the cyclical destruction of civilization by barbarism. For Howard this is not necessarily a bad thing; but even if it were, this is an inescapable process. The creators of both versions of *Lost Horizon* seem to fear that Howard's view that civilization will destroy itself might be right. They want to try to stop it. The film in particular makes an earnest plea for pacifism. Milius rebuts this plea in *Conan the Barbarian*.

Shangri-La is an isolated temple in the Himalayas which a lama has turned into a Library of Alexandria. The lama's plan is to wait out the anticipated civilization-ending war, and to keep safe "all things of beauty and culture." He tells the protagonist, an English diplomat and traumatized veteran of the First World War, that "when that day comes the world must begin to look for a new life. And it is our hope that they may find it here. For here we shall be with their books and their music and the way of life based on one simple rule: be kind" (*Lost Horizon*). He attempts to recruit the diplomat to replace him as guardian.

The lama is bent, shriveled, and extremely old. The halting delivery of his sermons is bizarre. He is a direct precursor to Yoda, the small green sage who first appeared in *The Empire Strikes Back* (1980). He even occasionally uses Yoda's inverted sentence structure: "What madness there is." Yoda is no pacifist—his philosophy is vaguely derived from the Bhagavad Gita and other Eastern scripture, just as the lama's philosophy is vaguely derived from the Gospels. However, most people would consider these fictional sages as basically "good" despite the differences in their inspiration.

John Milius is not most people. *Lost Horizon*'s most visually striking scene occurs after the lama dies. A great line of robed monks snakes through the giant set of the temple. Each monk holds a burning torch. Milius reverses this scene in his film to reverse the message of *Lost Horizon*.

In *Conan the Barbarian* the role of the lama is taken by the evil cult leader Thulsa Doom, played by James Earl Jones. Doom has a lot of young, pretty followers. In one scene Conan spies them having a mass orgy in a temple. What the hippie cultists are too drugged out to realize is not only the obvious fact that someone named "Thulsa Doom" may not be trustworthy, but also that members are periodically killed and mixed into a big vat of green stew in the temple basement. This stew is fed to the drugged cultists as hors d'oeuvres up at the orgy. Milius references the lama's funeral procession to oppose the morals of the counter-culture, which he equates with both the limp pacifism of *Lost Horizon* and the moronic docility of real-life cultists. Doom has his followers assemble outside the massive steps of his temple holding burning torches. After Conan stops listening to Doom's speeches and hacks his head off, the cultists sheepishly come forward with their torches and extinguish their flames in a pool, one by one. Conan burns down the temple, rescues the Patty Hearst–like princess, but refuses to become her new idol (apparently she has to learn to be her own princess), and heads off into the Spanish sunrise.

The film is not always portentous. Milius shows a light touch in several scenes. For example, he has Schwarzenegger emote to James Earl Jones, "You killed my mother! You killed my father! You killed my people! James Earl Jones smiles contentedly and sighs, "Ah. It must have been when I was younger."

However, an entire Conan film done in a campy style is an even worse than replacing Howard with Nietzsche. Director Richard Fleischer had made such successful epics as *20,000 Leagues Under the Sea* (1954) and *Tora! Tora! Tora!* (1970). However, his *Conan the Destroyer* (1984) owes more to the style of his *Soylent Green* (1973). That film infamously ends with Charlton Heston being carted away screaming that the food supplement everyone is eating in this dystopian future is less than savory: "It's people. Soylent Green is made out of people.... Soylent Green is people!" Unlike *Soylent Green, Conan the Destroyer* makes no attempt at social relevance, or much else. Wilt Chamberlain struts through the movie in a fur Viking helmet looking completely ridiculous as a rival to Conan named "Bombaata." The movie is a PG-rated attempt to make Conan accessible to children—a terrible idea.

Conan the Destroyer (1984) is a horrible movie, but the 2011 *Conan the Barbarian* is much worse. It attempts to replace the obsessions of Milius and the camp of Fleischer with digitized gore. The plot is far below that of an action movie or a comic book. It resembles the plot of a violent video game. It does not resemble anything written by Howard. The first appearance of Conan in the film is both vile and silly. It is representative of the whole film. A battle is taking place. The camera takes the viewpoint of Conan as a fetus. His mother's belly is stabbed. The blade misses fetus–Conan. Conan's mother gets her husband to give her a caesarian section with a sword. Conan's father howls as he lifts the bloody, computer-generated baby into the air where the title "Conan the Barbarian" is proudly shown. The filmmakers spent seventy million dollars on this critical and box office disaster.

The notion in the films that Conan had a traumatic childhood goes against everything Howard wrote about his character. He does not even show other Cimmerians in his stories, much less Conan's parents or Conan as a child. Barbarians are never children. Civilized characters in an action movie may have their sense of justice violated. They expect their world to be benign. A trauma such as their wife/child/parents being killed in front of them enrages them, and gives them license to kill or beat people for the rest of the film in an attempt to restore a sense of justice to the world. This allows action heroes to wade through buckets of fake or digital blood without seeming like unappealing psychopaths. The plot of the most recent movie implies that since Conan is so wronged (his parents were killed *and* he was attacked in his mother's womb!) that no amount of hacking and slashing is unjustified. Howard's Conan would never assume that the world is in any sense just—that would be civilized thinking. In both Howard's and Conan's eyes an essential quality of civilization is that it excuses its own atrocities.

The story of the civilized audience may be that it suffers and is redeemed by the violence of its fictional heroes. Conan does not need catharsis. Howard created the Hyborian Age out of his desires, his prejudices, and his pains. He could not even fantasize escaping them. Only a barbarian could do that.

It is possible for a good Conan film based on the works of Robert E. Howard to be made, but film might not be the best medium for the character. The fantasy world of the Hyborian Age is not just adornment, but is the core of the Conan stories. Six long, big-budget films (three *Lord of the Rings* films and another three based on *The Hobbit* and background material) will at least partially illuminate Tolkien's Middle-earth. Studios are unlikely to give the Hyborian Age even a fraction of those resources given the box office failures of the last two Conan films. Comic books, the children of the pulps, have proved a more effective medium for Conan. Talented writers and artists like Roy Thomas, Barry Windsor-Smith, John Buscema, and Kurt Busiek have produced Conan comic books from the 1970s to the twenty-first century. By the 1970s comic books had a long-established tradition of building their superhero stories around a detailed fantasy world. The Hyborian Age is not ignored in comic books, as it has been in films. However, the comic books have an understandable tendency to make Conan more like a superhero. This is not only alien to Howard's conception of the character, but also obscures his themes and much of what is interesting about the barbarian. Also, comic book creators have had to come up with Conan stories month after month for decades. This dilutes the quality of the work. Howard only had to worry about writing good Conan stories for a few years.

The ideal format to dramatize Conan today would be an HBO-style television series. Serialization suits a character from short stories better than a feature film. The success of the HBO fantasy series *Game of Thrones* (2010–present) proves that violent fantasy shows can succeed on television. John Milius himself co-created the HBO series *Rome* (2005–07). Schwarzenegger could play King Conan while other actors could play Conan at different ages. Such a series will have to wait. Fredrik Malmberg, CEO of Paradox Entertainment, announced a new Conan film in October 2012 (Fleming n.p.). He describes Conan as "that Nordic Viking mythic guy ... who has bedded more women than anyone.... He knows he'll be going to Valhalla, and wants to go out with a good battle." The long-suffering fans of Robert E. Howard's Conan have waited eighty years to see his version of the character filmed. They can wait longer.

Howard never imagined that critics would read his Conan stories. He had no reason to believe that Conan would live beyond the memories of the readers of *Weird Tales* in the 1930s—but Howard was not limited by reason. He may have dreamed that Conan would long survive him. He put his life into the tales, and wrote them with untutored skill. He was often quick to take offense in his letters, so it is easy to imagine that he would not have taken criticism of his barbarian quietly. He wrote instructions for any who dared to criticize his writing in an essay he circulated among his friends: "As always, those of you who object to my style, therefore, know right well that you have my cheerful permission to depart at once on your inevitable pilgrimage to the lower regions" (Howard "Eve" 55).

Any writer can appreciate that defiant quote. Defiance defines Howard—but not completely. He once consoled Novalyn Price when she despaired that her writing would never amount to anything. His words are a fitting epitaph for any writer—especially himself: "No writer or artist was ever satisfied with his masterpieces, but he did not destroy them because they were not perfect. He gave them to the world, and the world overlooked their faults, and enjoyed their points of excellence" (Howard *Letters* 3: 427).

V

Superman

Even if the good old days never existed, the fact that we can *conceive* of such a world is, in fact, an affirmation of the human spirit. That the imagination of man is capable of creating the myth of a more open, more generous time is not a sign of our folly.
—Orson Welles

They were definitely not supermen. Jerry Siegel (1914–1996) lived the childhood of a Jewish Charlie Brown: he was so unpopular at school that one year he only received a single Valentine at the class Valentine's Day party—from his teacher (Tye, chapter 1, paragraph 3). A budding writer, Siegel sent himself a card the next Valentine's Day in an attempt to appear less unpopular (Tye chapter 1, paragraph 3). Siegel loved *Weird Tales* magazine (Jones 29). He would have read many stories by Robert E. Howard. Writer Glen Wheldon calls Siegel an "ur-nerd" (Wheldon 9). Joe Shuster (1914–1992) "wore glasses that were incredibly thick. When it seemed that no one was looking, Joe put his face close—so close—down to the page, about two or three inches away, so he could finally see it" (Ricca). Together, they created one of the most popular characters of the twentieth century. They also created the superhero subgenre of fantasy. They started a process that would lead to the development of the largest fictional fantasy worlds in existence.

Shuster's family moved from Canada to a predominantly Jewish neighborhood in Cleveland, and became a friend of Siegel. Cleveland was a more populous city then—the fifth-largest city in United States (Jones 24). However, it was still no New York City, where the pair moved to work in a newly founded industry that had just started producing "comic books."

V. Superman

The young men's proposal for a feature starring their creation, Superman, made everyone at the publisher's office laugh. The staff found the idea ridiculous—even a man dressed as a circus strongman should not be able to lift a car over his head with ease (Simon 12). Siegel was an unpolished writer. His writing style was no more than adequate in comparison to those of other writers of comic books and far below the standards of the average writer of pulp magazine stories. It was not even worthy to be compared with the writing of talented pulp authors like Robert E. Howard.

The art was as crude as the dialogue. Joe Shuster couldn't even get a cartoon published in his school paper (Jones 71). Even after years of drawing the character, his draftsmanship was not impressive. Batman co-creator Bob Kane tells a story about Shuster that underlines Shuster's suspect artistic skills. Kane and Shuster were on vacation in Miami Beach. Kane was out looking for girls, while Shuster stayed at their hotel. He took a walk and saw a beautiful car on the street. He inspected the car closely, putting his head directly above it (so his myopic eyes could see the details of the vehicle). A police officer arrested him because he assumed that Shuster intended to break into the car, and brought him to a police station. Shuster protested his innocence and claimed that he was the artist of *Superman*. The skeptical police gave him paper and a pencil to prove his claim. Several officers examined the finished sketch, and concluded that it wasn't good enough to be drawn by a professional cartoonist. Shuster waited in jail until his publisher called the Miami Beach police department to verify his story. By that time, other artists were drawing the character in some of the comic books featuring Superman, as well as the popular *Superman* newspaper strip that followed the success of the comic book. More-skilled draftsmen had also produced countless advertisements and several high-profile animated film shorts featuring the first superhero.

Despite his original misgivings, Major Malcolm Wheeler-Nicholson, the publisher of National Comics (soon to be renamed DC Comics), decided to print the story starring Superman that Siegel and Shuster submitted to him. He may have been desperate for content, or he may not have cared much about the quality of the stories he published.

His decision to publish a story featuring Superman in *Action Comics* #1 (April 1938)[1] was one of the most profitable decisions in publishing history. However, it was not a profitable one for the major, or for Siegel and Shuster.

Wheeler-Nicholson cut a bizarre figure in 1930s Manhattan with his "beaver hat" and "mouthful of rust-colored teeth" (Simon 12). The major lived the real life of a fictional character from pulp magazines like *Adventure*. He commanded buffalo soldiers chasing Pancho Villa in Mexico. He fought Moro insurgents in the Philippines. He spied in Siberia. He wooed and won the hand of a Swedish aristocrat while in Paris (De Haven 46). He sabotaged his military career by writing a letter to President Harding that warned that the army was being undermined by a spirit of "Prussianism." By the late 1930s, he was reduced to working as a publisher of comic books. He did not belong to the era. Some of the young men who worked with him assumed he was a poseur who had never been in the military at all (Simon 12). He had been a hero in the army, but his military skills did not serve him well in the cut-throat business environment of the publishers of the first comic books.

A better businessman dispossessed Wheeler-Nicholson. Tom De Haven writes, "The Major's printer and distributor, unpaid for too long and fed up at last, finally went to court and got himself made Wheeler-Nicholson's legal partner. This would be Harry Donenfield, a short, animated, loudmouthed New York tough guy, a bootlegger back in the day, as ruthless as he was gregarious. After muscling in, he moved quickly to move the Major out" (De Haven 44). The long history of economic exploitation connected with Superman had begun. Businessmen and corporations would ensure that Siegel and Shuster made little of the hundreds of millions (now billions) that their creation generated.

The pair not only failed to secure a significant piece of the revenue from Superman, but were often treated with contempt by their corporate masters. Siegel and Shuster were at the wrong end of a class divide between working-class Jews and their upwardly mobile Jewish employers. Neal Gabler writes that Jewish studio moguls treated their itinerant Jewish employees (screenwriters, etc.) poorly in Hollywood because these journeymen reminded them of their (unsuccessful) working-class fathers. The bosses of film studios "had *luftmenshen* for fathers, men who shuttled from one job to another, from one place to another" (Gabler 4). The same relationships between Jewish businessmen and their creative underlings took place in the less prominent industry that published comic books. Jerry Siegel and Joe Shuster probably looked like *luftmenshen* to their bosses.

Cartoonist Art Spiegelman (*Maus*) described the interaction between the early comics creators and publishers in this way: "Soon, having run out of existing comics to reprint at low page rates, publishers turned to pulp illustrators and writers, down-at-the-heels painters, failed comic strip artists, and even green teenagers to fill their magazines with cheap new material" (Spiegelman 8). The phrase "even green teenagers" may refer to Siegel and Shuster. Authors of books on Superman often describe the duo as teens or boys; however, Siegel was 24 when *Action Comics* #1 went on sale, and Shuster was 23. The pair had moved away from their homes, and had careers in the big city. They were unlikely to have been the guileless naïfs that the sources sometimes imply.[2]

Whether capitalist or proletariat, almost everyone in the comic book field was Jewish. This remained true through the 1970s. Jews created or co-created most of the superheroes popular today: not just Superman and Batman; but Spider-Man, the Hulk, the X-Men, Captain America, Iron Man, Thor, etc. Jews probably dominated the field because for so long, no one else was interested. Jewish immigrants had entered the publishing industry in New York City in the nineteenth century because the established American printers did not use presses that could reproduce Yiddish characters, so Jews had an opportunity to develop a strong printing industry without competition from established gentile competitors. Jewish artists were well-positioned to take over the new field which the gentile-dominated (as well as more prestigious—and higher-paying) newspaper-strip industry ignored (Jones 19).

Comics writer Danny Fingeroth's book *Disguised as Clark Kent: Jews, Comics, and the Creation of the Superhero* examines the Jewish origins of Superman. Fingeroth quotes Pulitzer Prize–winning cartoonist Jules Feiffer on the subject: "Superman was the ultimate assimilationist fantasy.... Jerry Siegel's accomplishment was to chronicle the smart Jewish boy's American dream.... It wasn't Krypton that Superman came from; it was the planet Minsk or Lodz or Vilna or Warsaw" (Fingeroth 24).

The Superman story fits Feiffer's analogy. Superman leaves the exploding planet Krypton just as many Jews attempted to flee the Nazis from an "exploding" Europe in the 1930s. Superman arrives in America, just as Siegel's parents did. In fact, Superman arrives in Cleveland! (Siegel *Chronicles 1* 4). Unlike later origin stories, the original baby Superman does not arrive in Kansas, and is not raised by the loving Ma and Pa Kent. This Superman grows up in a city: first Cleveland, then New York City (fictionalized as Metropolis)—just like Siegel. Superman's hair is not blond like Flash Gordon's, but black—like Siegel's. Marc Tyler Nobleman gives a possible Hebrew translation for Superman's Kryptonian name "Kal-El" in his book *Boys of Steel: The Creators of Superman:* "all that is good" (Nobleman, afterword, paragraph 6).

Siegel and Shuster were outsiders even among the outsiders of the comics industry—they were from Cleveland. A single Bronx high school, DeWitt-Clinton High School, produced many of the most prominent creators of superheroes, including giants Bob Kane (Robert Kahn), Stan Lee (Stanley Martin Lieber), and Will Eisner (Fingeroth 66). This one New York City high school, just in its graduating classes of the 1930s, may have produced more influential members of the entertainment industry than Cleveland has in its history: Neil Simon (*The Odd Couple* 1965 and *The Goodbye Girl* 1977), Paddy Chayefsky (*Marty* 1955 and *Network* 1976), Stanley Kramer (*Inherit the Wind* 1960 and *Judgment at Nuremberg* 1961), Walter Mirisch (*The Magnificent Seven* 1960 and *In the Heat of the Night* 1967), Richard Condon (*The Manchurian Candidate* 1959 and *Prizzi's Honor* 1982), Burt Lancaster (*From Here to Eternity* 1953 and *Field of Dreams* 1989), Martin Balsam (*On the Waterfront* 1954 and *12 Angry Men* 1957), Don Adams (*Get Smart* 1965–1970), and Laurence Tisch (Loews Theaters and CBS 1987–1995) ("DeWitt-Clinton" n.p.).

The outsider from Cleveland wrote the story of the ultimate outsider—a hero who was not even from the planet Earth. Siegel's story of Superman is different from later versions. Not only is there no Ma and

V. Superman

Pa Kent, no Smallville, and no Metropolis, but Superman does not fly. So what is this Superman? Siegel tells the reader everything he needs to know about the character's motivations on the first page: "Champion of the oppressed. The physical marvel who had sworn his existence to helping those in need!" (Siegel *Chronicles 1* 4).

Supervillains were years away from being invented, as was kryptonite, so every encounter ended the same way—Superman wins! The villains of the early stories are mundane: Superman easily dispatches an uncaring governor, a munitions manufacturer, and a wife-beater. This Superman looks angry or stern in most every panel, except that he smiles when he is smashing something or hitting someone. The obtuse governor is shaken by his encounter with the hero. He sputters, "Thank heaven he's apparently on the side of law and order!" It is not clear that he *is* on the side of law and order in his introduction. He is on the "right" side of progressivism and the New Deal. Superman shows a munitions manufacturer the error of his ways. The merchant of death pleads, "Let me return to the U.S.—I've grown to hate war!" (Siegel *Chronicles 1* 29). Superman does not waste time reasoning with a wife-beater, but slams him into a wall, declaring, "You're not fighting a woman, now!" (Siegel *Chronicles 1* 20).

Early versions of Superman also lack some of the ethical standards that will later characterize him. He casually kills an evil aviator who is strafing civilians. His victim is on the *wrong side*—the villain's only dialogue before Superman knocks him out of his airplane is "Die! Like crawling ants!" (Siegel *Chronicles 1* 28). Siegel's Superman is interested in fighting for social justice, not in upholding the sanctity of life. This formula would be reversed in many future incarnations of the superhero.

Films influenced the creators of Superman. Siegel loved Douglas Fairbanks' *The Mark of Zorro* (1920) (Jones 27). The plot of that film is similar to the basic plot of every Siegel Superman story. In the film, the ineffectual Don Diego Vega annoys the beautiful Lolita Pulido, and is underestimated by everyone around him. He dons a costume and becomes the manly and dangerous Señor Zorro. He defeats his nemesis. In the comic book, the ineffectual Clark Kent annoys the beautiful Lois

137

Lane, and is underestimated by everyone around him. He dons a costume and becomes the manly and dangerous Superman. He defeats his nemesis. Joe Shuster was also influenced by the movies: his drawings of Clark Kent were based upon the appearance of comedian Harold Lloyd (Wheldon 14).

Shuster's art appears, at first glance, to be simultaneously sketchy and primal. However, his drawings may reflect neither weak draftsmanship nor intrinsic vitality. His work has an impressionistic quality. His drawings may have lacked sharp detail because his weak eyes could not see it. His Superman is a blur of lines in motion, as the world may have appeared to Shuster.

Siegel and Shuster had no successes after creating Superman. Critic Gerald Jones belittles the comics of Siegel's later career: "What is one to make of *Lars of Mars?*" (Jones 268). Shuster had no late career at all. The initial success of Superman did not depend on the talents of the young men from Cleveland, but neither was it a fluke. The pair unconsciously connected their own insecurities as awkward young introverts, the insecurity of Jews aware of the impending crisis for European Jewry, and, the anxieties of Americans stuck like Clark Kents in the Great Depression in a world of Hitlers and Stalins. Creators of comic books, radio and television programs, and films would find something mythic in the character—Superman would sometimes become a surrogate for American power or even a Christ figure. However, these interpretations were created many years after Jerry and Joe had been pushed aside. Siegel and Shuster drew upon their own anxieties in writing and drawing Superman. This made it possible for generations of young men to identify with an outsider trying to make good in an alien city, forced to hide his true identity—fighting the good fight and hoping to get his girl. However, the Superman stories of the 1930s are unique, much as the 1930s fantasies of Tolkien and Howard are unique, because they caught the zeitgeist of the age. The real power of the superhero comes from the mise-en-scène of Cleveland and a mythical New York City in the Depression era, not the yellow sun of Earth.

Neither Lex Luthor nor any supervillain appears in Siegel's early Superman stories. Superman is concerned with opponents of progressivism like strike-breakers. Above all, he fights corrupt politicians, who "sabotage ... the very foundations of Democratic government! When Superman finds the city of Metropolis infested by evil, conniving public officeholders, he begins a clean-up campaign" (Siegel *Chronicles 4* 145).

Grant Morrison, a notable contemporary author of Superman stories, claims that the superhero stood for something loftier, "an image of a fiercely human tomorrow that delivered the spectacle of triumphant individualism exercising its sovereignty over the implacable forces of industrial oppression" (Morrison, chapter 1, paragraph 10). This may be true. However, Siegel and Shuster's Superman expresses himself most often by punching people. Although the violence is in service of a progressive and community-oriented ethos, admiring critics of the early Superman need to remember that the original Superman spent most of his time in costume looking for people to beat up. If smacking people around (who seem to deserve it) is the triumphant individual "exercising sovereignty," then Superman did a lot of exercising of sovereignty in the stories from the 1930s.

Siegel knew from the start what he wanted to achieve. Right at the beginning, in his first proposal, he boasts that Superman will become the "greatest super-hero strip of all time!" (Jones 115). His stories achieved this almost immediately, and something more: they made an enormous amount of money for the company that employed him.

Superman did not slowly build to its current popularity: the character was a stunning success from the beginning. The first issue starring Superman went on sale in April. By the Christmas season, a Macy's department store drew a crowd of over 100,000 people for the opening of a Superman-themed display window (De Haven 59).

Competitors scrambled to capture some of this business. In doing so they set a process in motion that would lead to the creation of massive fictional fantasy universes. An out-of-work artist's mother wrote to a friend in March of 1939 of her efforts to help her son secure some of the super-windfall surrounding the superhero: "I'm going to spend all day tomorrow at the Public Library, doing some research work for Bill. He has to have a new character, for a strip ... to do in competition with the new one being syndicated—called the 'Superman' I think.... If you have any brilliant ideas for a competitive strip, for heaven's sake let us know" (Bell 28). Bill (Everett) did create a successful superhero—an anti-hero called Prince Namor, the Sub-Mariner, a paragon from the underwater kingdom of Atlantis. The Sub-Mariner was an original creation: he begins as an anti-hero, initially furious at "the surface world's" callous treatment of the world's oceans (Bell 1). However, his interest in a leggy American nurse, and the common threat of the Nazis to both the United States and Atlantis, conspire to turn Namor into a superhero who fights by the side of Captain America.

The real world would not spare even the creators of what was at the time (wrongly) assumed to be an ephemeral genre of fantastic escapism. The first cover of the superhero Captain America featured the red-white-and-blue superhero socking Hitler in the jaw—months before the United States and Germany were at war (Simon 44). The creator of Captain America, Joe Simon, noted that this angered many people at the time; the comic book was published almost a year before Hitler declared war on the United States, and the Germans had many supporters in the United States. Simon reports that his office received "raging hate mail and vicious, obscene telephone calls." He summarized the theme of the calls: "death to the Jews." Although the office received a lot of abuse initially, Captain America won many admirers—including a particularly high-profile supporter. Mayor Fiorello La Guardia was an avid reader of both newspaper comic strips and the new comic books, and he approved of the anti-fascist propaganda of *Captain America*. The mayor called the office that published the adventures of the patriotic superhero to congratulate and reassure Captain America's creators, that "you boys over there are doing a good job." He told them that he would take care of the situation, that "the City of New York will see that no harm will come to you." Simon noticed frequent police patrols of his office, after which the threats stopped (Simon 45).

Superman was born in a time of war. In April of 1938, when *Action Comics* #1 was published, although the Second World War had not officially started in Europe but the continent was at war. Generalissimo Franco's forces were pounding Republican forces in the Spanish Civil War. Superman would participate in the Second World War and, like the Sub-Mariner and Captain America, he fought Nazis before the United States entered the war. He was punching German submarines in September of 1941, and grappling with Swastika-wearing paratroopers the next month.

Superman would not only participate in both the Second World War and the Cold War in his comic books, he would also provoke America's real-life enemies: "Both during and after the war, political figures ranging from Hitler's minister of propaganda to Josef Stalin and Hirohito had commented on Superman's exploits, and most of them did not have kind words for the hero. A propagandist writing in Stalin's name once declared that Superman comics were 'designed to stir up revolt and revolution among ... peaceful people'" (*Superman Radio* 86).

Superman never fully used his abilities in wars. He did not participate in wars in later incarnations because by then the character's ethics had changed. In the 1930s and 1940s, the creators of Superman would have risked insulting real-life American soldiers if he had wiped out the enemies of the United States with his superpowers. Superman really participated in the war effort in our world: "During World War II, Superman's comic book incarnation was required military shipping, deemed an 'essential supply' to all Marine garrisons at Midway Island" (Rossen x).

Superman's impact on the American public in an era before television was considerable, and comic books sold well. David Hadjou estimates that 80–100 million copies of comic books were sold every week in the mid-1940s (Hadjou 5); therefore, in a country of roughly 132 million people, an estimated 4.16 billion comic book were sold every year. Superheroes are popular today, and Superman is well-known globally; however, the relative cultural impact of Superman and comics books was probably much higher in the 1930s and 1940s. Superman interacted with real-life events in the 1940s. In April of 1946, the *Adventures of Superman* radio program "took on the KKK in a sixteen-part adventure" (Scivally 21). As Bruce Scivally relates, "A Southern writer and journalist infiltrated a cell of the Klu Klux Klan, and passed the passwords on to the producers of the Superman radio show via the Anti-Defamation League. Samuel 'Doc' Green, Grand Dragon of Koven Number One of Atlanta, Georgia was not amused; every time he heard one of the passwords used on the show, he had to issue a new one" (Scivally 21).

The cultural impact of superheroes rapidly declined by the end of the 1940s. There are many possible reasons for this relative fall from grace, but the public campaign of crusading psychiatrist Dr. Fredric Wertham against the sale of comic books was an important factor. Wertham was an idealistic psychiatrist who had worked for the availability of mental health care for African-Americans: he established a free clinic in Harlem, and was friendly with Ralph Ellison and Richard Wright (De Haven 86). However, in the 1950s he and the nation shared an obsession with juvenile delinquency. Wertham decided that comic books were to blame for the break-down of society, and spent years trying to destroy the entire comic-book industry. He failed to eliminate the industry, but he did cripple it.

Wertham starts his book, *Seduction of the Innocent* (1953), with an obscure quotation from Sir Thomas Elyot (1490–1546): "And I verily do suppose that in the braines and hertes of children, whiche be membres spirituall, whiles they be tender, and the little slippes of reason begynne in them to bad, ther may happe by evil custome some pestiferous dewe of vice to perse the sayde members, and infecte and corrupt the softe and tender buddes" (Wertham 1). His selection of this passage tells the reader most of the information needed to evaluate the book: it is a pretentious and turgidly written attack on comic books; however, the author takes his subject seriously. Fortunately for Wertham, the doctor did not have to rely on his prose style to spread his anti-comics message. He was able to take some of the few pithy passages from his tome and use them to effectively lobby against comic books with the media and the government. He was ultimately the star witness in a congressional hearing on the relationship between comic books and juvenile delinquency.

Wertham writes about superheroes, "How did Nietzsche get into the nursery?" (Wertham 15). Although most comic-book-creators were Jewish, the psychiatrist persistently equated superheroes with Nazis, singling out "Superman (with the big S on his uniform—we should, I suppose, be thankful that it is not an S.S.)" (34). His comments about the creators of comic books are even more intemperate: "I think Hitler was a beginner compared to the comic-book industry.... They get the children much younger. They teach them race hatred at the age of four, before they can read" (Jones 264).

Wertham most hated comic books that collected "true crime" and horror stories, but he also despised superheroes. He is especially critical of characters that deviate from "normal" attitudes towards gender, stating, "The Batman type of story may stimulate children to homosexual fantasies.... We have inquired about Batman from overt homosexuals treated at the Readjustment Center" (Wertham 191) and "Superwoman (Wonder Woman) is always a horror type. She is physically very powerful, tortures men, has her own female following, is the cruel, 'phallic' woman. While she is a frightening figure for boys, she is an undesirable ideal for girls, being the exact opposite of what girls are supposed to want to be" (34).

Wertham demanded a ban on the sale of all comic books. He brushed aside arguments in favor of free speech (when applied to comic books), declaring that "people will have to learn that it is a distorted idea to think that democracy means giving good and evil an equal chance at expression. We must learn that freedom is not something that one can have, but is something that one must do" (Wertham 395).

The doctor was not unique in attacking comic books. There have been critics of comic book from the birth of the medium to today. However, the most common contemporary criticism is not that they damage society, but that they are infantile. Playwright David Mamet, author of *Glengarry Glen Ross* (1983) and *Speed-the-Plow* (1988), wrote of Superman, "The fantasy of omnipotence has, indeed, echoes of the psychology of someone who spends his life in his underwear: of the psychology of the infant" (Mamet 179).

Wertham never got the ban on comic books he desired. Governor Thomas Dewey of New York, loser of two presidential elections in the 1940s, vetoed the bill (Jones 327). However, Wertham "transformed a medium most people had considered merely disposable into something disreputable, even twisted ... church groups started up comic book burnings again in earnest; consumer groups urged parents to complain to their local grocers about the comics they stocked" (Wheldon 99).

American writer Sterling North, author of the best-selling children's novel *Rascal* (1963), was also disgusted by comic books. He complained, "Superman heroics, voluptuous females in scanty attire, blazing machine guns, hooded 'justice' and cheap political propaganda were to be found on almost every page" (Hadjou 40). Robert E. Southard, a Jesuit and a professor, wrote: "If our youth get the notion that it is heroic for a private person to 'take order' in matters of public order we are ready for a Hitler" (Jones 79). For him, proper authority resided with the Catholic Church and the state.

The readers of comic books felt differently. David Pace Wigransky probably expressed the opinion of many in a letter he wrote in May of 1948 to the *Saturday Review of Literature:* "Children ... should be kept in utter and complete ignorance of anything and everything except the innocuous and sterile world that the Dr. Werthams of the world prefer to keep them prisoner within from birth to maturity. The net result of all this, however, is that when they have to someday grow up, they will be thrust into an entirely different kind of world, a world of force and competition, an impersonal world in which they will have to fight their own battles, afraid, insecure, helpless" (Jones 114). Wigransky was 14.

Senator Estes Kefauver tried to use the issue of comic books and juvenile delinquency to aid his campaign to become President of the United States. Kefauver disdained machine politicians, and was distinguished-looking enough to make a good impression on television. He held the televised hearings that provided Dr. Wertham his moment in the sun. Harry Truman hated Kefauver, and intervened in the 1952 convention of the Democratic Party to keep the front-running Kefauver from becoming the Democratic nominee to face Eisenhower in the general election. The hearing was a sort of poor man's version of one of the hearings of Joseph McCarthy's House Committee on Un-American Activities. Although comic books were never banned, many comic-book-companies went out of business, and, the industry was frightened into giving prominence to a self-censoring panel, the Comics Code Authority (Jones 249).

The British government went further than the government of the United States and actually banned comic books in 1955 (Jones 303). This episode demonstrates that attacks on comic books were not limited to the political Right (or to the idiosyncratic Leftist, Frederic Wertham). Member of Parliament Peter Mauger, a regular contributor to Communist Party publications, led a temporarily successful effort against comic books, and the perceived cultural imperialism of the United States (302). Mauger wrote: "These magazines, which boast of spreading the American way of life throughout the globe, also deal in sadism, whippings, torture, and a rather vulgar form of visual pornography.... Comics glorify power.... Comics portray fantasies of the future, all fascist in character.... The lessons are that human nature is aggressive and ruthless" (302). Parliament passed a law in February of 1955 prescribing a penalty of up to four months in prison for distributors of comic books that "would tend to incite or encourage to the commission of crimes or acts of violence or cruelty, or otherwise to corrupt, a child or young person into whose hands it might fall" (303).

The decline in the popularity of comic books accelerated until the industry crashed in the late 1950s. At the beginning of 1957, Marvel Comics published 85 comic books. By April, the publisher produced only 16. According to Stan Lee, "Everybody was running scared" (Jones 327). The editor-in-chief of Marvel Comics survived the lean years for comics and helped to resurrect the superhero as a force in popular culture in the 1960s and 1970s. He co-created superheroes such as Spider-Man, Iron Man, the Hulk, Thor, the X-Men, and a resurrected Captain America.

Stan Lee essentially created the "Marvel Universe" of superheroes, supervillains, and their supporting cast—tens of thousands of corporately owned characters. Lee was following the originators of the genre. However, unlike J. R. R. Tolkien and Robert E. Howard, Jerry Siegel and Joe Shuster did not create their own fantasy world. Rather, they made possible the "DC Universe," as well as the "Marvel Universe"—every superhero ever invented.[3]

Only three superheroes survived the decline of the popularity of comic books in the late 1940s and 1950s: Superman, Batman, and Wonder Woman. This was an impressive feat. There were hundreds of superheroes in the "Golden Age of Comics" that Siegel and Shuster started, and to which Dr. Wertham put nearly the last nail in the coffin. Some DC Comics characters, such as Green Lantern and the Flash, were prominently resurrected in the early 1960s—the beginning of the "Silver Age of Comics." During this period, Stan Lee brought back Joe Simon's Captain America and Bill Everett's Sub-Mariner to join the superheroes he co-created, such as Spider-Man, in the "Marvel Universe." However, only comic-book-collectors and readers of obscure contemporary revivals of "Golden Age" superheroes remember the names of the hundreds of characters who did not survive: the Human Bomb, the Phantom Lady, Bulletman and Bulletgirl, Uncle Sam, Captain Freedom, Captain Battle, Captain Future, Miss Patriot, etc.

Even a summary of the characters of Batman and Wonder Woman would require books in themselves—a summary of Superman's adventures alone would require volumes. However, it is important to discuss briefly Batman and Wonder Woman in this examination of fantasy worlds created in the 1930s, because without them Superman would have been merely a cultural artifact like Buck Rogers or Popeye and not the progenitor of fictional universes.

Bob Kane was convinced of the centrality of his creation to the phenomenon of superheroes. "It was only after the arrival of Batman in 1939 that the deluge of superheroes began," he wrote. "Before the year was out, the Sandman, Blue Beetle, Amazing Man, the Human Torch, and Submariner hit the newsstands" (Kane *Batman* 99). Kane based his superhero more directly on films than Siegel did. Film versions of Dracula, the Scarlet Pimpernel, and Zorro are visible in Kane's drawings of Batman. Siegel, a writer, was the dominant force behind the creation of Superman, while Kane was an artist. As a consequence of Kane's greater interest in the visual arts rather than writing, the early stories of Batman often feature plots and dialogue that is even sketchier than Siegel's somewhat crude efforts. However, Kane's early Batman stories also feature superior and far more atmospheric drawings than the Superman comics.

Superman is often considered a simplistic character—suggestive, in David Mamet's words, of the psychology of an infant. This is a mistake: he is a hero who moves through simple plots, but the stories themselves are not simplistic. Writer Umberto Eco (b. 1932) has a more nuanced view of the character. Eco, who had hundreds of Superman comics stuffed into the cupboards of his residence, was the first person to write an academic article about Superman: "Il mito di Superman e la dissoluzione del tempo" (1962) discussed the psychology of the super-hero (Gabilliet xx). Eco wrote in 1972, "Clark Kent personifies fairly typically the average reader … an obvious process of identification [that] secretly feeds the hope that one day, from the slough of his actual personality, a superman can spring forth who is capable of redeeming years of mediocre existence" (Eco 15).

However, Siegel's Superman concerns more than power fantasies and action scenes: it also focuses on the dichotomy between Clark Kent and Superman; the love triangle between Lois Lane, Clark Kent, and Superman; and Siegel's championing of a muscular form of social justice. Kane's Batman is a far more limited character; unlike Superman, he is humorless. The Man of Steel often seems amused by his opponent's feeble attempts to defeat him. Joe Shuster drew Superman with a slight smirk every time some idiot hit him over the head with a crowbar. The superhero seems to be thinking: "Bullets just bounced off my chest, and you think you can beat me with a *crowbar?*" There is also some humor in Lois Lane's mistreatment of poor Clark Kent while mooning over Superman (although this subplot wears thin with endless repetition). In contrast, Kane's Batman speaks dialogue such as: "Tell me! Or I'll *kill* you!" (Kane *Chronicles* 22).

Superheroes would gain in psychological complexity. The process started in the 1960s and accelerated in the 1970s and 1980s. It is important to note that Siegel did not start out writing Superman stories for small children. A survey done by the *New York World-Telegram* in 1942 determined that the average reader of comic books was about twelve years old. This survey understates the average age of readers of comic books—millions of service members read Superman stories during the Second World War; they were clearly not 12 but were unavailable for the survey. The average age of comic book readers dropped in the 1950s because the stories of superheroes were infantilized to avoid attracting unwelcome attention from critics like Frederic Wertham, and ambitious politicians.

Moreover, since the late 1980s, comic books have been intended primarily for men in their 20s and 30s (Scivally 166). Film has taken over the job of entertaining children with superheroes. In consequence, the psychology of superheroes is more advanced in contemporary comics than in the superhero films. Batman is an easier character to write from a realistic perspective than Superman—if "realistic" is a word that should be used to describe a character who wears a cowl with horns and calls himself "Batman." In any case, while the psychology of contemporary versions of the character Batman will never be mistaken for a creation of Henry James or Austen or Shakespeare, the modern Batman is more psychologically complex than Ian Fleming's James Bond, or even many characters of Charles Dickens. Superman is much more difficult for a writer to psychologize: how can the reader relate to a man who can fly through volcanos? In the beginning, however, Superman was more complex than Batman. If Batman had been the first superhero, instead of Superman, as interesting as the character proved to be in later decades, there probably would not have been a second—there would have been no reason to copy a Batman who was basically an eccentric version of heroes like the Lone Ranger (created for radio in 1932). The character of Superman was unique enough to inspire thousands of imitators.

Mark White takes the characters of Superman and Batman seriously in his book, *Superman and Philosophy*, if not with deadly seriousness. (The book's subtitle is: "What Would Superman Do?") He writes, "Batman and Hobbes think that human nature with all its many imperfections is given and fixed, whereas Superman and Hegel believe that people can improve, but only within a society in which they can live together and which allows and enables everybody to recognize and be recognized by others" (White 202). Kevin Smith, director of *Clerks* (1994) and *Chasing Amy* (1997), puts this sentiment more succinctly: "Batman is about angst; Superman is about hope" (Scivally 169). Although the sidekick has always at least flirted with camp, the introduction of Robin in February of 1940 (over a year after Batman's 1939 debut) added some needed depth of character for Batman, as well as improving the visual palette of the comic book (Kane *Dark* 5).

Wonder Woman has always been a far less popular superhero than

Superman or Batman—hardly surprising, since whatever the age of the comic book audience, its gender has always been predominantly male. The character's story is less vital to the development of the superhero fantasy worlds, so it will be considered here only briefly. However, it would be a mistake to omit her story altogether. The character of Wonder Woman demonstrates, in a way nothing else could, the diversity of super-heroes and the diversity of the intentions of their creators. In addition, the story of the rationale behind the creation of Wonder Woman is fascinating and bizarre.

Psychologist William Moulton Marston created Wonder Woman to champion the empowerment of women, and also to share his bondage fetish. He explained in a magazine article explaining his reasons for creating a female superhero. "Superman and the army of male comics characters who resemble him satisfy the simple desire to be stronger and more powerful than anybody else. Wonder Woman satisfies the subconscious, elaborately disguised desire of males to be mastered by a woman who loves them" (Jones 78). *Wonder Woman #1* does not hide its message. The first line reads: "At last, in a world torn by the hatreds and wars of men, appears a *woman* to whom the problems and feats of men are mere child's play" (Marsten 4).

The origin of Superman is a science fiction story. The first Batman story is a stylized version of a hard-boiled detective story, combined with a revenge tragedy. Wonder Woman's origin story is a mythological tale. She (along with Marvel's Thor from the 1960s) is one of the only superheroes who really is a modern, commercial version of a myth, despite the conventional wisdom in much writing about comic books that superheroes are modern myths. Hercules tricks Queen Hippolyte of the Amazons into thinking that he is in love with her, then binds the queen so he can steal from her (Marsten 4). Aphrodite, the patron deity of the Amazons, feels for her people and frees them. She requires them to wear the cuffs of the manacles as a reminder to them of what happens to women who put themselves in men's power. Henceforth, if any Amazon is bound, she loses her superhuman vitality until she is freed. This is the origin of Wonder Woman's bullet-deflecting bracelets.

The identification of the character of Wonder Woman with bondage is not a cynical comment, or a humorous quip. Marston's obsession with bondage is on the surface of the early Wonder Woman stories. For example, in an issue published in December 1941, there is a scene depicting a comely blonde woman who is blindfolded, put on her hands and knees, and spanked. The episode has nothing to do with the plot of the story (Marston 89). Wonder Woman plays dominatrix in the stories by binding men with her Lasso of Truth. She often plays the submissive as she is bound by a villain (generally another female) and temporarily loses her powers. Marston transforms the "Clark Kent vs. Superman" dynamic of Superman comics into sexual role-playing: the submissive Diana Prince turns into the dominant Wonder Woman, and the aggressive Wonder Woman is bound and turned into the passive Diana Prince. Marston repeats the cycle over and over (sometimes several times in a single, brief story).

He also invented even more bizarre sub-plots, often featuring a recurring character, the morbidly obese Etta Candy. It not clear why Wonder Woman or her secret identity of Diana Prince has anything to do with Candy, who resides at (or, perhaps, presides over) a sorority house, surrounded by young co-eds. In one story, which the reader can reasonably assume was a personal favorite of Marston's, Etta Candy conducts sorority initiations (spanking), and gleefully punishes a wayward sister (more spanking) who has committed the sin of abandoning her sisters to go out on a date with a man (Marston 60). Again, this sub-plot has *nothing* to do with the action-adventure plot of the issue in which Wonder Woman triumphs over another malefactor in the style of Superman.

The character of Wonder Woman would develop over time, much as Batman transformed from a callow rich man playing a tough guy to a character with mystique and psychological complexity. When Marston stopped writing the stories, the obsession with bondage was dropped. Contemporary writers generally make Wonder Woman either a fierce warrior from Greek mythology (taking her quasi-mythological origin story seriously), or a physically powerful ambassador for peace to the troubled world of men (maintaining the more laudable aspects of Marston's first stories).

V. Superman

Far from being generic, the first superheroes were diverse because of the wildly different interests of their creators. The early superheroes were also diverse in their media. Superman expanded from its beginnings as a comic book to become a series of animated shorts, a live-action film serial, a radio program, and a television program—all in about fifteen years. Superman began the first transmedia fantasy worlds. An obscure few weeks of the popular Superman radio program *Adventures of Superman* (1940–51) changed the character and the development of fantasy worlds forever.

The producers of the radio program decided to spotlight a character other than Superman during a serial in late 1945. The villainess of the story, Southern socialite Dixie Lamar, was unremarkable. What was remarkable was that Batman (and Robin) were introduced to the radio audience, and worked together with Superman to solve the case (De Forest 170). This combining of superheroes was not done in the comic books until almost seven years after Superman was introduced. This seemingly obvious innovation was probably not tried because the Superman comic books were modeled after episodic newspaper comic strips, which only had a few panels each day in which to tell their story. Superman and Batman never met in their comics. Occasionally, they would be put together on the cover of a special comic book, but inside the issue they performed their heroic feats in discrete stories. The first pairing of National Comic' (later DC) two primary superheroes did not occur until 1952 (Hamilton and Swan "Superman").[4]

The simple expedient of placing superheroes together in the same story forced the evolution of simple stories into the miraculous creation of a massive fantasy world—aptly named a "universe." Superheroes could now leave their (until then) all-encompassing little fantasy cities to enter a larger world. If the Joker was defeating Batman in Gotham City, Superman could fly over and help out his pal. If Superman wanted to take care of a problem in outer space, he could have Batman dress up as Superman and hold down the fort in Metropolis. Robin could be amazed by Wonder Woman's beautiful Amazonian "sisters" during their visits to "the man's world." The hapless villains of each hero, tired of fighting their superhero alone and losing in every issue, could now band together in coalitions of villainy—they could at least fail to defeat their righteous enemies with greater dignity. The superheroes could band together to form groups, like the Justice League of America, to combat cosmic threats. These combinations of heroes and villains raised the stakes of the confrontations in the comics from Superman yawning through another bank robbery to the Man of Steel being forced to work with other heroes to defeat greater threats like massive alien invasions and demigods.

A fantasy universe was, for the first time, created through the effort of scores of writers and artists, building upon decades of earlier work. The expanding DC Universe was mimicked by the creators of Marvel Comics—effectively creating two, parallel realities hosting a multitude of stories in the same genre, but taking place in separate, competing universes. Jerry Siegel had developed the concept of what is today called "continuity"—the setting of each superhero story in the framework of the artificial history of the fictional "universe"—in a June 1939 story that referenced earlier adventures (Siegel *Chronicles 2* 4). Like the later teaming of Superman and Batman in the same story, this was a revolutionary development for the superhero genre. Comics creators developed this history with each new issue. Now the stories were not just separate tales, but building blocks that a comic book collector could horde like a stash of treasured baseball cards.

This changed the readers of comic books even more than the stories. Now they could amass not just the physical artifacts of low-quality, stapled-together newsprint, but also the intellectual treasure of knowledge about the living "history" of the superheroes. Devoted readers could top their friends with demonstrations of esoteric comic book lore. These were the first fantasy worlds created by accretion. The stories were improved through the sheer mass and collation of thousands of stories. Writers at the company who owned the copyright for a superhero could draw on countless earlier stories to overcome the limits of the generally straightforward plots of heroes inevitably triumphing over villains (a mandate by the Comics Code to reinforce the claims of real-world authority). Good ideas tended to survive, while bad plot-lines would magically sink, without the conscious efforts of the creators—a sort of Adam Smith–like "invisible hand" process for the super-hero set.

The DC Universe would become even more complicated than this because of developments in "continuity" caused by multiple authors creating fictional history in disconnected bits over decades. Endless complications ensued. For instance, the publishers could not allow Superman and Batman to age from roughly thirty-five in 1940 to roughly eighty in 1985. The artists' creative solution to this problem was to divide their DC Universe into separate sub-universes (Wheldon 213). For example, "Earth-1" was a fictional dimension featuring aged superheroes who had been in their prime during the 1940s, while "Earth-2" contained the "normal" superheroes as they were chronicled in current comic books. Matters became even more complex when the superheroes of "different Earths" crossed dimensional barriers and met each other in special stories: a silver-haired Superman could fight along-side his regular Superman counterpart. Writers also made different Earths for reasons rooted in the real-life comics business. "Earth-S" was a dimension within the DC Universe that contained the superheroes of a rival company, Fawcett Comics, which DC Comics had driven out of business with a copyright-infringement suit (Wheldon 213). DC Comics later claimed the rights to all of Fawcett's superheroes. Captain Mar-vel—a young boy who is magically transformed into a superhero when he yells "Shazam!"—was popular enough for the comics creators at DC to integrate into the primary fantasy world (Earth-2), which hosted the familiar versions of Superman and Batman and the main DC super-heroes.

This complexity made it hard for any but devoted initiates to under-stand these stories—but this, too, was part of the appeal for devoted readers of comic books. A fictional exchange of dialogue between boys in 1950s Oregon in director Rob Reiner's film *Stand by Me* (1986)—which was based on a story by Stephen King—dramatizes a simplified version of millions of actual conversations between young devotées of comic books:

VERN: Do you think Mighty Mouse could beat up Superman?
TEDDY: What are you, cracked?

VERN: Why not? I saw the other day. He was carrying five elephants in one hand!

TEDDY: Boy, you don't know nothing! Mighty Mouse is a cartoon. Superman's a real guy. There's no way a cartoon could beat up a real guy.

VERN: Yeah, maybe you're right. It'd be a good fight, though.

Filmmakers adapting superhero properties have only recently begun to understand the financial potential of stories featuring an entire superhero-fantasy world surrounding the featured superhero rather than making movies focusing exclusively on the star of the film. The makers of the first modern superhero movie, *Superman: The Movie* (1978), understandably focused on the main character—the first superhero in both the "real world" and the world of the film. However, the comic books that provide Hollywood with the grist for superhero films typically contain more than a single superhero. Both the "DC Universe" and the "Marvel Universe" have hundreds of superheroes active in their fantasy worlds at any one time. Superhero films that pretend their character is the only champion (or, often, the only competent adult) in the world lack plausibility. For example, when the Joker threatens mass slaughter in a Batman film, the viewers may ask themselves why Superman doesn't simply fly over from Metropolis to take care of the problem—or why some police officer doesn't shoot the maniac. The writers of comic books set in fantasy worlds have to answer these sorts of questions. This makes for better stories. The complexity of the plots in superhero films has not caught up to the increasing sophistication of their often-derided source material: the average superhero film of the twenty-first century has a plot comparable to a below-average comic from the 1980s.

Filmmakers have sometimes done worse than limit the environments of their films: they have often made their movies as if the action was taking place in the real world. This leads to some members of the audience wondering why, for instance, the characters wear spandex and tights. Making superhero films more "realistic" than their sources makes little sense: why make a fantasy film without a fantasy world?

It is not surprising that makers of superhero films have been slow to realize the financial and creative potential of using fantasy worlds in fantasy movies: creators at DC Comics and Marvel Comics took almost fifty years to realize this potential themselves. An early attempt to put a large number of superheroes interacting with each other in the same story was Marvel's *Contest of Champions* (1982): "Welcome, one and all, to mighty Marvel's very first *Limited Series*—a special, all-new kind of comic book series designed to run a finite number of issues," the editors wrote. "To kick off the new format, we have chosen a project that encompasses *all* of Marvel's stalwart super-stars in a single single-staggering epic ... the MARVEL SUPER HERO CONTEST OF CHAMPIONS!" (Gruenwald 1). The plot was rudimentary, although still better than the plot of the average twenty-first-century superhero film.

Filmmakers have finally started to apply the lessons of superhero comics to their big-budget film adaptations. Marvel Comics wisely decided to create their own film studio to adapt their superhero properties. Their first self-produced film—they had previously licensed their characters to established film studios—was *Iron Man* (2008), directed by Jon Favreau and starring Robert Downey, Jr. Marvel Studios, currently a subsidiary of the Walt Disney Company, used the film rights of their superheroes as collateral for a more than $500,000,000 bond issued through Merrill Lynch to amass a budget big enough to handle the portrayal of several superheroes in one film for *Marvel's The Avengers* (2012) (Gomez, paragraph 2). Their risk was rewarded: the film grossed 1.5 billion dollars and Disney earned $370 million in profits (McMillan, paragraph 2). Robert Downey, Jr., played the superhero Iron Man (1963), a member of the Marvel Comics team of superheroes, the Avengers (1963). After the surprising success of *Iron Man*, Downey re-negotiated his contract and was expected to make over 50 million dollars for playing the same superhero in *The Avengers* (Belloni "Marvel" paragraph 2).

Much of the narrative interest of superhero comic books comes from the aggregation of thousands of different stories. Good writers of comic books never write exactly the same story twice. It is impossible for even bad writers of comics to precisely replicate previous stories, so tiny changes are constantly introduced into their fantasy world. They accomplish character development and world-building through a sort of narrative crowd-sourcing: years of stories, scores of authors, and millions of readers create a fantasy world that a single author could not.

The Birth of Modern Fantasy

Superhero comics fall short of literary novels, but they have their own virtues. They are not inferior versions of novels produced for an infantile audience—the age of the reader of superhero stories is irrelevant, although, their audience (to a much greater degree than that of *The Lord of the Rings,* but similar to the readership of Robert E. Howard's stories) is predominantly male. Creators may use superhero fantasy worlds with more impressive results in the future.

Siegel created an embryonic fantasy world that required radio and generations of writers and artists to give it birth. The producers of the television program *Adventures of Superman* (1952–58) inherited the character, but were uninterested in developing a fantasy world for him to inhabit. Actor George Reeves was the face of Superman for a generation. *Hollywoodland* (2006), a film about Reeves' career and apparent suicide starring Ben Affleck, suggests that Reeves grew to hate being identified with the character of Superman. In the film, a spurned lover plays on Reeves' fears that his role as Superman has ruined his career, telling him, "George, that's all you were good for. Ten-year-olds and shut-ins. That was the best you were ever going to be. I knew that, why didn't you?" Glen Wheldon describes "The stubborn image of an embarrassed-looking George Reeves standing around like a burly trapeze artist on a smoke break" (Wheldon 186).

Reeves demonstrates that he has acting ability, even in his first performance as Superman, in the film *Superman and the Mole Men* (1951). However, even at the beginning of his career playing the superhero, he shows discomfort with the material. *Superman and the Mole Men* is a story for children, but it is also a parable about the evils of mob violence. The film comments on the environment that spawned the House Committee on Un-American Activities. HUAC (1938–69) was formed the year Superman was introduced. The environment of paranoia (which the film attacks) would later trouble Superman himself through Dr. Fredric Wertham's crusade against comic books in the 1950s. However, when—harkening back to Siegel's superhero—Superman is called upon to show righteous indignation (and a right hook) to the Enemies of Progress, Reeves sounds testy rather than joyfully indignant, as Siegel's Superman would have been: "Obviously, none of you can be trusted with guns, so I'm going to take them away from you."

Superman and the Mole Men was directed by Lee Sholem. The director was known as "Roll 'Em Sholem"—a tribute to his speed, to his determination to finish every scene according to the shooting schedule without ever taking any extra time ("Lee" paragraph 1). Neither Sholem nor Reeves was interested in the background and environment of the character. However, they were professionals. The nadir of Superman adaptations took place after Reeves' untimely death. Whitney Ellsworth, the producer of *Adventures of Superman,* decided to develop a new television program that retained the Superman brand without the bother of including Superman. *The Adventures of Superpup* (1958) features a canine version of Superman played by a little-person actor in a dog mask (*Superman: The Movie* 62). A pilot episode was produced and screened to an unsuspecting preview audience in a Los Angeles theater (Scivally 62).

The Adventures of Superpup is an extreme example of what happens when the fantasy world of a character is ignored, but it is not a rare phenomenon. *It's a Bird ... It's a Plane ... It's Superman* (1966) was a major Broadway musical by the creative team responsible for *Bye Bye Birdie* (1960). The villain of the play convinces Superman that he is actually "an egotist who performs his deeds out of a deep need to be loved, and breaks the superhero's heart when he turns the citizens of Metropolis against him" (Scivally 66).

Superman finally got his due in 1978 with *Superman: The Movie.* The film is an anomaly—in some ways the best of all Superman stories. The original screenplay for the film adaptation was written by Mario Puzo, a big name at the time because of the success of *The Godfather* (1972) and *The Godfather: Part II* (1974). Several other screenwriters wrote early drafts of the script that did not take the character seriously. One such scene featured Superman grabbing a man he believed to be the bald villain, Lex Luthor, but was actually Telly Savales. The bald actor famous for playing the television detective Kojak was to take his signature lollypop out of his mouth and deliver his catchphrase: "Superman! Who loves ya, baby?" (Wheldon 182). The producers initially took the casting no more seriously than the script: celebrities such as Neil Diamond were auditioned to play the Man of Steel. *Superman: The Movie* (1978) appeared as if it were going to be another low-quality film for children, perhaps enlivened by some novel special-effects-work—stagecraft had become fashionable again in films because of *Star Wars* (1977).

Richard Donner, born Richard Schwartzberg, changed the fate of the film, and created the sub-genre of superhero films. Donner had had a hit with *The Omen* (1976), but when hired to direct *Superman: The Movie* he was known primarily as a television director. He made many episodes of Westerns, including directing Richard Boone in *Have Gun—Will Travel* (1957–63), Steve McQueen in *Wanted: Dead or Alive* (1958–61), and Chuck Connors in *The Rifleman* (1958–63) ("Richard").[5] He was probably attractive to the producers because he was not an established film director who could demand a large fee. However, Donner brought something unexpected to the film—something that the producers would later rue when the director spent hours getting shots perfect for what, to them, was just a movie based on a cartoon. Donner was a true believer. He saw the character differently from anyone else in Hollywood: "We're dealing with American literature here. The British have their Shakespeare. We have our Superman" (Scivally 80).

Donner hired screenwriter Tom Mankiewicz to impose his vision of a Superman taken seriously upon the shooting script. Mankiewicz was the scion of a famous screenwriting family ("Tom"). His father, Joseph (1909–93), wrote the screenplays for films such as *All About Eve* (1950) and *Julius Caesar* (1953) ("Joseph"). His uncle Herman (1897–1953) wrote the screenplay for *Citizen Kane* (1941). Tom did the best work of his career in transforming the character from the likeable dolt of the original screenplay. Mankiewicz made Superman defiantly old-fashioned, and morally superior, to the other characters of the film—a subversively conservative hero.

Superman arrives in the film in a post–Vietnam, post–Watergate America. The newsroom in the film looks like the set of the *Washington Post* offices in *All the President's Men* (1976), but the reporters at the *Daily Planet* are foolish and arrogant rather than dashing and heroic

V. Superman

(like the reporters from *All the President's Men*). Clark Kent comes from a different (and implicitly superior) era than his colleagues—he missed the entire decade of the 1960s, as well as the first half of the 1970s, in seclusion ("journeying in time and space") with a didactic computer program based upon the personality of his father. He has avoided experiencing the draft for the Vietnam War, the social unrest of the 1960s, and Watergate. His fashion sense was suspended somewhere between the matinee idols of the 1930s and the pompadour-wearing icons of the 1950s—which explains his costume and hair. The voice of his father (Marlon Brando) chides him about his vanity: explaining that Superman's home planet was doomed by the arrogance of its inhabitants, and that if he had not been so proud his son would not have grown up without him. "Our destruction could have been avoided had it not been for the vanity of some who considered us indestructible. Were it not for vanity, why ... at this very moment ... I could embrace you in my arms. My son." Superman pretends to be square as Clark Kent, but he knows he is superior to any "Me Generation" reporter. Reeve's Superman is defiantly sincere, countering the dominant culture of the 1970s, which had been shaped by the counter-culture.

The key scene of the film is when girl reporter Lois Lane ("updated" from the character's 1930s origins to the 1970s—with outward confidence, but flaky insecurity) interviews Superman. She asks him why he has come to Earth. He answers, "I'm here to fight for truth and justice and the American way." Lois laughs at Superman and walks away, saying, "You're gonna end up fighting every elected official in this country!" Superman chuckles politely, and chides her, "I'm sure you don't really mean that, Lois." She then wonders aloud at the naiveté of this man: "I don't believe this." Superman's voice changes and he says her name sharply. She turns to face him. He speaks with controlled anger: "I never lie." He chooses, as Clark Kent, to put up with the abuse of his urban co-workers, but as Superman he will not allow his values to be questioned.

Director Richard Donner explained in a documentary what he saw in the character of Superman: "He's a lot of what America once was a long time ago. I'm a very liberal human being in my philosophies and

159

my politics and I find myself in an odd sort of way looking and respecting the conservative attitude of what Superman stands for now because I think I see a lot of my philosophies in application now and I'm not very happy with them and I almost wish I could go back to what once was and what America once was" (*Making Superman*).

Film critic Roger Ebert (1942–2013) wrote, "Superman is a pure delight, a wondrous combination of all the old-fashioned things we never really get tired of: adventure and romance" (Ebert, paragraph 1). Of course, some film critics were tired of adventure and romance or, perhaps, tired of old-fashioned things. Pauline Kael (1919–2001) was hoping for a different type of Superman film: "It would be more fun to see him putting out a fire while kids threw stones at him, or arresting a mugger and being surrounded by an angry, booing crowd, or tackling the garbage problem." She found that the film had a "sour and scared undertone," but the core of her critique of the movie was that it "doesn't bring any ambiguity into this portrait of an outsize F.B.I. man from space" (Kael 526). However, Kael did approve of the lead actor of the film, Christopher Reeve (1952–2004).

Reeve, like Donner, took the character seriously. He explained why he approached the role in this way in an interview in which he recounted visiting children suffering from cancer, dressed as the superhero: "It's not Superman the tongue-in-cheek cartoon character they're connecting with; they're connecting with something very basic: the ability to overcome obstacles, the ability to persevere, the ability to understand difficulty and to turn your back on it." The editor responsible for writing the headlines in the *Time* magazine titled the interview "Up, Up, and Awaaay!!!" (Scivally 90).

The actor would need to overcome obstacles himself. A riding accident in 1995 paralyzed him. He worked the last nine years of his life as an advocate for the disabled, and for increased funding for research into spinal cord injuries. He spoke at the 1996 Democratic National Convention, saying, "Over the last few years, we've heard a lot about something called family values. And like many of you, I've struggled to figure out what that means. But since my accident, I've found a definition that seems to make sense. I think it means that we're all family, that we all have value.... If we can conquer outer space, we should be able to conquer inner space, too: the frontier of the brain, the central nervous system, and all the afflictions of the body that destroy so many lives and rob our country of so much potential" (Reeve 287).

Superman: The Movie demonstrates that fantasy worlds are never divorced from the real worlds inhabited by their authors. Superman, like the hobbits and Conan, was born in the 1930s. Unlike Middle-earth and the Hyborian Age, the fantasy worlds inhabited by Superman (and, even more so, the larger DC and Marvel fantasy "universes") are not the vision of a single man—although they originate from the dreams of Jerry Siegel. The Superman of Donner, Mankiewicz, and Reeve is as iconic as any version of the Man of Steel.

There are many versions of Superman, but there are some aspects of his character that remain constant. Many critics seem to miss one of his most important characteristics: he works for what he perceives as the greater good and is not subservient to political authority. His first appearance in 1938 shows him threatening the governor of New York when the official balks at staying the execution of an innocent man (Siegel *Chronicles 1* 7). In the film *Man of Steel* (2013), Superman snaps the manacles in which the post–9/11 military authorities have placed him and says, "Let's put our cards on the table: you want to control me, and you can't. But that doesn't make me your enemy." Robert E. Howard would have approved.

The character of Superman is a rebuttal of Lord Acton's famous dictum: he has absolute power, but it does not corrupt him. Rather, his powers grant him freedom from fear. This freedom allows him to be a superman, and to realize his potential by helping others.

VI

The Inheritors

The common people pray for rain, healthy children, and a
summer that never ends.... It is no matter to them if the high
lords play their game of thrones....
        —George R.R. Martin, *A Game of Thrones*

Tolkien, Howard, and Siegel were not the only creators of fantasy
worlds in the 1930s. Theodor Geisel finished a picture-book on the
return voyage of a trip to visit to relatives in Nazi Germany (MacDonald
3). The book was both a colorful celebration of a child's imagination
and a somber rumination on the power of adults to stifle that imagination. *And to Think That I Saw It on Mulberry Street* (1937) was the book
that established the pattern for decades of Dr. Seuss's books. The boy
imagines many spectacular sights as he walks home, but is troubled by
his father's injunction to "stop turning minnows into whales" (Geisel
n.p.).

Ruth K. MacDonald writes of Geisel's (1904–1991) childhood shame
of his German heritage: "Nicknamed the Kaiser, and sometimes called
the Drunken Kaiser, since the senior Geisel was part owner and eventual
president of a brewery, Kuhlnbach and Geisel, the boy was occasionally
pelted by rocks as he made his way to and from school" (MacDonald 1).
His books may have been intended partly as escapes for other children
disenchanted with reality.

Like Tolkien, Geisel loved languages. He was especially interested
in Latin, which he said "allows you to adore words—take them apart
and find out where they come from" (Macdonald 3).

In many ways, the most popular creator of fantasy worlds in the
1930s was Walt Disney. Like Tolkien's, his creative career spanned

decades. Unlike Tolkien's, however, his fantasy world originated in the 1920s. In the 1920s he was a pioneer in animation, making the original Mickey Mouse cartoons. In the 1950s he built the physical fantasy world of Disneyland. However, his work in the 1930s was significant—he created the world's first feature-length animated film, *Snow White and the Seven Dwarfs*, in 1937. This led to decades of animated features, and through Pixar Studios the Walt Disney Corporation still dominates the field in the twenty-first century.

Tolkien, Howard, and Siegel inspired generations of creators of fantasy worlds. One of the best fantasy writers to follow Tolkien was Lloyd Alexander (1924–2007). Alexander was drafted into the army during the Second World War. The army sent him to be an artilleryman, but he kept dropping shells. The army then assigned him to be a medic, but he fainted at the sight of blood. The army next sent him to be a member of an army band, but he could not play a musical instrument. He then was put to work scrubbing dishes—until he saw a sign in the kitchen asking for people who spoke a foreign language. He demonstrated that he knew French and escaped kitchen duty. He was immediately sent to a base in Wales. Six weeks later, the army smuggled him into France to act as an intelligence operative with orders to make contact with the French Resistance (May 5). This experience of comedic misadventure set against a background of danger would influence Alexander's later writing.

He admired the Welsh countryside and was inspired to consider his own Welsh ancestry. He found Wales "far more ancient than England, wilder and rougher hewn.... Wales to my eyes appeared still a realm of bards and heroes; even coal-tips towered like dark fortresses" (May 6). Two decades later he would write a fantasy series inspired by *The Lord of the Rings*. *The Prydain Chronicles* (1964–1973) are set in a small fantasy world derived from Welsh legend. Unlike *The Lord of the Rings,* these novels were written for children.

Alexander stayed on in Paris after the war ended. He looked up Gertrude Stein in a phone book, and was granted an audience. He gave her a manuscript to read. She warned him that the life of a writer was not an easy one, but supported his hopes: "When I confessed I hoped to be a writer, she nodded and answered, 'Yes, if that's what you really want, then you will be'" (May 7).

Alexander also called upon the Surrealist poet Paul Éluard. The meeting led to Alexander's translating the works of Éluard into English. As a result of this meeting, Alexander also translated Jean-Paul Sartre's *Nausea* (1938)—creating the preferred English translation of the work (May 7). Existentialism is the hidden heart of the *Chronicles of Prydain*. Prydain is a fictional kingdom that serves as Alexander's medieval fantasy world.

He wrote his *Prydain Chronicles* during the Vietnam War. Tolkien hated war, and had his hero Frodo move toward pacifism at the end of *The Lord of the Rings*. However, Tolkien was not a pacifist—Alexander was. He was horrified by the Vietnam War. He wrote in 1968, "Each day of war is taking us further from all we could hope to be or to do.... Our lives erode and diminish, our children see no future except a calendar of anguish and death. Our only hope for tomorrow is peace now" (May 9).

The best book of the series, *Taran Wanderer* (1968), shows the protagonist forsaking the path of an epic hero. Taran strives to abandon the path of the sword. He works to find his calling by attempting to complete an apprenticeship in a peaceful craft. Much like Alexander's experience in the army, Taran cannot find a trade sutiable to his skills. The climax of the novel comes when Taran is told to seek an enchanted pool to learn of his true self (Alexander *Taran* 112). The "Mirror of Llunet" recalls the passage from *The Lord of the Rings* in which the fleeing Frodo gazes into an ancient pool (Tolkien *Lord* 334). Taran's pool is different. He looks into the pool, and sees himself. "I saw ... strength—and frailty," he says. "Pride and vanity, courage and fear.... Of intentions, many good ones; but many more left undone.... Now I know who I am: myself and no other. I am Taran" (Alexander *Taran* 270). Taran later rejects the dreams of his youth: "Once, I hoped for a glorious destiny.... That dream has vanished with my childhood; and though a pleasant dream it was fit only for a child. I am well-content as an Assistant Pig-Keeper" (Alexander *High* 292).

Taran is raised by Dallben, the Gandalf figure of the series. Alexan-

VI. *The Inheritors*

der reveals Dallben's origin in a short story in 1973 (Alexander *Foundling*). The young Dallben finds the omniscient Book of Three (whose title refers to the past, present, and future) and is intoxicated by the knowledge of the world that he finds within it. However, his knowledge soon turns to horror as he reads further in the book: "For now the book told him of other ways of the world; of cruelty, suffering, and death. He read of greed, hatred and war; of men striving against one another with fire and sword … of harvests lost and lives cut short" (26). He stops reading, but the knowledge has already aged him from a youth to an old man "his hands gnarled and knotted, his eyes pale as if their color has been wept away" (27). He despairs that the price of knowledge is so high but resolves to finish what he started. Picking up the book again, he reads "not only of death, but of birth as well; how the earth turns in its own time and in its own way gives back what is given to it; how things lost may be found again; and how one day ends for another to begin. He learned that the lives of men are short and filled with pain, yet each one a priceless treasure, whether it be that of a prince or a pig-keeper" (27).

A prophecy in the series states that the high king will be "one who chose a kingdom of sorrow over a kingdom of happiness" (Alexander *High*). Taran makes this choice, and becomes king in the final volume of the series. He chooses a path consistent with existentialism when he forgoes eternal life in the "summer country" to remain in the world of human suffering. This is a sort of happy ending, although a happy ending is not a necessary component of a modern fantasy story. As author Fletcher Pratt (1897–1956) wrote, "Imaginative fiction has no connection either for or against the happy end" (Pratt 18).

Ursula Le Guin also took modern fantasy, and modern fantasy worlds, in a new direction during the period of the Vietnam War. Although her *Earthsea Trilogy* (1968–1972) was written for children in the style of Tolkien's books, she had a different perspective on the form. "The novel is a fundamentally unheroic kind of story.... That is why I like novels: instead of heroes they have people in them" (Cadden 86). Le Guin (b. 1929) is the child of anthropologists Theodora Kroeber (1897–1979) and Alfred Kroeber (1876–1960) and the brother of literary critic Karl Kroeber (1926–2009) ("Ursula" paragraph 1). Her mother wrote *Ishi* (1961)—the account of the last member of a American Indian tribe who was discovered in California in 1911 (Le Guin "Biographical" paragraph 1).

Le Guin's background in anthropology led her to develop a different cultural setting for her fantasy world. She infused the Earthsea books with a non–Western ethos. Amy Clarke writes, "The emphasis on Taoist balance was unusual in Western fantasy up until that time" (Clarke 49). Le Guin gives the foundation for the religion of Ged's people: "In the Creation of Eá which is the oldest song, it is said, 'Only in silence the word, only in dark the light, only in dying life: bright the hawk's flight on the empty sky'" (Le Guin *Earthsea* 65).

The series recounts events in the life of Ged, a wizard in a fantasy world composed of islands and archipelagoes. The cultures of the world of Eá are reminiscent of those of Bronze Age Greek society. However, the complexion and hair color of Ged resemble those of a American Indian in our world.

Le Guin writes with an anthropological sensibility, but the books focus on the interior life of Ged. Thematically, these bildungsromans deal with both life-affirming and destructive responses to the fear of death. The villain of the last volume is a wizard who is so afraid of dying that he has placed the world in a listless state, without magic or vitality, in a futile attempt to cheat death. Ged sacrifices his magic powers, and heals the world, thinking, "It is time to be done with power. To drop the old toys, and go on…. There is no kingdom like the forests. It is time I went there, went in silence, went alone. And maybe there I would learn at last what no act, or power can teach me, what I have never learned …" (Le Guin *Earthsea* 441).

Le Guin won even greater acclaim for her "New Wave" science fiction novels, such as *The Left Hand of Darkness* (1969) and *The Dispossed* (1974). Another American who made his reputation in the New Wave movement of 1960s science fiction was Roger Zelazny (1937–1995). He also created his own fantasy world in two linked fantasy series known collectively as *The Chronicles of Amber* (1970–1991).

Zelazny uses some of the conventions of Tolkien's fantasy, infusing them with elements from the American pulp tradition. Zelazny nodded to writers like Robert E. Howard, but his work seems to be inspired primarily by the detective stories of Dashiel Hammett and other authors from the pulp magazine *Black Mask,* as well as the Philip Marlowe novels of Raymond Chandler. *Nine Princes in Amber* (1970) starts with the first-person narrative of a man with amnesia. Zelazny gradually reveals that the protagonist is a superhuman member of a cosmic ruling family. The members of the clan are immortal, but are not divine. They belong to a squabbling, dysfunctional royal family who reside at the Platonic center of all reality: everything else, including our Earth, is just a shadow of the one true world of Amber. Zelazny mixes genres to tell a saga, alternately a mind-bending fantasy and a struggle waged by ruthless brothers and sisters to seize a cosmic throne. The heroes, Corwin and his son Merlin, think and speak in a manner far removed from Tolkien's characters: for example, "It is a pain in the ass waiting around for someone to try to kill you" (Zelazny 579).

The series blends a pulp adventure with psychological family dynamics and philosophy. Zelazny's main theme is that people, even superhuman heirs to a cosmic dynasty, are not the center of the universe. This fits comfortably with Tolkien's theme in *The Lord of the Rings* despite the fact that the authors had radically different backgrounds. Zelazny was no Oxford Professor, but a Social Security clerk in Baltimore who spent his nights after work in the 1960s writing his science fiction stories (Kovacs n.p.).

In a fascinating scene, Corwin ends up creating his own universe based upon his memories of living during the Belle Époque. (He is an immortal who had been stranded, with amnesia, in our world for the last few centuries.) Like Proust in *Swann's Way* (1913), Zelazny is concerned with issues of memory. Corwin uses his memory of his time in Paris to form the pattern of a new world, building a "fantasy world" himself within Zelazny's fantasy world. He writes of "the play of the fountains in the Place de la Concorde.... And down the Rue de la Seine and along the quais, the smell of the old books, the smell of the river.... The smell of chestnut blossoms..." (Zelazny 541).

Zelazny was a mentor to the most successful contemporary creator of a fantasy world, George R.R. Martin. Martin is currently writing his fantasy series *A Song of Ice and Fire* (1996-present). The books are being adapted in an HBO television series, *Game of Thrones* (2011-present). Martin wrote of Zelazny that he was "one hell of a writer ... one hell of a friend" (Martin, "Memoriam" paragraph 6).

Martin is a synthesis of the giants of the modern fantasy tradition. He describes his response to the author of *The Lord of the Rings*: "I admire Tolkien greatly. His books had enormous influence on me ... but I think ultimately the battle between good and evil is weighed within the individual human heart.... When I look at the world, I see that most real living breathing human beings are grey" (Martin "Admire" paragraph 1). In 2013 he recommended to his readers that they search out the stories of Robert E. Howard (Martin "Reading" paragraph 3). He has also been influenced by superheroes. He enlisted Roger Zelazny to write a short story for his fantasy world. *Wild Cards* (1987) is a superhero saga set in a world in which an alien virus is released over New York City in 1946. Most people infected with the virus die—but some are turned into monsters, while a fortunate few gain superpowers.

Martin's sprawling *A Song of Ice and Fire* combines the sensibilities of modern fantasy and historical fiction: he has also extolled the virtues of Sir Walter Scott's *Ivanhoe* (Jackson, paragraph 8). Martin is also a devotée of Rod Serling: his earlier career was as a television writer during the 1980s revival of *The Twilight Zone*. Martin is still developing his fantasy world of Westeros in *A Song of Ice and Fire*, but the series is already the most popular contemporary fantasy franchise.

An examination of *A Song of Ice and Fire* is beyond the scope of this book—the series is still being produced on both the page and television. However, Martin's work is the most prominent representative of literary modern fantasy. The influences of Tolkien, Howard, and Zelazny are obvious. Modern fantasy from the 1930s is still with use in twenty-first-century books, film, and television.

Conclusion

The fantasy worlds derived from the 1930s are still with us, and will be for the foreseeable future. Behind these fantastic tales will always be the lives and times of the men who created the first modern fantasy worlds—who themselves hailed from the lost worlds of Oxford, Cleveland, and Cross Plains, Texas of the 1930s. Films will continue to dramatize the deeds of the original heroes of modern fantasy for decades to come: Frodo will sail away from Middle-earth with the last of the elves departing from our world, Conan will rely on his own mighty limbs to cleave his way to new treasures in exotic lands, Superman will streak through the sky on his way to save another life—until the inhabitants of Earth can learn to save themselves.

Chapter Notes

Chapter I

1. This date is not likely to have been a coincidence, but it is an obscure detail in an appendix of a novel of over a thousand pages. It is further complicated by Tolkien's use of multiple invented calendars (those of the Hobbits, the Elves, and the Dwarves, for example) in the body of *The Lord of the Rings*. Whereas his friend C.S. Lewis had Father Christmas running around in his fantasy world, Tolkien kept the details of Middle-earth consistent to that setting. A character in *The Lord of the Rings* would never reference "March" because the Gregorian calendar does not exist in Middle-earth.

2. They are somewhat incurious about the status and ultimate origin of their friend, but, after all, they are on a world-ending quest with a lot to keep them busy.

3. "I cordially dislike allegory in all its manifestations, and always have done so since I grew old and wary enough to detect its presence. I much prefer history, true or feigned, with its varied applicability to the thought and experience of readers. I think that many confuse 'applicability' with 'allegory'; but the one resides in the freedom of the reader, and the other in the purposed domination of the author" (Tolkien *Lord* xxiv).

4. The films imply that some sort of genetic engineering has been used.

5. "Me gusta mucho Lewis Carroll, pero me encuentro desconcertado por Tolkien" (Hadis 116).

6. The word "God" is never used. Other names in languages of Middle-earth are used, such as "Eru" (Tolkien *Silmarillion* 13).

Chapter II

1. The Hobbit does have two relationships between an adult character and a father figure: those between Bilbo and Gandalf, and Bilbo and Thorin—but these two are eclipsed by the many relationships between adult characters and their father figures in *The Lord of the Rings*, as Croft writes.

2. Fantasy is distinct from science fiction. The two genres are related, but distinct. In particular, *The Lord of the Rings* has less in common with science fiction than even many mainstream works—almost nothing.

3. $1,554,983.23 in 2013 dollars based on £104,000 in 1969.

Chapter III

1. A film of this famous prizefight is currently viewable on YouTube (Motion Pictures). It is silent, so it is impossible to tell if Howard was exaggerating about the sound of the final blow. He claims in

the letter that the fight so excited him that it triggered a heart irregularity which caused him to collapse in the theater.

2. The song "Dark Town Cabaret" was published in 1913 and is about the reaction to Emancipation Day. The chorus is "Down in Georgia lan with my honey man" (Detroit Public Library).

3. At least he did in the magazine serial. The *Adventure* serial is a punchier, American version of the English novel. The opening of the novel suggests a more insistently English version of piracy: "Peter Blood, bachelor of medicine and several other things besides, smoked a pipe and tended the geraniums boxed on the sill of his window" (Sabatini 1). This approach of moving from bucolic England to foreign adventure and back to England was symbolically used by Tolkien in both *The Hobbit* and *The Lord of the Rings*.

4. Southerner Randall Wallace's screenplay for *Braveheart* (1995) portrays William Wallace as a hero fighting an imperial occupier. The English villains of the screenplay are at times more reminiscent of versions of Union forces from Southern folklore than anything from medieval legend. This vision was popular: the film won the Academy Award for Best Picture, and Mel Gibson won the Academy Award for Best Director.

5. A point of the second letter is to suggest the "Pennsylvania Dutch" as antagonists in a horror story to his correspondent, H.P. Lovecraft. Lovecraft was a racist and eugenicist, and Howard is likely trying to impress him, but this is does not lessen the ridiculousness of the reference and the thought process behind it.

6. Dickens gets off easy compared to Oliver Goldsmith. He discusses "one of the most abominable books ever penned"—*The Vicar of Wakefield*: "The

old cuss in the book has one daughter seduced, if I'm not mistaken, and the other abducted by the same egg. So he stood around mouthing pious platitudes—the old jackass" (Howard *Letters* 2: 470).

7. However, Howard might well have viewed an American who moved to the heart of the British Empire with suspicion.

8. De Camp is probably referring to the work of Lynn White (which did not exist when he was a young college graduate) who started the "Great Stirrup Controversy." However, White argued for humility in his groundbreaking 1940 article given the difficulty of determining anything precisely about medieval technology. He warned, "The perfectionists had better stay in the shadow of Notre Dame, where their vanity will be less vulnerable" (White 157). De Camp did not heed this advice.

9. Howard was wary of the phrase "blood and thunder." He wrote, "One problem in writing bloody literature is to present it in such a manner as to avoid a suggestion of cheap blood-and-thunder melodrama—which is what some people will always call action, regardless of how realistic and true it is" (2: 411).

10. According to footnote 254, Insull is Samuel Insull, a Chicago capitalist. His fortune had collapsed spectacularly by the time Howard wrote this letter. Howard was not sympathetic. Orson Welles claimed that Insull was a model for the character of Charles Foster Kane (Welles 49).

Chapter IV

1. At his death, Howard owned twelve books by Sir Arthur Conan Doyle (Burke).

2. These place names are pedestrian compared to Lovecraftian personal names—most famously, "Cthulhu."

3. For example, the *Star Wars* and *The Lord of the Rings* films have Nazi-like villains. *Raiders of the Lost Ark* double-dips by featuring both snakes and Nazis.

4. Lovecraft is recognized today as a major figure in the American horror genre. A Library of America edition of his works was published in 2005.

Chapter V

1. The cover date was June 1938, but like most comic books it was actually released on the newsstand two months before.

2. The probable reason for this frequent mistake is that many general writers on Superman are eager to portray the pair as young to make their feat of creating an iconic character more impressive. Many writers who write books specifically about the comics field wish to make the contrast between inexperienced men being taken advantage of by businessmen and corporate lawyers as stark as possible.

3. Other companies and artists have created characters similar to superheroes, but the term itself is a joint copyright of DC Comics (now owned by Time Warner) and Marvel Comics (purchased in 2009 by the Walt Disney Corporation).

4. The plot of the first Superman/Batman team-up had little to do with heroics: Lois Lane uses her feminine wiles and pretends to like Batman to make Superman jealous.

5. His most notable work is probably "Nightmare at 20,000 Feet," a 1963 *Twilight Zone* episode starring William Shatner as a mental patient flying home after a stay in an institution who cannot convince anyone else on his plane that there is a real gremlin on board attempting to crash the aircraft.

Works Cited

Adventure. 3 July 1921. *Internet Archive.* Web.

Aldington, Richard. "Whitechapel." *London: A History in Verse.* Ed. Mark Ford. Cambridge: Belknap, 2012. Print.

Alexander, Lloyd. *The Foundling and Other Tales of Prydain.* New York: Puffin, 1990. Print.

_____. *The High King.* New York: Yearling, 1990. Print.

_____. *Taran Wanderer.* New York: Holt, 1975. Print.

Anderson, Douglas A. "Humphrey Carter (1946–2005)." *Tolkien Studies: An Annual Scholarly Review* 2 (2005): 217–24. Print.

Apocalypse Now. Dir. Francis Ford Coppola. Screenplay by John Milius and Francis Ford Coppola. Perf. Marlon Brando. Paramount, 1979. Film.

Auden, W.H. "At the End of the Quest, Victory." Rev. of *The Return of the King* by J.R.R. Tolkien. *The New York Times.* New York Times 22 Jan. 1956, Books Section. Web.

Authorized King James Version of the Holy Bible. Nashville: Thomas Nelson, 1990. Print.

Beagle, Peter. "Tolkien's Magic Ring." Introduction. *The Tolkien Reader.* By J.R.R. Tolkien. New York: Ballantine, 1966. ix–xvii. Print.

Belk, Patrick Scott. "*Adventure* Magazine: America's No. 1 Pulp." *Pulp mags.org.* The Pulp Magazine Project: An Archive of All-Fiction Pulpwood Magazines from 1896–1946. Web.

Bell, Blake. *Fire & Water: Bill Everett, the Sub-Mariner, and the Birth of Marvel Comics.* Seattle: Fantagraphic, 2010. Print.

Belloni, Matthew. "Marvel Moolah: Robert Downey, Jr. 'Avengers' Pay Set to Hit $50 Million." *The Hollywood Reporter.* The Hollywood Reporter, 15 May 2012. Web.

_____. "Tolkien Estate Sues Warner Bros. Over 'Lord of the Rings' Slot Machines (Exclusive)." *The Hollywood Reporter.* The Hollywood Reporter, 19 Nov. 2012. Web.

Blavatsky, H.P. *The Secret Doctrine: The Synthesis of Science, Religion, and Philosophy.* 1888. *Theosociety.org.* Theosophical University Press Online Edition. Web.

Bloom, Harold. Introduction. *J.R.R. Tolkien's The Lord of the Rings.* Ed. Bloom. Philadelphia: Chelsea House, 2000. 1. Print.

Booker, M. Keith. "The Other Side of History." *The Cambridge Companion to the Twentieth-Century English Novel.* Ed. Robert L. Caserio. Cambridge: Cambridge University Press, 2009. 251–65. Print.

Bradley, Marion Zimmer. "Men, Halflings, and Hero Worship." *Tolkien and the*

Index

Critics: Essays on J. R. R. Tolkien's The Lord of the Rings. Ed. Neil D. Isaacs and Rose A. Zimbardo. Notre Dame: Notre Dame University Press, 1968. Print.

Bratman, David. "The Inklings: Their Lives and Works." *The Company They Keep: C.S. Lewis and J. R. R. Tolkien as Writers in Community*. By Diana Glyer. Kent, Ohio: Kent State University Press, 2007. 230–43. Print.

Braveheart. Dir. Mel Gibson. Screenplay by Randall Wallace. Paramount, 1995. Film.

Brooker, Will. *Star Wars*. Basingstoke: Palgrave Macmillan, 2009. Print.

Brooks, Peter. Rev. of *The Black Count: Glory, Revolution, Betrayal, and the Real Count of Monte Cristo* by Tom Reiss. *The New York Review of Books* 23 May 2013: 33. Print.

Buhle, Paul. *Jews and American Comics: An Illustrated History of an American Art Form*. New York: New Press, 2008. Print.

Burke, Rusty. "The Robert E. Howard Bookshelf." *The Robert E. Howard Bookshelf*. The Robert E. Howard United Press Association, 1998. Web.

Butler, Charles. *Four British Fantasists: Place and Culture in the Children's Fantasies of Penelope Lively, Alan Garner, Diana Wynne Jones, and Susan Cooper*. Lanham, Maryland: Scarecrow, 2006. Print.

Cadden, Michael. *Ursula K. Le Guin Beyond Genre: Fiction for Children and Adults*. New York: Routledge, 2005. Print.

Caldecott, Stratford. *The Power of the Ring: The Spiritual Vision Behind The Lord of the Rings*. New York: Crossroad, 2005. Print.

"Can't See the Wood." Editorial. *The Times* n.d.: n. pag. *The Times*. The Times, 3 Feb. 2011. Web.

Captain Blood. Dir. Michael Curtiz. Perf. Errol Flynn. Warner Bros., 1935. Film.

"Captain Blood (1924)." *IMDb*. The Internet Movie Database, 1990–2013. Web.

"Captain Blood (1935)." *IMDb*. The Internet Movie Database, 1990–2013. Web.

Carpenter, Humphrey. *Tolkien: A Biography*. Boston: Houghton Mifflin, 1977. Print.

Cavalier, Bill. "REHupa." *Robert E. Howard Days 2012*. REHupa, 30 May 2012. Web.

Clarke, Amy M. *Ursula K. Le Guin's Journey to Post-Feminism*. Jefferson, N.C.: McFarland, 2010. Print.

Coleridge, Samuel Taylor. *Biographia Literaria*. 1817. *Project Gutenberg*. Project Gutenberg, 2004. Web.

"Commentary." Perf. Richard Donner. *The Superman Motion Picture Anthology*. Warner Brothers, 2011. Blu-ray.

Conan Doyle, Arthur. *The War in South Africa: Its Cause and Conduct*. London: G. Bell & Sons, 1902. Kindle.

Conan the Barbarian. Dir. John Milius. Screenplay by Milius and Oliver Stone. Perf. Arnold Schwarzenegger and James Earl Jones. 1982. Universal, 2003. DVD.

Conan the Barbarian. Dir. Marcus Nispel. Lionsgate, 2011. Film.

"Conan the Barbarian (2011)." IMDb. The Internet Movie Database, 1990–2013. Web.

Conan the Destroyer. Dir. Richard Fleischer. Perf. Arnold Schwarzenegger and Wilt Chamberlain. 1984. Universal, 2003. DVD.

Conrad, Joseph. *Heart of Darkness and The Secret Sharer*. New York: Bantam, 1981. Print.

Cooper, James Fenimore. *The Last of the Mohicans*. Ebookslib, 2004. Kindle.

"CPI Inflation Calculator." *U.S. Bureau of Labor Statistics*. United States Department of Labor. Web.

Croft, Janet Brennan. "Three Rings for

Hollywood: Scripts for the Lord of the Rings by Zimmerman, Boorman, and Beagle." *Fantasy Fiction into Film: Essays.* Ed. Leslie Stratyner and James R. Keller. Jefferson, N.C.: McFarland, 2007. 7–20. Print.

_____. *War and the Works of J.R.R. Tolkien.* Westport, CT: Praeger, 2004. Print.

Davie, Donald. *Thomas Hardy and British Poetry.* London: Routledge, 1973. Print.

De Camp, L. Sprague. *The Miscast Barbarian: A Biography of Robert E. Howard (1906–1936).* Saddle River, N.J.: Gerry De La Ree, 1975. Print.

De Camp, L. Sprague, and Catherine Crook De Camp. *Time & Chance: An Autobiography.* Hampton Falls, N.H.: D.M. Grant, 1996. Print.

De Camp, L. Sprague, Catherine Crook De Camp, and Jane Whittington Griffin. *Dark Valley Destiny: The Life of Robert E. Howard.* New York: Bluejay, 1983. Print.

De Haven, Tom. *Our Hero: Superman on Earth.* New Haven: Yale University Press, 2010. Print.

DeForest, Tim. *Storytelling in the Pulps, Comics, and Radio: How Technology Changed Popular Fiction in America.* Jefferson, N.C.: McFarland, 2004. Print.

"DeWitt Clinton High School." *Wikipedia.* Wikimedia, 2013. Web.

Dickens, Charles. *Our Mutual Friend.* New York: Random House, 1992. Modern Library. Kindle.

Ebert, Roger. "Superman." Rev. of *Superman: The Movie. The Chicago Sun-Times* 15 Dec. 1978: n. pag. *Roger Ebert.com.* Web.

Eco, Umberto. Trans. Natalie Chilton. "The Myth of Superman." *Diacritics* 2.1 (1972): 14–22. *JSTOR.* Web.

Ellis, Novalyne Price. *One Who Walked Alone: Robert E. Howard, the Final Years.* West Kingston, R.I.: D.M. Grant, 1986. Print.

The Empire Strikes Back. Dir. Irvin Kershner. Screenplay by Leigh Brackett, Lawrence Kasdan, and George Lucas. Prod. Lucas. Perf. Frank Oz. Twentieth Century–Fox, 1980. Film.

"Empiricism." *The Catholic Encyclopedia.* New York: Robert Appleton, 1907. *Catholic.org.* Catholic Online. Web.

Faulkner, William. *Light in August.* New York: Random House, 2012. Print.

The Fellowship of the Ring. Dir. Peter Jackson. Comp. Howard Shore. New Line, 2001. DVD.

Fingeroth, Danny. *Disguised as Clark Kent: Jews, Comics, and the Creation of the Superhero.* New York: Continuum, 2007. Print.

Finn, Mark. *Blood & Thunder: The Life & Art of Robert E. Howard.* Austin: MonkeyBrain, 2006. Print.

Fleming, Mike. "Arnold and 'Conan the Barbarian' Reunited: Universal Reboots Action Franchise with Schwarzenegger." Deadline.com.Variety, 25 Oct. 2012. Web.

Ford, Judy Ann. "The White City: The Lord of the Rings as an Early Medieval Myth of the Restoration of the Roman Empire." *Tolkien Studies: An Annual Scholarly Review* 2 (2005): 53–74. Print.

Gabilliet, Jean-Paul. *Of Comics and Men: A Cultural History of American Comic Books.* Jackson: University Press of Mississippi, 2010. Print.

Gabler, Neal. *An Empire of Their Own: How the Jews Invented Hollywood.* New York: Crown, 1988. Print.

Gallagher, Robert S. "Me for Ma—and I Ain't Got a Dern Thing Against Pa." *American Heritage* Oct. 1966. *American Heritage.* Web.

Garth, John. *Tolkien and the Great War: The Threshold of Middle-Earth.* Boston: Houghton Mifflin, 2003. Print.

Geisel, Theodor. *And to Think That I*

Saw It on Mulberry Street. New York: Vanguard, 1937. Print.

Gomez, Jeff, and Fabian Nicieza. "6 Reasons 'The Avengers' Is Crushing It at the Box Office." *Business Insider*. Business Insider, Inc., 15 May 2012. Web.

The Good, the Bad and the Ugly. Dir. Sergio Leone. Perf. Clint Eastwood. MGM, 1966. DVD.

Gray, William. *Fantasy, Myth and the Measure of Truth: Tales of Pullman, Lewis, Tolkien, MacDonald and Hoffmann*. Basingstoke: Palgrave Macmillan, 2009. Print.

Greenberger, Robert. *Star Trek: The Complete Unauthorized History*. Minneapolis: Voyageur, 2012. Print.

Gruenwald, Mark, Bill Mantlo, and Steven Grant. *Contest of Champions #1*. New York: Marvel Comics, 1982. Print.

Hadis, Martin. "Prodigios y ficciones: coincidencias y descencuentros entre Borges y Tolkien." *Hispamérica* 38.112 (2009): 115–21. Web.

Haining, Peter. "Introduction to a Legend." *Weird Tales: A Selection, in Facsimile, of the Best from the World's Most Famous Fantasy Magazine*. Ed. Haining. New York: Carroll & Graf, 1990. 7–19. Print.

Hajdu, David. *The Ten-Cent Plague: The Great Comic-Book Scare and How It Changed America*. New York: Farrar, Straus and Giroux, 2008. Print.

Hamilton, Edmond. "The Man Who Returnedt." Ed. Farnsworth Wright. *Weird Tales: A Selection, in Facsimile, of the Best from the World's Most Famous Fantasy Magazine*. Ed. Peter Haining. New York: Carroll & Graf, 1990. 21–30. Print.

_____, and Curt Swan. "Superman #76." *Superman: A Celebration of 75 Years*. New York: DC Comics, 2013. 64–76. Print..

Herodotus. *The Landmark Herodotus:*

The Histories. Ed. Robert B. Strassler. Trans. Andrea L. Purvis. New York: Pantheon, 2007. Print.

Herron, Don. "The Dark Barbarian." *The Dark Barbarian: The Writings of Robert E. Howard, a Critical Anthology*. Ed. Herron. Westport, CT: Greenwood, 1984. 149–81. Print.

Herzog, Basel, H. "History of Tuberculosis." *Respiration* 65.1 (1998): 5–15. Karger.com. S. Karger AG. Web.

Hilton, James. *Lost Horizon*. New York: Harper Perennial, 2004. Print.

"Historical Rates." *Historical Exchange Rates from 1953 with Graph and Charts*. Laurent PELE. Web.

The Hobbit: An Unexpected Journey. Dir. Peter Jackson. Screenplay by Fran Walsh, Philippa Boyens, Jackson, and Guillermo Del Toro. By J. R. R. Tolkien. New Line and MGM, 2012. Film.

Hollywoodland. Dir. Allen Coulter. Screenplay by Paul Bernbaum. Miramax, 2006. Film.

Howard, Robert E. "Beyond the Black River." *Wikisource*. Wikisource, 18 Apr. 2012. Web.

_____. "The Black Stranger." *The Conquering Sword of Conan*. Ed. Patrice Louinet and Rusty Burke. New York: Del Rey/Ballantine, 2003. 101–73. Print.

_____. *The Collected Letters of Robert E. Howard*. Ed. Rob Roehm and Rusty Burke. 3 Vols. Plano, Texas: Robert E. Howard Foundation, 2007–2008. Print.

_____. "The God in the Bowl." *The Coming of Conan the Cimmerian*. Ed. Patrice Louinet and Rusty Burke. New York: Del Rey/Ballantine, 2003. 39–58. Print.

_____. "The Hour of the Dragon." *Wikisource*. Wikisource, 9 Feb. 2014. Web.

_____. "The Hyborian Age." *The Coming of Conan the Cimmerian*. Ed. Patrice Louinet and Rusty Burke. New York:

Del Rey/Ballantine, 2003. 381–98. Print.

_____. "Maps of the Hyborian Age." Map. *The Coming of Conan the Cimmerian.* Ed. Patrice Louinet and Rusty Burke. New York: Del Rey/Ballantine, 2003. 423+. Print.

_____. "The Phoenix on the Sword." *Wikisource.* Wikisource, 9 Nov. 2012. Web.

_____. *Post Oaks and Sand Roughs.* Hampton Falls, N.H.: D.M. Grant, 1990. Print.

_____. "Queen of the Black Coast." *Wikisource.* Wikisource, 24 Nov. 2012. Web.

_____. "Red Nails." *The Conquering Sword of Conan.* Ed. Patrice Louinet and Rusty Burke. New York: Del Rey/Ballantine, 2003. 211–81. Print.

_____. "Rogues in the House." *Wikisource.* Wikisource, 13 Apr. 2012. Web.

_____. "The Scarlet Citadel." *Wikisource.* Wikisource, 9 Nov 2012. Web.

_____. "Something About Eve." *The Spell of Conan.* Ed. L. Sprague de Camp. New York: Ace, 1980. 55–57. Print.

_____. "The Tower of the Elephant." *Wikisource.* Wikisource, 10 Nov. 2012. Web.

_____. "A Witch Shall Be Born." *Wikisource.* Wikisource, 9 May 2011. Web.

Hunt, Peter. "Fantasy and Alternative Worlds." Introduction. *Alternative Worlds in Fantasy Fiction.* Ed. Hunt and Millicent Lenz. London: Continuum, 2001. 1–41. Print.

"Interview with Leigh Brackett & Edmund Hamilton." Interview by Dave Truesdale and Paul McGuire, III. *Tangent Online.* Tangent Online, 12 Dec. 2009. Web.

Isaacs, Neil D. "On the Possibilities of Writing Tolkien Criticism." *Tolkien and the Critics: Essays on J.R.R. Tolkien's The Lord of the Rings.* Ed. Isaacs and Rose A. Zimbardo. Notre Dame: Notre Dame University Press, 1968. Print.

Jackson, Matthew. "George R.R. Martin Recommends Books You'll Like If You Like Thrones." *Blastr.* Syfy Channel, 26 Mar. 2013. Web.

James, Henry. *Daisy Miller: A Study in Two Parts.* 1879. Project Gutenberg, 3 July 2008. Web.

"John Boorman." *IMDb.* The Internet Movie Database, 1990–2013. Web.

"John Milius." *IMDb.* The Internet Movie Database, 1990–2013. Web.

Jones, Gerard. *Men of Tomorrow.* New York: Basic, 2004. Print.

"Joseph L. Mankiewicz." *IMDb.* The Internet Movie Database, 1990–2013. Web.

Kael, Pauline. "The Package." Review. *The New Yorker.* The New Yorker 1 Jan. 1979: n. pag. Web.

Kane, Bob. *Batman: The Dark Knight Archives.* Vol. 3. New York: Archive Editions, 1992. Print.

_____. *The Batman Chronicles.* Vol. 1. New York: DC Comics, 2005. Print.

_____, and Tom Andrae. *Batman & Me: An Autobiography.* Forestville, Cal.: Eclipse, 1989. Print.

Knight, George. "Robert E. Howard: Hard-Boiled Heroic Fantasist." *The Dark Barbarian: The Writings of Robert E. Howard, a Critical Anthology.* Ed. Don Herron. Westport, CT: Greenwood, 1984. 117–36. Print.

Kovacs, Christopher S. "...And Call Me Roger." Introduction. *Threshhold: The Collected Stories of Roger Zelazny,* Vol. 1. By Roger Zelazny. Framingham, Mass.: NESFA, 2009. N. pag. Print.

Lamb, Harold. *The Grand Cham.* [Rockville]: Wildside, 2003. Print.

_____, and Howard Andrew Jones. "Harold Lamb: Master of Surprise." Introduction. *The Grand Cham.* [Rockville]: Wildside, 2003. 5–6. Print.

The Last of the Mohicans. Dir. George B. Seitz. Perf. Randolph Scott and Binnie Barnes. United Artists, 1936. Film.

The Last of the Mohicans. Dir. Michael

Mann. Perf. Daniel Day-Lewis and Madeleine Stowe. 1992. Twentieth Century–Fox, 2010. DVD.

Le Guin, Ursula. *The Earthsea Quartet.* New York: Penguin, 1992. Print.

_____. "Ursula K. Le Guin: Biographical Sketch." *Ursula K. Le Guin's Web Site.* Aug. 2011. Web.

"Leatherstocking (1924)." *IMDb.* The Internet Movie Database, 1990–2013. Web.

"Lee Sholem." *IMDb.* The Internet Movie Database, 1990–2013. Web.

Lewis, C.S. "The Dethronement of Power." *Tolkien and the Critics: Essays on J.R.R. Tolkien's The Lord of the Rings.* Ed. Neil D. Isaacs and Rose A. Zimbardo. Notre Dame: Notre Dame University Press, 1968. Print.

_____. *The Lion, the Witch, and the Wardrobe.* London: Collins, 1978. Print.

_____. *Surprised by Joy.* London: Collins, 2012. Print.

Lobdell, Jared. "Defining the Lord of the Rings: An Adventure Story in the Edwardian Mode." *J.R.R. Tolkien's The Lord of the Rings.* Ed. Harold Bloom. Philadelphia: Chelsea House, 2000. 121–22. Print.

_____. *The Rise of Tolkienian Fantasy.* Chicago: Open Court, 2005. Print.

The Lord of the Rings. Dir. Ralph Bakshi. Warner Brothers, 1978. Film.

The Lord of the Rings: The Fellowship of the Ring (Extended Edition). Dir. Peter Jackson. Screenplay by Fran Walsh, Philippa Boyens, and Jackson. By J.R.R. Tolkien. New Line, 2012. Film.

The Lord of the Rings: The Return of the King (Extended Edition). Dir. Peter Jackson. Screenplay by Fran Walsh, Philippa Boyens, and Jackson. By J.R.R. Tolkien. New Line, 2012. Film.

The Lord of the Rings: The Two Towers (Extended Edition). Dir. Peter Jackson. Screenplay by Fran Walsh, Philippa Boyens, and Jackson. By J.R.R. Tolkien. New Line, 2012. Film.

"The Lord of the Rings (1978)." *IMDb.* The Internet Movie Database, 1990–2013. Web.

Lost Horizon. Dir. Frank Capra. Columbia, 1937. Film.

Louinet, Patrice. "Hyborian Genesis." *The Coming of Conan the Cimmerian.* Ed. Louinet and Rusty Burke. By Robert E. Howard. New York: Del Rey/Ballantine, 2003. 429–52. Print.

_____. Introduction. *The Coming of Conan the Cimmerian.* By Robert E. Howard. Ed. Louinet and Rusty Burke. New York: Del Rey/Ballantine, 2003. xix–xv. Print.

_____. Introduction. *The Conquering Sword of Conan.* By Robert E. Howard. Ed. Louinet and Rusty Burke. New York: Del Rey/Ballantine, 2003. xvii–xi. Print.

MacDonald, Ruth K. *Dr. Seuss.* Boston: Twayne, 1988. Print.

Macintyre, Ben. "Bilbo Baggins Was Born in the Somme Mud." *The Times.* The Times, 14 Dec. 2012. Web.

"The Making of Superman: The Movie". *Superman: The Movie.* Dir. Iain Johnstone. Warner Brothers, 2011. Blu-ray.

Mamet, David. "Kryptonite." *Some Freaks.* New York: Viking, 1989. Print.

Man of Steel. Dir. Zak Snyder. Screenplay by David S. Goyer. Perf. Henry Cavill. Warner Brothers, 2013. Film.

"Marcello, I'm Bored (1966), 16mm, 9 Min." Dir. John Milius. *Cross Town Rivals: Films from USC and UCLA in the 1960s.* Ray Stark Family Theater, George Lucas Building, USC School of Cinematic Arts Complex, Los Angeles. 19 Apr. 2012.

The Mark of Zorro. Dir. Fred Niblo. Perf. Douglas Fairbanks. United Artists, 1920. Film.

Marsten, William Moulten. *The Wonder Woman Chronicles.* Vol. 1. New York: DC Comics, 2010. Print.

Martin, George R.R. "I Admire Tolkien

Greatly." *Goodreads*. Goodreads, 2013. Web.

_____. "In Memoriam: Roger Zelazny." *George R.R. Martin*. George R.R. Martin, June 1995. Web.

_____. "Reading Recommendations." *George R.R. Martin*. George R.R. Martin, 13 Mar. 2013. Web.

_____. *Wild Cards I*. New York: Tor, 2010. Kindle.

Matheson, Richard. "Nightmare at 20,000 Feet." *The Twilight Zone*. CBS. 11 Oct. 1963. Television.

May, Jill P. *Lloyd Alexander*. Boston: Twayne, 1991. Print.

McMillan, Graeme. "How Much Did Disney/Marvel Make from AVENGERS?" *Newsarama*. Tech Media Network, 24 Sept. 2012. Web.

Moore, Alan, and Curt Swan. *Superman: Whatever Happened to the Man of Tomorrow?* New York: DC Comics, 2009. Print.

Morris, May. Introduction. *House of the Wolfings*. By William Morris. London: Longmans, Green, 1912. xv–xxix. Print.

Morris, William. *The House of the Wolfings*. London: Longmans, Green, 1912. Print.

Morrison, Grant. *Supergods: Our World in the Age of the Superhero*. London: Jonathan Cape, 2011. Kindle.

Mortimer, Patchen. "Tolkien and Modernism." *Tolkien Studies: An Annual Scholarly Review* 2 (2005): 113–30. Print.

Motion Pictures of the Heavyweight Boxing Contest Held at Yankee Stadium New York, New York July 21, 1927. Perf. Jack Dempsey and Jack Sharkey. Blackhawk Films, 1927. Film. *You Tube*. 100 Years of Boxing, 20 May 2010. Web.

Nassan, Bill. "The Battle of Paardeberg 1900." *Battlefields: Exploring the Arenas of War, 1805–1945*. By Michael Rayner. London: New Holland, 2009. 92–95. Print.

Nielsen, Leon. *Robert E. Howard: A Collector's Descriptive Bibliography*. Jefferson, N.C.: McFarland, 2007. Print.

Nietzsche, Friedrich. *Twilight of the Idols*. 1889. Grtbooks.com. Great Books and Classics. Web.

"1930 Texas Population Schedule, Reel 2416." *Archives.gov*. United States Bureau of the Census. Web.

Nobleman, Marc Tyler, and Ross MacDonald. *Boys of Steel: The Creators of Superman*. New York: Knopf, 2008. Print.

The Outlaw Josey Wales. Dir. Clint Eastwood. By Forrest Carter. Screenplay by Philip Potter, Kaufman and Sonia Chernus. Perf. Eastwood. Warner Bros., 1976. Film.

Pakenham, Thomas. *The Boer War*. New York: Avon, 1992. Print.

Potter, Charles, Ferd. E. Mierisch, Hattie Harlowe, and Ed. Moebus. "Darktown Cabaret." Jos. W. Stern, 1913. *19th & 20th Century Sheet Music of Negro Themes*. The E. Azalia Hackley Collection of the Detroit Public Library. Web.

Pratt, Fletcher. *World of Wonder: An Introduction to Imaginative Literature*. New York: Twayne, 1951. Print.

"Pre–Ice Age Complex Found Off Bahamas Coast." *Edgarcayce.org*. Edgar Cayce's Association for Research and Enlightenment. 17 Aug. 2011. Web.

Raffel, Burton. "The Lord of the Rings as Literature." *J. R. R. Tolkien's The Lord of the Rings*. Ed. Harold Bloom. Philadelphia: Chelsea House, 2000. 11–26. Print.

Raiders of the Lost Ark. Dir. Steven Spielberg. Prod. George Lucas. Screenplay by Lawrence Kasdan. Perf. Harrison Ford. Paramount, 1981. Film.

Rateliff, John D. *The History of the Hobbit: Part One, Mr. Baggins*. London: HarperCollins, 2007. Print.

Reeve, Christopher. *Still Me*. New York: Random House, 1998. Print.

Reid, Robin Anne. "Tree and Flower, Leaf and Grass." *Fantasy Fiction into Film: Essays.* Ed. Leslie Stratyner and James R. Keller. Jefferson, N.C.: McFarland, 2007. 35–54. Print.

Rérolle, Raphaëlle. "My Father's 'Eviscerated' Work—Son Of Hobbit Scribe J.R.R. Tolkien Finally Speaks Out." *Wordcrunch.* Wordcrunch, 9 July 2012. Web.

Ricca, Brad. *Super Boys: The Amazing Adventures of Jerry Siegel and Joe Shuster, the Creators of Superman.* New York: Macmillan, 2013. Print.

"Robert E. Howard." *Modern Fantasy Writers.* Ed. Harold Bloom. Philadelphia: Chelsea House, 1995. 57–70. Print.

Rosebury, Brian. *Tolkien: A Cultural Phenomenon.* Basingstoke: Palgrave Macmillan, 2003. Print.

Ross, Alex, and Paul Dini. *Superman: Peace on Earth.* New York: DC Comics, 1999. Print.

Rossen, Jake. *Superman vs. Hollywood: How Fiendish Producers, Devious Directors, and Warring Writers Grounded an American Icon.* Chicago: Chicago Review, 2008. Print.

Rutledge, Fleming. *The Battle for Middle-Earth: Tolkien's Divine Design in Lord of the Rings.* Grand Rapids: William B. Eerdmans, 2003. Print.

Sabatini, Rafael. *Captain Blood.* Project Gutenberg, 26 Sept. 2008. Web.

Sale, Roger. *Modern Heroism: Essays on D.H. Lawrence, William Empson, & J.R.R. Tolkien.* Berkeley: California University Press, 1973. Print.

_____. "Tolkien and Frodo Baggins." *Tolkien and the Critics: Essays on J.R.R. Tolkien's The Lord of the Rings.* Ed. Neil D. Isaacs and Rose A. Zimbardo. Notre Dame: Notre Dame University Press, 1968. Print.

Sammons, Martha C. *War of the Fantasy Worlds: C.S. Lewis and J.R.R. Tolkien on Art and Imagination.* Santa Barbara: Praeger, 2010. Print.

Scithers, George H. "Balthus of Cross Plains." *The Spell of Conan.* Ed. L. Sprague de Camp. New York: Ace, 1980. 51–54. Print.

Scivally, Bruce. *Superman on Film, Television, Radio, and Broadway.* Jefferson, N.C.: McFarland, 2008. Print.

Scott, Walter. *Ivanhoe.* London: Penguin, 2009. Kindle.

Scull, Christina, and Wayne G. Hammond. *The J.R.R. Tolkien Companion & Guide: Chronology.* Boston: Houghton Mifflin, 2006. Print.

The Searchers. Dir. John Ford. By Alan Le May. Screenplay by Frank S. Nugent. Perf. John Wayne. 1956. Warner Bros., 2006. DVD.

Serling, Rod. "A Stop at Willoughby." *The Twilight Zone.* CBS. 6 May 1960. Television.

Shippey, Tom. *J.R.R. Tolkien: Author of the Century.* Boston: Houghton Mifflin, 2001. Print.

_____. *The Road to Middle-Earth: Revised and Expanded Edition.* Boston: Houghton Mifflin, 2003. Print.

Siegel, Jerry, and Joe Shuster. *The Superman Chronicles.* Vol. 1. New York: DC Comics, 2006. Print.

_____. *The Superman Chronicles.* Vol. 2. New York: DC Comics, 2007. Print.

_____. *The Superman Chronicles.* Vol. 4. New York: DC Comics, 2008. Print.

_____. *The Superman Chronicles.* Vol. 6. New York: DC Comics, 2009. Print.

_____. *The Superman Chronicles.* Vol. 7. New York: DC Comics, 2009. Print.

Simon, Joe, and Jim Simon. *The Comic Book Makers.* New York: Vanguard, 2003. Print.

Sparks, Patricia Meyer. "Power and Meaning in *The Lord of the Rings.*" *Tolkien and the Critics: Essays on J.R.R. Tolkien's The Lord of the Rings.* Ed. Neil D. Isaacs and Rose A. Zimbardo.

Notre Dame: Notre Dame University Press, 1968. Print.

Spiegelman, Art, and Françoise Mouly. *The Toon Treasury of Classic Children's Comics.* New York: Abrams ComicArts, 2009. Print.

Stevenson, Robert Louis. *Treasure Island.* New York: Scribner, 2007. Print.

Superman and the Mole Men. Dir. Lee Sholem. Screenplay by Richard Fielding. *The Superman Motion Picture Anthology.* Warner Brothers, 2011. Blu-ray.

The Superman Radio Scripts. New York: Watson-Guptill, 2001. Print.

Superman: The Movie. Dir. Richard Donner. Screenplay by Mario Puzo, David Newman, Leslie Newman, Robert Benton and Tom Mankiewicz. Perf. Christopher Reeve. *The Superman Motion Picture Anthology.* Warner Brothers, 2011. Blu-ray.

Superman II. Dir. Richard Lester. Screenplay by Mario Puzo, David Newman and Leslie Newman. Perf. Christopher Reeve. *The Superman Motion Picture Anthology.* Warner Brothers, 2011. Blu-ray.

Superman II: The Richard Donner Cut. Dir. Richard Donner. Screenplay by Mario Puzo, David Newman and Leslie Newman. Perf. Christopher Reeve. *The Superman Motion Picture Anthology.* Warner Brothers, 2011. Blu-ray.

Superman III. Dir. Richard Lester. Screenplay by David Newman and Leslie Newman. Perf. Christopher Reeve. *The Superman Motion Picture Anthology.* Warner Brothers, 2011. Blu-ray.

Superman IV: The Quest for Peace. Dir. Sidney J. Furie. Story by Christopher Reeve and Lawrence Konner and Mark Rosenthal. Screenplay by Lawrence Konner and Mark Rosenthal. Perf. Christopher Reeve. *The Su-perman Motion Picture Anthology.* Warner Brothers, 2011. Blu-ray.

Superman Returns. Dir. Bryan Singer. Screenplay by Michael Dougherty and Dan Harris. Perf. Brandon Routh. *The Superman Motion Picture Anthology.* Warner Brothers, 2011. Blu-ray.

Swinfen, Ann. *In Defense of Fantasy: A Study of the Genre in English and American Literature Since 1945.* London: Routledge, 1984. Print.

Thirkell, Angela. *Three Houses.* London: Allison & Busby, 2012. Print.

Tolkien, Christopher. *The Return of the Shadow.* Boston: Houghton Mifflin, 1988. Print.

Tolkien, J.R.R. *The Hobbit, Or, There and Back Again.* Illus. Michael Hague. Boston: Houghton Mifflin, 1984. Print.

_____. *The Letters of J. R. R. Tolkien: A Selection.* Ed. Humphrey Carpenter. Boston: Houghton Mifflin, 2000. Print.

_____. "Lord of the Hobbits." *Tolkien and the Critics: Essays on J. R. R. Tolkien's The Lord of the Rings.* Ed. Neil D. Isaacs and Rose A. Zimbardo. Notre Dame: Notre Dame University Press, 1968. Print.

_____. *The Lord of the Rings.* Boston: Houghton Mifflin, 2004. Print.

_____. "On Fairy Stories." *The Tolkien Reader.* New York: Ballantine, 1966. 31–99. Print.

_____. *The Silmarillion.* Boston: Houghton Mifflin, 1977. Print.

"Tom Mankiewicz." *IMDb.* The Internet Movie Database, 1990–2013. Web.

Tunnel, Michael O. *The Prydain Companion.* New York: Holt, 2003. Print.

Tye, Larry. *Superman: The High-Flying History of America's Most Enduring Hero.* New York: Random House, 2012. Kindle.

"Ursula K. Le Guin." *Wikipedia.* Wikimedia Foundation, n.d. Web.

Walker, Steve. *The Power of Tolkien's*

Prose: Middle-Earth's Magical Style. New York: Palgrave Macmillan, 2009. Print.

Weinberg, Robert E. *The Weird Tales Story.* West Linn: FAX Collector's Editions, 1977. Print.

"weird, adj." *OED Online.* Oxford University Press, Sept. 2012. Web.

Welles, Orson, and Peter Bogdanovich. *This Is Orson Welles.* Ed. Jonathan Rosenbaum. New York: Da Capo, 1998. Print.

Wells, H.G. *The Invisible Man.* New York: Dover Publications, 1992. Print.

_____. *The Outline of History, Being a Plain History of Life and Mankind.* New York: Macmillan, 1921. *Internet Archive.* Web.

Wertham, Fredric. *Seduction of the Innocent.* New York: Rinehart, 1954. Print.

Wheldon, Glen. *Superman: The Unauthorized Biography.* New York: Wiley, 2013. Print.

Whitaker, Albert Keith. "California Dreamin' in the Postmodern Academy." *Journal of Education* 184.2 (2003): 123. *Albert Keith Whitaker.* Boston College. Web.

White, Donna R. *A Century of Welsh Myth in Children's Literature.* Westport, CT: Greenwood, 1998. Print.

White, Lynn. "Technology and Invention in the Middle Ages." *Speculum* 15.2 (1940): 141–59. *JSTOR.* Web. 21 Oct. 2012.

White, Mark D., ed. *Superman and Philosophy: What Would the Man of Steel Do?* Malden, Mass.: Wiley, 2013. Print.

"Who Was Edgar Cayce? Psychic and Medical Clairvoyant." *Edgarcayce.org.* Edgar Cayce's Association for Research and Enlightenment. Web.

The Whole Wide World. Dir. Dan Ireland. By Novalyn Price Ellis. Screenplay by Michael Scott Myers. Perf. Vincent D'Onofrio and Renée Zellweger. Sony Pictures Classic, 1996. DVD.

Wicks, Robert. "Friedrich Nietzsche." *Stanford Encyclopedia of Philosophy.* Ed. Edward N. Zalta. Stanford University, 29 Apr. 2011. Web.

Williams, Tennessee. "The Vengeance of Nitocris." *Wikisource, the Free Online Library.* 16 May 2012. Web.

_____. "Williams' Wells of Violence." *New York Times* 8 Mar. 1959, Drama sec. *Proquest.* Web.

The Wizard (Fox, 1927) Lobby Card. Advertisement. HA.com. Heritage Auctions, July 2008. Web.

"The Wizard (1927)." *IMDb.* The Internet Movie Database, 1990–2013. Web.

Zelazny, Roger. *The Great Book of Amber: The Complete Amber Chronicles.* New York: Avon, 1999. Print.

Index

Action Comics #1 134
Adventure 61–67, 71, 90, 134, 172
Adventures of Superman 156, 157
The Adventures of Superpup 157
Aldington, Richard 54
Alexander, Lloyd 163–165
American Indians 57, 59, 77, 115, 118, 119, 123, 166
And to Think That I Saw It on Mulberry Street 162
Anglicanism 4, 6, 11
Aquilonia 60, 108, 114, 115, 117–119, 121
Aragorn 10, 20, 21, 32, 41, 49, 50, 53–55
Arwen 32
Atlantis 60, 103–105, 108, 140
atomic bomb 37, 38
Auden, W.H. 11, 39, 46, 47
Augustinian 6, 47
Aule 31
The Avengers 155

Baggins, Bilbo 33, 34, 44–47, 53, 171
Baggins, Frodo 8–10, 17–21, 24, 32, 35, 36, 44, 46–52, 57, 164
Balthus 114, 115, 117, 118, 122–124
Batman 133, 135, 143, 145–154, 173
Beowulf 18, 19, 42, 55, 90, 101
Beren and Luthein 32, 33
"Beyond the Black River" 102, 108, 113–124
Bible 6, 7, 9, 31, 61
Birmingham 13
"The Black Stranger" 102
Blavatsky, Madame Helena 105
Bloemfontein 4
Bloom, Harold 41, 42, 56
Boer War 3–5, 17, 56
Bombadil, Tom 49

Boromir 18–21
Brando, Marlon 120, 159

Captain America 135, 140, 141, 145, 146
Carpenter, Humphrey 3, 4, 11, 14, 33, 39
Carter, Linwood Vrooman 85
Catholicism 1, 3, 5, 6, 8–11, 13–15, 18, 25, 41, 46, 53
Cayce, Edgar 105
Christianity 6–8, 22, 48
The Chronicles of Amber 166, 167
Churchill, Winston 38
Cimmerian 60, 108, 109, 112, 123, 129
Civil War 59, 60, 67, 87, 88, 116
Cold War 141, 145
Coleridge, Samuel Taylor 29
comic books 85, 86, 114, 130–138, 140–156, 173
Comics Code 144, 152
Conan 1, 2, 5, 60, 67, 69, 73–76, 80–88, 90, 95–131
Conan Doyle, Arthur 5, 76, 172
Conan the Barbarian 120, 124–129
Conan the Barbarian (2011) 129, 130
Conan the Destroyer 129
concentration camps 5
Costigan, Steve 67–73
Cross Plains, Texas 58, 59, 61, 62, 64, 69, 74, 80, 81, 86, 87, 89, 92, 105, 108, 124

Daily Planet 158, 159
Dark Valley Destiny 81
DC Comics 133, 134, 146, 151–154, 173
Dead Marshes 21
De Camp, L. Sprague 61, 67, 74, 77, 81–86, 107, 114, 117, 172
Demetrio 97, 98, 101
Denethor 9, 24

Index

Dickens, Charles 71, 73, 148, 172
Disney, Walt 162, 163
Dr. Seuss 162
Donenfield, Harry 134, 135
Donner, Richard 158–161
Doom, Thulsa 126–128
dwarf 33, 34, 38, 39, 50, 52, 54, 171
Dyson, Hugo 15

Earthsea Trilogy 165, 166
Ebert, Roger 160
Eco, Umberto 146, 147
elf 13, 14, 20, 21, 24–27, 32, 35, 36, 38, 39, 48–52, 54, 57, 106
Eluard, Paul 164
The Empire Strikes Back 91, 127
Ents 51, 52
Existentialism 164, 165

Faerie 26–28
fantasy world 1, 2, 6, 23, 30, 36, 43, 60, 69, 73, 80, 86, 90, 95–97, 107, 113, 117, 119, 120, 126, 130, 152–157, 161–168, 171
Faramir 20, 21, 36
Faulkner, William 87, 91
Ferguson, Ma and Pa 115, 116
Fingeroth, Danny 135, 136
Finn, Mark 67, 77, 83, 86
The Flash 146
Fleischer, Richard 128, 129
Franco, Generalissimo Francisco 140

Galadriel 48
Game of Thrones 130, 168
Gamgee, Samwise 17, 18, 20, 21, 36, 37, 51–53, 57, 110
Gandalf 6–11, 21, 24, 25, 47–49, 52, 164, 171
Generalissimo Franco see Franco, Generalissimo Francisco
Gilson, Rob 15
God 1, 6–8, 11, 17, 18, 23, 25, 28, 31, 32, 47, 110, 117
"The God in the Bowl" 97, 98
Gollum 8–10, 21, 37, 48
The Good, the Bad and the Ugly 126
Gotham City 151
"The Grand Cham" 64, 65
Great Depression 2, 48, 61, 73, 95, 109
Green Lantern 146

Henneberger, Clark 92, 93
Hirohito 141
Hitler, Adolf 25, 37, 48, 138, 140–142, 144
hobbit 9, 11, 12, 17, 19–24, 34, 48–50, 53–55, 57, 161
The Hobbit 6, 8, 26, 30, 31, 33–37, 40, 41–45, 56
Hollywoodland 156
Holy Spirit 9
The Hour of the Dragon 98–102
Howard, Hester Irvin 58, 69, 77, 80–82, 88, 96, 107, 113
Howard, Isaac Mordecai 53, 58, 77, 81–83
The Hulk 135, 145
Hyborian Age 1, 43, 73, 86–90, 97–108, 111–114, 117–122, 126, 130

Inklings 15
Iron Man 135, 145, 155

Jackson, Peter 7, 54, 56
James, Henry 76
Jesus 7, 11, 106, 138
Jews 2, 11, 37, 132–138, 140, 142
Johnson, Lyndon Baines 116
Jones, James Earl 126, 128
Justice League of America 152

Kael, Pauline 160
Kal-El 136
Kane, Bob 133, 136, 146, 147
Kefauver, Estes 144
Kent, Clark 135–138, 147, 150, 159
Kent, Ma, and Pa 136, 137
Kipling, Rudyard 70
Kitchener, Major-General Horatio Herbert 4, 5
Krypton 136

La Guardia, Fiorello 127, 140
Lamb, Harold 64, 65
Lane, Lois 137, 147, 159, 173
Lee, Stan 136, 144–146
Legolas 21
Le Guin, Ursula 165, 166
Lewis, C.S. 8, 10, 15, 17, 18, 22, 28, 39, 44, 171
Lloyd, Harold 138
Lord of the Rings 1, 3, 6–13, 16–18, 21–28, 30–57, 106, 107, 110, 111, 118, 120, 130, 156, 163–164, 168, 171, 172

Lord of the Rings: Fellowship of the Ring 7
Lord of the Rings: Return of the King 22, 55
Lord of the Rings: The Two Towers 40, 54
Lost Horizon 127, 128
Lovecraft, H.P. 66, 103, 112, 113, 122, 172, 173
Lucas, George 101, 120, 124
Luthor, Lex 138, 157

Madame Blavatsky *see* Blavatsky, Madame Helena
magic 6–8, 27–29, 44, 45, 51, 105, 118, 120, 152, 153, 166
Man of Steel 161
Mankiewicz, Tom 158, 161
The Mark of Zorro 137, 138, 146
Marston, William Moulton 149, 150
Martin, George R.R. 168
Marvel Comics 144–146, 149, 152, 154, 155, 161, 173
McCarthy, Joseph 144
Melkor 31, 32
Metropolis 136, 137, 139, 151, 154, 157
Mickey Mouse 163
Middle-earth 6–15, 18–20, 25, 31, 32, 36, 27, 42–46, 49–53, 56, 103, 106, 119, 120, 130
Milius, John 120, 124–131
Minas Tirith 20, 24
Modernism 12, 25, 26, 42, 76, 77
Mordor 19
Mundy, Talbot 65, 66
Munsey, Frank 90
Mussolini, Benito 61, 62

Namor, Prince *see* Prince Namor
National Comics 133, 134, 151
Native Americans *see* American Indians
Nazis 2, 37, 48, 101, 105, 136, 140–142, 162, 173
Nemedia 60
"The Nemedian Chronicles" 60
Nietzsche, Friedrich 125, 128, 142

"On Fairy-stories" 26–28
One Ring 7, 10, 19, 32, 44, 48, 50, 51
One Who Walked Alone 74–81
orc 20, 21, 50, 51, 54, 56

Paardeberg, Battle of 4, 5, 17
Patches 123, 124
Picts 108, 115, 117–124
Post Oaks and Sand Roughs 67–73, 102
Price, Novalyn 74–81, 112, 115, 131
Prince Namor 140
Prohibition 72, 103, 115
The Prydain Chronicles 163–165
pulp magazines 61, 62, 66, 73, 74, 80–84, 90–94, 104, 105, 114, 133–135, 167

"Queen of the Black Coast" 99, 102

Raiders of the Lost Ark 101, 173
Reconstruction 87, 88, 172
"Red Nails" 101
Reeve, Christopher 159–161
Reeves, George 156, 157
The Return of Conan 84
Robin 148, 151
"Rogues in the House" 98, 99
Roosevelt, Franklin Delano 116
Roosevelt, Theodore 64, 90

Sabatini, Rafael 64
Sartre, Jean-Paul 164
Saruman 9, 11, 40, 51
Satan 18, 25, 31
Sauron 6, 7, 9, 11, 19, 20, 24, 25, 31, 34, 35, 46, 48–53, 55
"The Scarlet Citadel" 99, 102
Schwarzenegger, Arnold 124, 126, 128, 131
Seduction of the Innocent 142–145
Serling, Rod 71, 168
Shakespeare, William 14, 26, 42, 52, 56
Shangri-La 127, 128
The Shire 21, 24, 35, 43, 48, 49, 110
Shuster, Joe 2, 132–139, 145–147
Siegel, Jerry 2, 132–139, 145–147, 152, 156, 161
The Silmarillion 6–8, 11, 25, 30–33, 45, 111, 171
Smallville 137
Smith, Geoffrey Bache 15, 17
Snow White and the Seven Dwarfs 163
Somme, Battle of 15, 17
A Song of Ice and Fire 168
South Africa 3–5, 30
Spanish Civil War 140
Spider-Man 135, 145, 146
Spiegelman, Art 135

Index

Spielberg, Steven 101, 124
Stalin, Josef 138, 141
Stand by Me 153, 154
Star Trek 40
Star Wars 40, 55, 91, 120, 158, 173
Stein, Gertrude 163, 164
Superman 2, 132–154, 156–161
Superman and the Mole Men 156, 157
Superman: The Movie 154, 157–160
Supervillains 137, 138, 145

Taran Wanderer 164
Tauran 114
Taurus 111, 113
T.C.B.S. 14–17
"Tea Club and Barrovian Society" *see* T.C.B.S.
Texas 1, 2, 58–62, 67, 68, 79, 82, 86–89, 92, 114–116, 121
Thor 135, 145, 149
Tolkien, Christopher 15, 16, 30, 44
Tolkien, Edith 1, 11, 15, 33, 39, 56
Took, Pippin 35
"The Tower of the Elephant" 102, 108– 113, 115, 124
Treebeard 51, 52
Twilight of the Idols 125
Twilight Zone 71, 168

Vanity Fair 80
"The Vengeance of Nitocris" 93–95
Vietnam War 158, 159, 164, 165

Watergate 158, 159
"weird" 90, 101, 107, 112, 114, 120, 127
Weird Tales 67, 83, 90–96, 102, 105, 108, 112, 118, 131, 132
Wells, H. G. 45, 46
Wertham, Fredric 142–147, 156
Wheeler-Nicholson, Major Malcolm 133, 134
"Whitechapel" 54
The Whole Wide World 78
Williams, Tennessee 93–95
Wiseman, Christopher 15, 17
"A Witch Shall Be Born" 100
wizard 6, 11, 34, 51, 164, 166
Wonder Woman 143, 146, 148–151
World War I 1, 3–5, 15–18, 21, 23, 30, 37, 43, 44, 54, 92, 110, 127
World War II 3, 4, 16, 21, 37, 38, 40–45, 47, 48, 61, 140, 141, 147, 163
Wright, Farnsworth 92, 93, 95, 96

X-men 135, 145

Yoda 127, 128

Zamora 60, 108, 111, 112
Zelazny, Roger 166–168